Speaking Volumes

Speaking Volumes

Narrative and intertext in Ovid and other Latin poets

Alessandro Barchiesi

Edited and translated by
Matt Fox and Simone Marchesi

Duckworth

First published in 2001 by
Gerald Duckworth & Co. Ltd.
61 Frith Street, London W1D 3JL
Tel: 020 7434 4242
Fax: 020 7434 4420
Email: enquiries@duckworth-publishers.co.uk
www.ducknet.co.uk

A catalogue record for this book is available
from the British Library

ISBN 0 7156 3027 X

Typeset by Ray Davies
Printed in Great Britain by
Bookcraft (Bath) Ltd, Midsomer Norton, Avon

Contents

Preface

I begin by offering short summaries of the individual papers that now form the eight chapters of this book. In square brackets after the chapter title I give the place of original publication.

1. Continuities [*MD* 16, 1986]
The basic condition for Ovid's poetics is a sense of continuity and co-existence, between stories as between texts.

2. Narrativity and convention in the Heroides [*MD* 19, 1987]
The *Heroides* construct a world where the oscillation and equivocation between elegiac convention and non-elegiac plot is a source of contrast and irony.

3. Voices and narrative 'instances' in the Metamorphoses [*MD* 23, 1989]
The presence of internal narrators in the *Metamorphoses*, far from being an inert structural device, creates implications and ironies.

4. Teaching Augustus through allusion [*MD* 31, 1993]
In two poems where different authors, Horace and Ovid, address the emperor, the role of allusion is strategic and suggests a delicate balance between addressee and audience.

5. Future reflexive [*HCSP* 1993 (in English)]
The Alexandrian idea of positioning a story as a forerunner of its traditional background becomes a systematic approach in the *Heroides*, whereby tradition is both forestalled and acknowledged.

6. Tropes of intertextuality in Roman epic [*Lexis* 13, 1995]
Epic objectivity is a restriction for Roman self-reflexivity, but also stimulates 'tropes', that is mediated figures and images of literary self-consciousness: dreams, oracles, memories, artifacts and echoes.

7. Some points on a map of shipwrecks [*MD* 39, 1997]
Contemporary problems and perspectives in the study of literary memory and intertextuality: a summing-up.

8. Allusion and society: Ovid the censor [*AJAH* 13, 1997 (in English)]
One final case-study presents a poetic text facing political, not literary
intertextuality, and advocates a sociology of allusion.

Speaking Volumes is a collection of papers previously published in various
journals over a decade: two of them in English, six in Italian. The Italian
chapters have been translated and revised by Matthew Fox and Simone
Marchesi (at the time, both graduate students of Princeton University). I
have updated the references and made changes when possible, but I have
refrained from reformulating the arguments. Taken together, the papers
seek to describe the Ovidian poetics of allusion as a crucial moment in the
history of Roman intertextuality, and offer perspectives on other texts of
Roman and Alexandrian literature. The trajectory of the collection starts
from a paper where the focus is on textual problems and ends with a paper
that foregrounds the problem of how far an intertextual approach to
literature can deal with discourses, not just texts. The intermediate chapters aim to explore links between intertextuality and genre (2), narrative
(3 and 6), power (4), literary history (5), while Chapter 7 attempts a more
comprehensive snapshot of Roman intertextuality, as seen in and through
the research of my generation of Latinists. Yet I imagine that the issues of
genre, narrative, and allusion will be found to be ubiquitous throughout
the book.

The title, as will be clearer at the end of Chapter 1, is based on the
striking, prophetic image of *Tristia* 1.1.105-20, where the Ovidian books
communicate with each other inside the bookcase of Ovid's Collected
Works. *Speaking Volumes* is also a reminder of the way in which allusion
reanimates previous works of literature, and even (through a different
kind of ambiguity) of the issues of 'voice', 'polysemy', and 'levels of communication' raised at several points of my analysis.

Some of the friends who have contributed ideas and comments for the
individual papers will receive thanks *suo loco*, but here I feel I must name
at least Stephen Hinds, who gave an unforgettable reading of the speaking
volumes by Ovid in Hinds (1985).

The book as a whole owes much to Susanna Braund, who suggested the
idea of the collection, and to the editorial advice of Deborah Blake. I am
equally grateful to the translators and to the advice of Ilaria Cortesi
(Rutgers University), the four of us working together in the familiar
atmosphere of the historical 'Bagni La Rina' in Cecina Mare on the
Tyrrhenian Sea (summer of 2000).

Arezzo, 17 November 2000*   A.B.

---

*The anniversary of my parents Lilli and Marino (they were born on the same day, month,
and year), to whom the collection is now dedicated in gratitude.

1

Continuities

The observations gathered here are not the result of systematic research on Ovid's poetics and on the mechanics of the art of allusion, subjects on which much has been written recently and with success. They are, instead, marginal notes, linked to the preparation of a commentary on Ovid. Each individual contribution is a response to specific uncertainties of text and interpretation and should be judged on its own merits, the more so as the whole lacks any unity of intent from a textual-critical point of view. These responses include choosing between variant readings, defending textual transmissions, and endorsing conjectural emendations.

From another point of view, I admit that this assortment, in comparison to a real assembly of *atakta*, will seem a bit more organized. The textual problems I confront one by one are also intertextual problems, inasmuch as editorial choices imply the presence of underlying models that call for our recognition, models both for expression and of narrative. And the way in which the Ovidian text implies its models allows one to glimpse certain characteristic and coherent threads that can be traced back to a narrative poetics. What is more, it seems to me that this poetics has to do with a particular way of viewing literature. This is why it will be necessary at times to pass from individual problems to certain aspects of Ovid's poetics, and to one in particular: the way in which Ovid represents his narrative texts and their possible interconnections, those points of passage, or liminal zones, in which one text seems to lose itself in another.

Studies of this poet are particularly exposed to the danger of a move somewhat tautological and circular: they end up explaining to what degree Ovid is intimately and typically Ovidian. We also run the risk of over-emphasizing the recurrence of certain allusive schemes and the predictable coherence of the intertextual 'imagination'. My brief final comment will try to lay the responsibility for these insistences on Ovid himself. This should at least serve to recall the importance of Ovid's *explicit* poetics, an aspect that otherwise (bound as we are to the narrow compass of individual contexts) might find few occasions for its proper significance to be assessed.

1. The misfortunes of Briseis: *Heroides* 3.44

Briseis has been taken by Agamemnon and Achilles abandons her to her fate. At this point she calls to mind her painful past:

> Qua merui culpa fieri tibi vilis, Achille?
> quo levis a nobis tam cito fugit amor?
> An miseros tristis fortuna tenaciter urget
> nec venit inceptis mollior hora meis?
> Diruta Marte tuo Lyrnesia moenia vidi ...
> *(Her.* 3.41-5)

Judging from the most recent editions, the textual status of v. 44 must be considered stable. Dörrie accepts *meis*, the consensus in the manuscript tradition, and records in the apparatus: *malis Planudes Housman Palmer*.[1] In fact, the correction of *meis* to *malis* had a rather turbulent fate in the second half of the nineteenth century.

Some clarification is in order here. It is true that the Palmer-Purser edition proposes *malis*, accompanying this choice with an enthusiastic note in the apparatus: *malis Housman, quod mirifice confirmat Planudes, meis libri*.[2] It is true also that the version of the thirteenth-century monk makes one think that his model had offered *inceptis ... malis*: *ameinôn hôra tois hupêrgmenois kakois oukoun epeisin?* (p. 171 Palm.). Nevertheless, Housman did not publish the conjecture *malis* as his own. In his 1899 review of Palmer-Purser, he limits himself to noting that *malis* is one of the better contributions to the Ovidian text derivable from Planudes, and that it amounts to a new and independent argument in favour of this conjecture – which Housman correctly assigns to its true author, Karl Lehrs.[3] The comment of Palmer-Purser at 3.44 is also precise (and again enthusiastic): 'This confirmation of Lehrs' conjecture is probably the most signal service rendered to the criticism of Ovid by the version of Planudes' (p. 300).

This clarification might seem pedantic (and it is by now common knowledge that our modern apparatus are used to robbing from the poor to give to the rich), so much so that the conjecture *malis* has lost credibility without even receiving the honour of an explicit refutation. Once the initial excitement at the novelty of the Byzantine version had worn off, modern editors tranquilly turned back to the vulgate text, which seems irreproachable as far as sense is concerned, presenting as it does a use of *inceptum* as a noun that sounds *difficilior* when compared to the combination *inceptis malis*.

After all, the conjecture had been presented in a very laconic manner even before this silent eclipse. Lehrs proposed it in a short note of a work, on the whole not very successful and little followed, aimed at discovering the many interpolations and falsifications in the text of Ovid's epistles.[4] His argument wholly rested upon two – actually quite relevant – Ovidian parallels: *Pont.* 4.14.50: *non potuit nostris lenior esse malis*, and *Her.* 15.59: *an gravis inceptum peragit fortuna tenorem?*[5] On the other side, nobody, as far as I know, has raised explicit objections to *inceptis ...meis*.

But one strong objection arises from the entire context of Ovid's epistle, and from the larger context of Homeric narratives that it implicates. Briseis has reason to complain, and is actually the object of a persistent persecution by fortune. As she is about to tell – in vv. 45-52, right after the pentameter in question – she was an eminent person in her city. Achilles has destroyed the city, slaughtering her husband and her three brothers, and has made her a slave. Once taken, Briseis has found a certain consolation in the love of her master. But a new abduction, this time by Agamemnon, has worsened her condition yet again. Now she has been enslaved twice and twice made a captive. A Trojan woman in the hands of Greeks, she does not attempt escape for fear of falling into the hands of the Trojans (cf. vv. 17ff.). She has undergone the *servitium* – and the *servitium amoris* – of Achilles, and now the new, most unwelcome *servitium* of Agamemnon. The particular thrust of the whole epistle arises precisely from the *passivity* to which Briseis has been bound. The heroine feels she is a genuine hostage of misfortune: at the beginning of the epistle she speaks of herself as a *munus*. Ovid boldly converts into the first person the designation of Briseis as a *geras*, a fundamental motif in Homer's narration of the wrath of Achilles.

In reality Ovid is giving voice to a 'person-object', the consummate example of the passive figure in Homer. Briseis has never been able to act or choose: the love of Achilles, the wrath of Achilles, both have irrevocably decided her destiny. It is not at all understood to which personal *incepta* of her own Briseis might be referring. *Inceptum* – also in an erotic context – is a very strong and binding word. Leander calls *incepta* his fearless deed of diving into the stormy Hellespont (*Her.* 18.35: *obstitit inceptis tumidum iuvenalibus aequor*). Surely Briseis sees her destiny not as a series of endeavours and frustrated personal plans, but rather, more simply, as a chain of disgraces that from the moment it begins never leaves her.

This is precisely the sense of the Homeric model that Ovid is reinterpreting. I have already hinted at the story of her first misfortune, the destruction of Lyrnessus:

> Diruta Marte tuo Lyrnesia moenia vidi
> et fueram patriae pars ego magna meae.
> Vidi consortes pariter generisque necisque
> tres cecidisse: tribus, quae mihi, mater erat.
> Vidi, quantus erat, fusum tellure cruenta
> pectora iactantem sanguinolenta virum.
> Tot tamen amissis te compensavimus unum:
> Tu dominus, tu vir, tu mihi frater eras.
>
> (*Her.* 3.45-52)

This recalls Briseis' lament in *Iliad* 19:

ἄνδρα μὲν ᾧ ἔδοσάν με πατὴρ καὶ πότνια μήτηρ
εἶδον πρὸ πτόλιος δεδαϊγμένον ὀξέι χαλκῷ,
τρεῖς τε κασιγνήτους, τούς μοι μία γείνατο μήτηρ,
κηδείους, οἳ πάντες ὀλέθριον ἦμαρ ἐπέσπον.
οὐδὲ μὲν οὐδέ μ᾽ ἔασκες, ὅτ᾽ ἄνδρ᾽ ἐμὸν ὠκὺς Ἀχιλλεὺς
ἔκτεινεν, πέρσεν δὲ πόλιν θείοιο Μύνητος,
κλαίειν, ἀλλά μ᾽ ἔφασκες Ἀχιλλῆος θείοιο
κουριδίην ἄλοχον θήσειν, ἄξειν τ᾽ ἐνὶ νηυσὶν
ἐς Φθίην, δαίσειν δὲ γάμον μετὰ Μυρμιδόνεσσι.

(Il. 19.291-9)

But her memories of disaster, just as in Ovid, arise from a new disaster, the death of Patroclus, whom Briseis is mourning. Let us now compare the two verses, in Ovid and in Homer, which introduce the transition from present misfortune (the rape by Agamemnon, the death of Patroclus) to her sorrowful recollection:

3.44 nec venit inceptis mollior hora malis
19.290 ὥς μοι δέχεται κακὸν ἐκ κακοῦ αἰεί

The allusion is clear, and the point of view of the Homeric Briseis – for whom a new *kakon* always follows a previous original *kakon* – compels us to print *malis* in Ovid. (Now the nicely alliterative pair *mollior* / *malis* echoes and balances the pair *miseros* / *tristis* with which the couplet begins, juxtaposing at the same time an antithesis with a redundancy. Finally, the arrival of the *mollior hora*, by forceful hyperbaton, seems to interrupt abruptly the series of her disgraces.) Ovid's reader knows that this chain of *mala* is not over yet. Briseis' letter is written after the embassy to Achilles, and before, of course, his wrath has ceased.[6] Briseis has a friend in Achilles' tent, a gentle man who has always tried to comfort her (cf. *Her*. 3.23-4; *Il*. 19.287ff. and 295ff.). Those familiar with Homer know that this dear and only friend of Briseis is going to fall in battle – better yet, is *about to fall*, if one looks, as Ovid forces us to, at the temporal situation and the dramatic framework of the epistle. Briseis is on the verge of losing Patroclus also. And this new *kakon* will be but another link in the chain of *mala* which Ovid's Briseis already knows how to read in her destiny as a slave.

2. Circe's promise: *Remedia Amoris* 281ff.

Circe is making her last attempt to detain the departing Ulysses. After she has failed as an enchantress (cf. *Ars* 2.103) she resorts to the arts of verbal persuasion:

'Quae tibi causa fugae? non hic nova Troia resurgit,
   non aliquis socios Rhesus ad arma vocat.
Hic amor et pax est, in qua male vulneror una,
   totaque sub regno terra futura tuo est'.
Illa loquebatur, navem solvebat Ulixes:
   inrita cum velis verba tulere Noti.

                                            (*Rem.* 281-6)

The outcome of the plot is predictable. Faced with a similar attempt in the *Odyssey*, Odysseus went so far as to turn down the promise of immortality (cf. Calypso's words in Homer, *Od.* 5.208-9).

Most editors of the *Remedia* since Heinsius have printed – and continue to print – *non aliquis socios Rhesus ad arma vocat* at v. 282.[7] This reading, *Rhesus*, has long remained unchallenged, together with such reassuring glosses as 'Rhesus, king of Thrace, Trojan ally', until one asks with the utmost clarity what the overall sense of v. 282 would be in this case, and to what it is referring. It is indeed inevitable that Circe is alluding here to something known, which Odysseus, and of course also Ovid's readers, are able to interpret without effort. The merit of having shown how poorly Rhesus fits the context goes to E.J. Kenney, who more than once (though very briefly) has made the point that one should accept the variant reading *rursus*, and has explained v. 282 as a periphrasis referring to *Agamemnon*.[8] It is my contention however that, starting from the text proposed by Kenney, it may be useful to add another reference, namely some sort of ironic addition relevant both to the reading *rursus* (not irrelevant, given the fact that Rhesus continues to have supporters),[9] and to highlight an allusive web that stretches through the entire context and, incidentally, makes it much more entertaining than Ovidian commentators suppose.

In its rhetorical momentum Circe's plea, as has long been noted,[10] is closer in tone to the *Heroides* than to the *Remedia*. Circe is not trying to tame or to ease her love for Odysseus – in this, as Ovid explained in vv. 263ff., her magical arts had already failed – but to convince her beloved to stay and, if possible, to love her back. Circe's speech becomes a kind of 'micro-Heroid' which at times breaks out of the didactic framework of the *Remedia*. Strong parallels in situation, and thus in argument, connect this text particularly to Dido's letter to Aeneas. Like Dido, Circe insists that the conditions of the sea are not yet favourable; she asks merely for a delay, ostentatiously renouncing any hope for marriage. Dido promises Aeneas, among other things, that Africa will provide him with a kingdom not only pacified but also, if he wishes, belligerent (*nequid desit, praebebimus hostem; / hic pacis leges, hic locus arma capit*: *Her.* 7.157-8). Readers of Virgil know very well what this promise alludes to. In the *Aeneid*, after Mercury reproached Aeneas, he lamented that by staying in Carthage he was going to deprive Iulus of great conquests (*Aen.* 4.354ff.). The dialogic nature of Ovid's text incorporates this argument. In reply, Ovid's Dido offers both the peace which the wandering Trojans desire so much and also, in an amusing agnostic gesture so typical of Ovid's erotic ideology, as many wars and triumphs as he wishes.

Circe instead makes a single offer: 'in this land there is peace without risks of danger for you: another war could not possibly break out!' The Ovidian context presupposes that this is an argument that – at least as far as Circe is concerned – might appeal to Odysseus, just as Dido's promises to Aeneas are likely to evoke a predictable response from him (that is, in the composite image that the reader constructs of Aeneas by combining the character of the letter's implied addressee with the traditional character of Aeneas, i.e., Virgil's Aeneas). Thus one might expect that Circe's offer, in order to be effective, is motivated by the figure of the addressee. This problem has been noticed by G.P. Goold who, however, adopts a very different interpretation.[11] In his view, Circe's argument is completely wrong, even counterproductive, and is meant to elicit irony for the reader. Odysseus is the quintessential hero who thirsts for dangers and novelties: peace and safety are unsuitable offers to a man who finds them boring. (Goold corrects *tota* to *tuta* in v. 284, following Bentley.)[12]

I find Goold's reasoning forced. He presupposes and takes for granted that Odysseus is only after adventure and dangers, a kind of romantic Odysseus. But Odysseus in Homer is not like this, and the end of all his wanderings will be peace and tranquillity (*Od.* 24.486), just like the peace Circe promises here. Ovid's Ulysses (a character whose frequent reappearance in the erotic works and the *Metamorphoses* has its own unique coherence) is never that idealized. At any rate, the matter in question here is wars, not adventures and travels. And where do we ever find a Ulysses as a character eager for war? Dousa, on the contrary, got it right. The notion that 'no one here is summoning the allies to wage war against Troy' is pertinent and meaningful, not because Odysseus is deaf to these kinds of promises, but for the opposite reason: because it is addressed to someone who went so far as to feign madness to avoid going when that famous levy came calling. (Ovid himself narrates the story in *Met.* 13.34ff.: *timidi commenta retexit / Naupliades* [Palamedes] *animi vitataque traxit ad arma.*)

The argument is designed ad hoc to appeal to the most famous draft-dodger in antiquity. Still Ulysses does not pay attention; while she is still talking, he casts off. And ironically – this is truly the irony of the present passage – he does well to refuse Circe's promises and leave.

We are perhaps over-personalizing the narrative situation, and the next step will be even worse. I will ask Ovid's text a rationalistic question, one of those questions which serious critics find ridiculous and pedantic. Some explanation is in order that will deal with a general feature of Ovidian poetics. We know that Ovid's imagination is, so to speak, intertextual and systematic. His devotion to deceptive illusions consists in taking too seriously fictional texts (both literary and mythical) and their explicit or merely potential interconnections. Ovid's gaze favours those spaces in

fictional texts that we might call liminal, those where he sees the possibility for a bridge of communication between different narratives. The
Metamorphoses is for us the most impressive document of this sensibility,
moving as it does from Callimachean 'modernity' to reach well beyond
Callimachus himself.

Any telling of a story is partial, made up of stories and diverse, autonomous parts thereof. The Muse at the beginning of the *Odyssey* is asked to
tell from somewhere (*hamothen*: v. 10) in the macro-text of Odysseus'
heroic adventures. At the beginning of the *Iliad*, the Muse will tell from
where (*ex hou*: v. 6) a partial story begins. This is how one narrates. But
the story has no end; it has many tentacles, branches, joints, interruptions
and incessant continuations. Ovid knows the whole treasure of ancient
fables. He knows the doors that conjoin them, allowing passage from one
to another. He chooses this or that path in the web of possible pathways,
but always aims at showing himself able to map out the great labyrinth of
adjoining rooms. He has mastered all the narratives and now knows how
to rewire and how to short-circuit them.

This game has its restrictive rules. The pleasure of reading consists in
the fact that Ovid does not appear to force the stories to fit. They are
perpetual by their own nature, even if their border zones, their points of
contact, do not strike the reader's eye. Transitions are thus unpredictable,
but never capricious and arbitrary. Each fictional text is taken for what it
is and each text has its own appropriate themes. These themes can be
woven together around analogies that overcome their differences in space
and time. Any narrative text offers itself already loaded with its own
peculiar space and time. If one takes these two categories at their word –
literally – (an intellectual gesture of which Ovid is master) areas of contact
can arise, marked by coincidences of time and space. These two strategies
act almost in opposite directions. On the one hand, analogy can create
large and sudden leaps in space and time, or even anachronisms.[13] On the
other hand, spatial and temporal continuity can mark the irreconcilability
of subject matters (or irreconcilabilities even more profound, for example
between the real and the imaginary, just as in that recent novel that stages
a meeting between Freud and Sherlock Holmes).

It is not by chance that Ovid is a great lover of literary chronologies. To
be sure, what interest him are the chronologies internal to literature, not
the erudite critical discourse surrounding the production of literary works.
It is rather because of the perversely synoptical nature of his intertextual
fantasy that Ovid loves most of all to be able to arrange precisely any
single mythical or literary event within a relative chronology and geo-
graphy. The narrative continuity of the *Metamorphoses* is therefore but the
final limit towards which Ovid pushes his rationalistic art of illusion. Not
having read Valéry's statement, 'a myth is that which dies from a little
added precision', Ovid requires each myth to take its place in relation to
the others and to declare its own coordinates of space and time. This does

not make of Ovid an Enlightenment polemicist. He does not hide his
doubts about the chronology for stories of Bacchus.[14] His is clearly not a
rationalistic critique of the anthropomorphic chronology, but only a sign of
a heightened sensibility that arises when one experiences and tests the
whole mythical tradition all at once.

There are texts that seem to be predestined to undergo these sorts of
combinatory tests. Two great epic texts of antiquity each narrate the deeds
of a hero who has survived the war at Troy. We know that the more recent
one, the *Aeneid*, is largely patterned on the first, the *Odyssey*; but this is
not what concerns us here. The point is rather that the *Aeneid* 'evades' the
Odyssey: it behaves as if it were autonomous. The reader is allowed to
glimpse the possibility that Aeneas and Odysseus might meet. In the
tradition that Virgil had before him, this encounter on Italian soil actually
happened, at least in one branch of the tradition.[15] But Virgil has arranged
everything in order to avoid this encounter. He has not fully exploited the
possible permutations provided by this spatial and temporal proximity.
(We can also elaborate on the reason why he chose not to do this, in the
same terms applied earlier to Ovid. Thematic analogy and spatio-temporal
continuity are, when taken together, two forces that exert too powerful an
attraction. The *Aeneid* is already too close to the *Odyssey* in its thematic
structure to sustain a spatio-temporal intersection. Virgil decided to avoid
the opening up of an endless reciprocal mirroring which would have
undermined his transformation of the Homeric model.) The more the plot
of Virgil's poem seems to take Aeneas to the threshold of the *Odyssey*, the
more his behaviour diverges from that of Odysseus. Virgil, who so often
has his hero openly resemble Odysseus, distinguishes him strongly from
the model wherever the place and time of their separate adventures attain
nearly perfect coincidence. Aeneas curses Ithaca, reversing the gestures
and words of Odysseus upon his homecoming.[16] He rescues from the
danger of the Cyclops not only his own companions, but a companion of
Odysseus as well. He steers clear of the Phaeacians, Scylla, the Sirens and
Circe. In the places where Aeneas could 'meet' Ulysses or 'repeat' Odysseus
(two occasions that Virgil perceives as similarly threatening to the autonomy of his narrative) Aeneas is providentially steered away.

When the *Aeneid* joined the ranks of great classical narratives, it raised
new questions for educated readers of epic. The relative chronologies of
myths and of narratives had long since occupied the minds of erudite
Greeks; Homer and the tragedians offered an ideal hunting ground for
synchronies and anachronisms. As a consequence, Roman commentators
took very seriously the question of whether, and to what degree, the
individual adventures of Aeneas and Odysseus might have been contem-
poraneous (cf. Serv. Dan. on *Aeneid* 3.590). The basis on which to begin a
synchronized reading of the two poems was clear: Homer tells us that
Odysseus wandered for a total of *ten* years, and Virgil repeatedly mentions

a *seven*-year period (though not in the clearest of ways, but that is another question).[17]

Pedantries, such as who first visited the cave of Polyphemus, do not amuse us today, but Ovid knew how to take advantage of them. In *Aeneid* 9, Virgil presents the curious story of transformation of the Trojan ships into sea nymphs (a story that many have considered one of his most 'Ovidian' productions). Naturally Virgil does not say what happened to these creatures afterwards. The metamorphosis is already for him a strong concession to the fantastic, and to describe the feelings of a character who is, in a certain sense, an ex-ship, and in turn an ex-tree, is an undertaking too improbable to interest him. But Ovid goes all the way. According to the *Metamophoses*, in which this metamorphosis is duly recorded, the Naiads remember their past as vessels, retaining pity for sailors and keeping them afloat during storms. They make an exception, however, for the Greeks since – inasmuch as they are ex-trees – the Naiads are still natives of Trojan Ida. It is on account of their patriotism that the nymphs witness with great satisfaction the shipwreck of Odysseus' raft (*Od.* 5.368ff.).[18] The assumption making this play possible is that some of Odysseus' wanderings logically ought to have occurred later than the shorter voyage of Aeneas. Homer's complicated internal chronology lends plausibility to the roving of the nymphs between book 9 of the *Aeneid* and book 5 of the *Odyssey*. Against all the appearances of the real chronology, the world of Virgil is contemporary and sometimes even prior to that narrated by Homer. For this to be the case, one need only take the texts, and the connections between them, at their word.

Hence it is possible that the scene between Odysseus and Circe in the *Remedia* allows one to make a rationalistic inference of this kind – in so far as one accepts the possibility of asking the text questions of where and when (after all, Ovid might have done so countless times, interrogating literary and mythological texts destined to flow together in the making of the *Metamorphoses*, the *Fasti*, and already in the *Heroides*). We are on the shores of Latium – where every literate person of this age, Greek and Roman, in particular Virgil, imagined Circe's home to be[19] – in an unspecified year of the heroic era. As far as dating goes, we can do better than this. Without a doubt, we are in a year *post Troiam captam*: Odysseus has been wandering for ten years after the fall of the city, and his adventure with Circe (as is clear from Homer) occurs at an advanced stage of his travels. Another hero, himself a veteran and survivor of the war at Troy, will reach the shores of Latium roughly seven years after the capture of the city. This hero will bring with him, and bring about, a new Troy. Circe might well insist:

> ... *non hic* nova Troia *resurgit*

while Aeneas, knowing better, is certain of the opposite:

> tendimus in Latium ...
> ... *illic* fas regna *resurgere* Troiae
> (*Aen.* 1.205ff.)[20]

But there is more. Our present passage clearly rules out not only a new
Troy, but a new Trojan War as well. This, as everyone knows, is the primary
theme of the second half of the *Aeneid*, in which the war in Latium is
repeatedly, and from shifting perspectives, presented as a replay of the
Trojan War. It is unnecessary here to recall relevant passages in the
Aeneid. It is quite easy to imagine how uncomfortable Odysseus, the Greek
most hated by the Trojans, would feel in this situation. Ancient Italy as a
whole – which, as Circe very aptly points out, has 'so far' been a peaceful
land – is about to be embroiled in a war: *ardet inexcita Ausonia et
immobilis ante* ... (*Aeneid* 7.623). Not only will the Italians be called to
arms, repeating the role of the Greek alliance against the new Troy; the
Greek heroes will be called back to arms as well – at least those who are
available on location in Italy. Diomedes, Odysseus' companion in many
adventures, will be recalled *ad arma*:

> muris *iterum* imminet hostis
> *nascentis Troiae* nec non *excercitus alter*
> atque *iterum* in Teucros Aetolis surgit ab Arpis
> Tydides ...
>
> (*Aen.* 10.26ff.)

In Virgil's repeated *iterum*, Ovid's *rursus* finds both its reason for being
and its oxymoronic complement,[21] just as Aeneas' confident *illic* undermines Circe's *non hic*. Similarly, the gesture of calling allies to arms takes
on new meaning when projected onto the future, and the empty, generic
periphrasis *non aliquis* provides the best possible setup for a sudden ironic
completion. From the same perspective it is also ironic that Circe guarantees Odysseus dominion over the 'entire' kingdom of undisturbed peace.[22]

Finally, it is odd that a goddess famous for her clairvoyance turns into
such an unreliable prophetess. (Is it for sheer interest? Or is it rather
because – which would be a very Ovidian move – she is so in love as to be
blinded?) Circe's words, borne off by the winds (*inrita cum ventis verba
tulere Noti*),[23] turn out to be empty promises, contradicted by a future
already given over to the great national epic – a future, in sum, already
written.

3. Ariadne and her future: *Heroides* 10.81-98

If there is a distinctive mode of Ovidian allusion, it is that it is organized,
so to speak, in retrospect. By this I mean those well-known cases where an
Ovidian character recalls and repeats another past self, and quotes an
outside text as part of his or her own subjective memory. Ariadne, in *Fasti*

3.469ff., complains of Bacchus' infidelity. Since she sees in it a replay of Theseus' infidelity, it is perfectly fitting for Ariadne to quote literally her former reproach to Theseus, i.e. the very same words 'she herself' uttered in Catullus 64. As G.B. Conte wrote, 'Ariadne, Ovid's character, has "lived" her experience as a poetic persona in Catullus' epyllion, and remembers the tears she cried then: the tears and laments of Catullus' Ariadne. *Memini* is the marker of remembrance, of the difference between the present moment and the distant past.'[24] One could say that the replay has the effect upon the reader of a momentary wavering of perception. The repetition of an identical situation has something frustrating about it, as though the deepest and most persistent ideological assumption about literature has fallen into crisis, the assumption that literature is the crystallization into memorable forms of unique and unrepeatable moments. But the crisis that arises is resolved at once in the literal quotation, which, paradoxically, reaffirms the uniqueness of literary utterances.

In cases like these, the ironic flash triggered by the literary operation is fostered by memory, which is the only ground shared by the author, the audience, and the character to whom the text entrusts the role of remembering and the responsibility for the retrospective quotation. For this reason, clearly, the most effective and celebrated examples of this technique concern texts taken up again and cited as *past* presuppositions of the present narrative situation. But what would happen if, on the contrary, the text alluded to is eerily projected into the *future*? This type of situation, at first sight, presents greater difficulties. If the responsibility of foretelling were delegated to the narrator, the intertextual play is deprived of the implicit irony so typical of Ovid. A foretelling offered from the 'outside', in the narrator's voice, would destroy the delicate balance between reality and literary fiction. If one wants, finally, to make the character responsible for the 'foretelling allusion', one runs into problems of verisimilitude. The character must be presented and accepted as prophetic, or at least as endowed with extremely clear sight, a fact that in turn risks undermining any irony. Indeed, one could imagine a character who might foretell by chance, haphazardly and indirectly, something that he or she could not reasonably know. But in this case the allusion becomes delicate and very difficult to handle (cf. examples cited above in n. 13).

For these and other reasons, the most appealing intertextual prefigurements are those which are *wrong*, just as Circe's foresight that 'the war at Troy will not be repeated' is wrong. Ovid had a free hand in achieving these kinds of effects in composing the *Heroides*. Each letter is meant to occur at a precise temporal intersection, a 'pregnant moment' taking its place in a narrative continuum, a continuum guaranteed by the recall of known models, of literary and (more generally) mythological texts. For obvious reasons of dramatic economy, the letters are much more interesting if they are allowed to play not only with the past but also with a still undecided future. If Medea were to write to Jason after having killed their sons, the letter would lack any dramatic tension. For a similar reason, Ovid does not appreciate his heroines having too much information about the future. A letter by Cassandra (as the case of Lycophron shows) might turn out rather monotonous. Of Ovid's heroines, at least one, Oenone, is singled out in the tradition as a prophetic character. But Ovid's Oenone has very confused ideas, and when she writes to her beloved she is not capable of clairvoyance. In sum, Ovid has designed his epistles so that they might have a wide intertextual *limen* opened toward the future. In this matter chronology can be of further assistance. We have already seen how important the internal chronology of the *Iliad* and the *Odyssey* is to the epistles of Briseis and Penelope (cf. above, n. 6). But it is not necessary for the frame to be provided by a literary text. It is natural to think that less formalized texts – the more generic plots, or 'scripts', of mythology – might also function in a similar manner. What will change in this case are the specific techniques of poetic allusion.

But let us come back to Ariadne. It is not hard to imagine that the Ariadne of the *Heroides*, writing to Theseus 'live' from the barren wastes of Naxos' shores, is deeply imbued with her Catullan antecedent, just as the Ariadne of the *Fasti* was. Obviously there are no longer any temporal discrepancies between the time-frames, and Ovid is careful to achieve a perfect alignment with the situation of his model. Catullus' Ariadne foresees, in a pseudo-Homeric style, being abandoned and left as prey to birds and beasts:

> dilaceranda feris dabor alitibusque
> praeda ...
>
> (64.152ff.)

Ovid disassembles the traditional model into a series of well-distinguished dangers, 'a collage of picturesque death sequences ... a collage which has no precedent in extant Latin or Greek literature'.[25] *Destituor rapidis praeda cibusque feris* (v. 96)[26] functions both as the matrix for the entire amplification, and as an allusive signpost, because it reiterates the epic-tragic tone of its model.

As for the rest, her letter has appeared to many as merely hypertrophic and poorly connected amplification:

> nunc ego non tantum quae sum passura recordor,
>   sed quaecumque potest ulla relicta pati.   80
> Occurrunt animo pereundi mille figurae,
>   morsque minus poenae quam mora mortis habet.
> Iam iam venturos aut hac aut suspicor illac,
>   qui lanient avido viscera dente, lupos;
> forsitan et fulvos tellus alat ista leones?   85
>   Quis scit an haec saevas tigridas insula habet?
> Et freta dicuntur magnas expellere phocas;
>   quis vetat et gladios per latus ire meum?

Tantum ne religer dura captiva catena
   neve traham serva grandia pensa manu,   90
cui pater est Minos, cui mater filia Phoebi,
   quodque magis memini, quae tibi pacta fui.
Si mare, si terras porrectaque litora vidi,
   multa mihi terrae, multa minantur aquae.
Caelum restabat: timeo simulacra deorum;   95
   destituor rapidis praeda cibusque feris.
Sive colunt habitantque viri, diffidimus illis;
   externos didici laesa timere viros.

                      (10.79-98)

This passage has heaped upon itself so many and such great suspicions that the most direct remedy offered recently (after many more conservative attempts, such as the deletion of the 'bestiary' of vv. 83-8) has been mass deletion of vv. 86-95. Thus, M.D. Reeve has proposed a lacuna of indefinite length.[27] Reeve's intervention in the text also has the merit of condensing and listing all the difficult points that crowd around these few lines. In pointing them out I will follow him closely.

(a) v. 86 is corrupt, and none of the proposed emendations are able to solve all the difficulties; (b) whose swords are mentioned in v. 88? (c) how does the fear of being a slave fit the context? (d) what are the *simulacra deorum*? (e) how can v. 95 be reconciled with the context? (f) v. 97 offers a use of *sive* without a correlative; (g) v. 97 also contains two verbs lacking objects.

In my view, some of these points admit of individual answers, while others – in particular (d) and (e) – require more extensive treatment, and must be linked to a general argument that I would like to develop. Thus I can propose the following provisional answers: (a) I agree that v. 86, if genuine at all, is certainly corrupt;[28] but I would not agree with excessive conflation of individual corruptions and problems of authenticity. In general, tying together different kinds of problems is dangerous. In a highly notorious transmission such as that of the *Heroides*, a single crux in a fifteen-line passage does not constitute a stumbling block, and moreover, should not be treated in the same manner as other sorts of difficulties with which I will deal shortly. (b) Who is brandishing the swords? Reeve cunningly suggests swordfish. But who, one might respond, is brandishing the swords that Ovid fears so greatly in *Tr.* 1.1.43-4: *ego perditus ensem / haesurum iugulo iam puto iamque meo*? In the end, unnamed dangers always grip the heart a little tighter. After all, if one follows the deeper train of thought in Ariadne's anxious logic, v. 60, *non hominum video, non ego facta boum*, was already a warning sign; cautious Odysseus had made the same observation (*Od.* 10.98: *entha men oute boôn out' andrôn phaineto erga*) right before running into the Laestrygonians. (c) The motif conveys first of all Ariadne's pride in being a *virgo regia* (cf. Catullus 64.86-7) not without a cunning, last-minute change of course (*quodque magis memini* ...). In the *Heroides,* Ovid pays scrupulous attention to the varying social statuses of his heroines, as with Briseis in 3.75ff. But above all, there is a variation on the theme of Catullus 64.160ff., where Ariadne says that, had she been allowed to stay with Theseus, she would have agreed to be his slave and to carry out the most lowly of tasks.[29] (f) This usage is rare but attested in Ovid (as Reeve himself acknowledges). It is typical of poetic language (cf. Kühner-Stegmann II, 437ff.); it is coherent with the broken and monodic style of the whole speech; in particular, it is prompted by the contextual opposition between *viri* and *feris* in the preceding line.[30] (g) The island is so prevalent in all Ariadne's anxieties that the ellipsis after v. 85 does not seem intolerable, even if it is objectively harsh when compared, e.g., with *Aen.* 1.530ff. (= 3.163-6) *Est locus* ... / *Oenotri coluere viri.* The suspicion of a lacuna is difficult to dispel, but it is not the same as suspecting a long interpolation.

All this said, the fundamental motive behind the scandal these lines provoke is rather their overall and blatant pointlessness. The list of dangers is random and vexing – which perhaps could be forgiven, since the monologues of heroines in distress often contain this operatic stylization. Horace's Europa also fantasizes about many ways of dying (*Carm.* 3.27.50-66). But how can one accept Ariadne saying, 'I know, off the top of my head, not only what will happen to me, but also what might happen to any abandoned maiden', thus exposing a background of systematic rationalism that is the generating mechanism for this entire chaotic enumeration. This truly seems a *reductio ad absurdum* of the traditional motif, since Ariadne (clearly aware of the Catullan model) finds herself to be part of the paradigm of the abandoned woman (*ulla* ... *relicta*), which is then articulated in a series of particular instances. But indeed the *reductio ad absurdum* of traditional topoi is a procedure unsurprising in Ovid. An expert in declamatory techniques, correctly noting the importance of this line, has argued that Ovid is here admitting, in a naïve way, his debt to rhetorical ethopoiea: it is the figure of *tinas an eipoi logous ho deina* that shines through in Ariadne's words. Catalogues of dangers, evoked to illustrate a certain situation, are also typical of *suasoriae.* But Bonner speaks of 'naïve admission',[31] and the charge of naivety does not seem to fit a poet like Ovid. One could say, rather, that the initial utterance ironically undermines the entire parade of dangers, revealing their substance to be illusory, and resulting from a calculated projection too systematic for us to be satisfied by a mere *ostentant omnia letum* (Cat. 64.186). *Occurrunt animo pereundi mille figurae* clearly calls for a long list of *schemata.* We ought not to trust then attempts to cut down the list by taking out some of the most outrageous deaths. But one detail continues to be disturbing. With a sort of systematic compulsion, Ariadne adds to the threats of land and sea those of the *sky: caelum restabat: timeo simulacra deorum.* This verse poses serious problems. Attempts have been made to get around them by referring to *Met.* 8.185ff.: *'terras licet'* inquit *'et undas*

/ *obstruat, at caelum certe patet'*; but this sentence is spoken by Daedalus when persecuted by Minos. He, unlike Ariadne, has concrete plans to be first in flight.[32] If Ariadne really intended to fly away, she should have said it more clearly, as Ovid himself does at *Tr.* 3.8.1ff. (Triptolemos, Daedalus, Medea). I prefer to draw attention to two other places in Ovid containing the same figure of invective curse. At *Met.* 8.97, Minos – who is on the worst of terms with Ariadne as well – inveighs against Scylla: *tellus tibi pontusque negetur.* A little later, Scylla is turned into a bird. At *Her.* 6.161, Hypsipyle wishes upon Medea that she might have no place in the world, so much so that she will be forced to 'take to the pathways of the sky' after exhausting those of land and sea. The hyperbolic curse is humorous to those who recall that Medea's future holds in store for her the winged chariot of Helios. In both cases, the exhaustive series land / sea / sky is used to set up an ironic expectation for the reader, a space that is easily filled for those who know the fantastic outcome of the story. If one looks at the structure of the myths, both Scylla and Medea seem to be fitting fellow travellers for Ariadne. The tercet thus formed is of women who commit treachery for the love of foreigners.

It is clear, if we want to stop at the literal level of the expression, that Ariadne has no great expectations from the sky either. It is not hard to imagine why, since she has betrayed her homeland and helped to kill one of her relatives, as unpleasant as he may have been: she would thus have good reason to fear divine vengeance (cf. vv. 67ff.). But from whatever point of view we look at it, *simulacra deorum* remains an enigmatic reference. Of course *simulacra* may be the most frightful apparitions: phantasms, ghosts, shades of the dead. But it is not a term commonly used to designate 'divine apparitions', however one wants to conceive of them. On the contrary, when associated with *deorum* and similar terms, it usually refers to 'statues of the gods' (e.g. cf. *Met.* 10.964). Perhaps Ariadne does not know exactly what she is afraid of. With regards to the sky, *simulacrum* has another common technical sense: it is one of the Latin terms for the constellations (cf. e.g. *Met.* 2.194, [Phaethon] *vastarumque videt trepidus simulacra ferarum*; fr. 1.4 s. Mor. *tot numero talique deus simulacra figura / imposuit caelo*; and for the genitive *deorum* in a reference to the constellations, cf. esp. *Met.* 1.73, *astra tenent caeleste solum formaeque deorum*). We will soon come back to this not too logical connection.

Let us return for the last time to the question of the future. Unlike many other heroines in the *Heroides*, Ariadne seems completely cut off from her future. In her situation of total *amêchaniê*, Ariadne can do nothing more than guess. Other heroines, though desperate or coerced into inaction, are at least somehow able to discern the outline of their future fate. They are faced with a choice of possible alternatives, or a situation toward which the epistle can orient itself, actively proposing some solution (depending on whether in the individual poem the deliberative tone prevails over the suasorial). As a consequence of her total lack of escape, Ariadne's words do not constitute a true letter, but a monologue. Aiming her speech at Theseus is here, more than anywhere else in Ovid's work, purely phatic, and the epistolary disguise is profoundly unrealistic.[33] The darkness enveloping her future corresponds to the particular literary model that Ovid has in mind. Usually the *Heroides* are presented as 'incisions' into continuous models, 'cuts' into their narrative bodies. Homer and Virgil, the tragedians and Hellenistic poets, offer some master plots that Ovid freezes, so to speak, at a precise instant. But *Heroides* 10 is an exception. It has a model that is, already on its own, 'cut' according to the poetics of the *Heroides*. The horizon of the letter coincides precisely with the one projected in Catullus 64.

But, as everyone knows, Ariadne still has a future. The end of the adventure on Naxos is illustrated by the myth and confirmed by a wide-spread iconographic tradition.[34] Catullus, who is reshaping an object of art in narrative terms, makes recourse to this information: and indeed he mentions, as an epilogue to Ariadne's lament, the imminent epiphany of Bacchus (64.251ff.: *at parte ex alia florens volitabat ...*). Ovid, who operates through a true and proper dramatic monologue and accepts its constraints of perspective, cannot – nor does he want to – do the same. Everything must be conveyed in the voice and through the consciousness of the abandoned Ariadne. It is here that the perversely exhaustive inventory of the *pereundi mille figurae* is grafted (once again, we can appreciate the strategic importance of this formula). Such a lengthy montage of images is useful for concealing something that Ariadne cannot reasonably foresee, but that the reader will respond to with an inward *credo quia absurdum*. Wolves, lions, and even creatures of the sea,[35] are fauna one would expect to encounter on the shores of an unknown and savage land. But what characters of Greek myth have ever even thought of being threatened by *tigers*? Perhaps only Horace's delirious Europa (*Carm.* 3.27.56).

Tigers, exotic animals, were first seen in the flesh around 11 BCE (Pliny *NH* 8.65). Before the games of the circus became a literary topos, Roman poets mention tigers only in a specific mythological context, the same in which their Greek predecessors mention panthers instead: the retinue of the god Bacchus.[36] Some of the strangest of Ariadne's fears will soon turn out to be true, but they will appear with their valence reversed, in light of an incredible rescue:

> iam deus in curru, quem summum texerat uvis,
>   tigribus adiunctis aurea lora dabat.
> Et color et Theseus et vox abiere puellae
>   terque fugam petiit terque retenta metu est.
>
> 'Pone metum. Bacchi, Gnosias, uxor eris!
> munus habe caelum; caelo spectabere sidus ...
> Dixit et e curru, ne tigres illa timeret,
>   desilit ...
>
> (*Ars* 1.547ff.)

'*Quid mihi fiet?*'[37] was the simple question Ariadne asked in the *Ars* (vv. 534ff.); '*Heaven will be your new home*', her saviour responds.[38] A heavenly being will come on his chariot drawn by tigers and the terrifying chariot will bear Ariadne to the heavens and the eternal honour of a constellation.[39] Instead of being a *captiva* and *serva* (cf. vv. 91-2, a couplet that seems to have escaped suspicion), she will become the goddess the Romans invoke by the name of *Libera*.

4. Ovid's intertextual imagination: some provisional observations

Ariadne and Briseis, who probe their futures on the margins of an outside text, and the unrealistic moment at which Odysseus might 'step into' the *Aeneid* – these are topics that have detained us for too long. If we have dealt with them longer than necessary for contributions to textual criticism, this is because there is some method in Ovid's passion for the contacts between texts. The contacts between *alien* texts are involved in this passion – such as the *Odyssey* and the *Aeneid*, which in the whole compass of Ovid's works frequently come together only to separate again – and also the contacts between Ovid's texts and those of other authors. In the latter case, as with Briseis and Ariadne, the poet not only insists on implicating the voice of his models (this would be mere 'Alexandrianism'), but also highlights the junctures between what is his own and what belongs to others. Retrieving the designs of these intertextual thresholds is made easier by plotting the coordinates that draw the texts closer to one another, be they spatial and temporal, or analogical.

The telling of many different stories entails one constant feature in Ovid's experience as a narrator. The movement of his narrative from time to time touches upon and meets the texts of many other poets, each one a partial realization of a story (the focus here, in fact, is on stories, not on the words of the poets). Ovid often behaves as if there were a universal repository in which every narrative already textualized is stored – a place through which every new story must constantly pass. He is drawing closer to the risky enterprise of producing a text that can stage the whole continuum of stories already told, or rather, that will stage one among the many possible uninterrupted tracks, not, of course, an inconceivable *aleph* of narrativity. This will be a massive *carmen perpetuum* from the beginning of time until the present, from myths of origin to contemporary reality. Every story, in becoming a narrated text, by imposing a beginning and an end, cuts across and into the continuum of narratable story. But where a text leaves off, one can imagine the story continuing as the origin of another text. The natural continuity of narratives challenged Ovid to produce a text that could transform every ending into a point of transition. A text such as the *Heroides*, which emphasizes in its poetics the arbitrary nature of beginnings and endings, comes very close to evoking the 'continuous' poetics of the *Metamorphoses*. But while the poetics of the *Metamorphoses* are a symptom too conspicuous to be analysed here, there are still some collateral observations that deserve to be made.

The idea of poetry as a road or a path trodden by the poet is a familiar one. But there is something uncannily literal in the idea that roads and pathways may connect *one text to another*. Ovid is the poet who stands out for his use of this image: *ecquis ad haec* [the *Fasti*, in which this line is inserted] *illinc* [from his past poetry of erotic elegy] *crederet esse viam?* (*Fast.* 2.8). But if one thinks of poetry not only as a road or pathway but also, more literally, as a passage from text to text, new possibilities open up. Then there arises, insidiously, the idea of a pathway heading backwards, from the text that is 'now' being made and read, to texts already written and known. Ovid often plays with this type of imagery in the *Tristia*.

Moreover, Ovid is perhaps the most daring of ancient poets in personifying texts and animating books.[40] We know that a book of poetry can be described in great physical detail, and that each detail can resonate on the level of a poetic programme (Catullus 1). At other times, a book can become a person, appropriating feelings and human mutability. One can also attempt to make delicate and subtle compromises between these two strategies (Horace in *Ep.* 1.20). The book, in sum, can become either the icon of a poetic programme, or a personified messenger. It all depends on whether one insists on a naturalistic register or an allegorical image. But can one have it both ways? Ovid in the first book of the *Tristia* seems to think so. The book of *Tristia* is sad, shabby, unrefined, lacking polish. As a messenger it is maimed, the protagonist in a fearful and uncertain repatriation. The two metaphorical levels are simply juxtaposed, and the reader is not spared a doubly destabilizing effect.

Another innovation is of greater interest here. A classical simplicity establishes that a book should open and speak as a text to its readers, revealing something directly about its author (Hor. *Ep.* 1.20.20ff.) – in a nutshell, a model of literary communication. But a book by Ovid, as a text, has among its duties that of communicating *with other texts*. *Tristia* 1.1 has received precise instructions on this point (vv. 105ff.). When it will have arrived in its humble home, the bookcase of Ovid's works, the book will have to deal with his senior colleagues.[41] It will have to avoid any contact with the books of the *Ars*, unfortunate and involuntary parricides (Ovid recalls Oedipus and Telegonus) which have undone their author. 'Flee them', the poet tells the book of the *Tristia*. He has indeed avoided in his new work any mingling with the genre of happy erotic elegy. More surprisingly is the contact between the new arrival and the fifteen rolls of the *Metamorphoses*: there is a message for them (v. 119ff. *his mando dicas*: *inter mutata referri / fortunae vultum corpora posse meae*). Here we have a new transformation for the book of *Metamorphoses*, with *mutata ... corpora*, along with *mutatae ...formae*, assuring us of the juxtaposition of the works. If one regards the books as texts, we are dealing with a true addition. Given Ovid's chronological programme (*ad mea perpetuum deducite tempora carmen*) we know also where this new branch is to be grafted: it can stand only at the end, there where the poet, having arrived at the *tempus* in which the work was written, foretold for his name irresistible success. From the point of view of the poet of the *Tristia*, the *Metamorphoses* and its transformations are not over yet. A new, depressing and saddening epilogue will be their necessary continuation, as if the very text of the *Tristia* should reread, in its own key, the other text already completed.

New texts reread their predecessors. This extraordinary image, of volumes conversing while locked in their cabinet, gives us perhaps the extreme example of Ovid's intertextual imagination. But the 'tristifying' of the *Metamorphoses* is taken further in elegy 1.7. Here Ovid recounts how, before leaving, he burned a copy of his poem. But the work, or so it seems, survives and circulates, reaffirming the seal that wants to be imperishable and resistant to fire (*Met.* 15.871: *...nec ignis ...*). Thus there is need for a new testimony, one which the text of the *Tristia* delivers so as to have it inscribed on the front of the *Metamorphoses*:

> hos quoque sex versus, in prima fronte libelli
>   si praeponendos esse putabis, habe:
> 'orba parente suo quicumque volumina tangis,
>   his saltem vestra detur in Urbe locus.
> quoque magis faveas, non haec sunt edita ab ipso,
>   sed quasi de domini funere rapta sui.
> quicquid in his igitur vitii rude carmen habebit,
>   emendaturus, si licuisset erat'.

(1.7.33-8)

The idea of a new epilogue is followed by a concrete proposal of a new protasis: six lines that, already in their elegiac meter (at this point conceived by Ovid as a melancholy limping), will denounce the sad change. (Ironically, by adding these lines to the old proem, the *Metamorphoses* will finally have a protasis of acceptable length: ten lines, like the *Odyssey*, instead of only four.) This new implant produces the strongest of antibodies. It is the same work which proudly foresaw itself being read in every land reached by the name of Rome (15.871), that now humbly asks to find hospitality in Rome, at least for itself, following a centripetal path reversing the one just traced. The *perpetuum carmen* that enclosed in its perfect circle every story from primeval chaos to the present is now a *rude carmen*: just as the heap of chaos from which Ovid began to weave his order had been *rudis* (*Met.* 1.7), and like the earth which in the beginning was amorphous, *rudis et sine imagine* (*Met.* 1.87).[42] Above all, the promise of immortality in the epilogue – *vivam* – is now inscribed in a funereal reality; the voice of the orphaned *Metamorphoses* reaches us *de domini funere*. Thus, in a few exquisite strokes, the *Metamorphoses* have now been rewritten. The text of the *Tristia* does not only speak about itself; it must also, as it were, reform its predecessor.

The complex relationships between the *Tristia* and preceding Ovidian poetry deserve more than cursory treatment. All this is of interest here only indirectly, as the mark of a poetics that remains, surprisingly, internal to the imaginary systems Ovid had already created for himself. Now, at the moment when an incurable fracture tears through the life of the poet, narrative continuity and continuation of texts surface more explicitly than ever. The depressing annexation of the *Metamorphoses* by the *Tristia* presupposes, it is now clear, an intense sensibility for those dead zones created by the contacts between texts. When carefully combined, texts classically closed and delimited, apparently impermeable, can open themselves up to new avenues of meaning. It is evident that this sensibility plays a role in the poetics of the *Metamorphoses*, the *Fasti* and the *Heroides*, where stories that have already been told are retold in surprising combinations, or where the consciousness of a previous textuality adds new connotations to the individual scene. There is no reason why Ovid should stop this web of connections at the threshold of his own works, now that he has written so much that he can find in them a copious universe of texts waiting to be explored and mapped out. Now begins for him the most depressing of intertextual journeys, the backward path of retracing his own writing in light of his present misery, and seeing the sadness of the outcome as the last metamorphosis to be narrated.

2

Narrativity and Convention
in the *Heroides*

I

In the *Heroides* Ovid imposes upon himself an apparent law of composition: that each individual epistle be autonomous. This law of autonomy consists in the fact that each epistle must provide by itself all the necessary information (along with all the implicit signals that it can supply; more on this below). Above all, the epistles are shaped in such a way as not to call for any response or supplement. Also on account of this, it is no accident that the first piece in the collection is Penelope's epistle.[1]

Penelope writes a letter, but states explicitly that she does not want a reply from Odysseus (*nil mihi rescribas tu tamen ...*). She wants her husband home right away (*... ipse veni*), and in closing her letter adds sorrowfully 'even if you come back right away, I will look like an old woman' (1.116). Right away? Of course the letter does not expect to elicit either a response or a positive outcome. And for an eminently practical reason: it is sent to an unknown address. Penelope intends to entrust it to some foreigner passing through Ithaca, in the hope that he might by chance contact Odysseus. It is almost a message in a bottle. But there is a second reason. The letter will never be answered, for at the very moment of writing *Odysseus is already in Ithaca*.[2] Ovid's epistle fits perfectly into the plot of the *Odyssey*, a universally known text the entire factual framework of which Ovid intends to respect. Penelope had many years to think about writing letters and indeed, as Ovid takes care to inform us in vv. 59-62, she has written many, entrusting them to sailors passing through. But *this* letter is not placed at a random point in her monotonously prolonged wait. The letter is clearly 'dated' on the day Telemachus returned from Sparta and reported to his mother some uncertain news about his father.[3] In Lessing's terms, this is a truly pregnant moment in the plot. On that day – how could one forget Homer – the house of Penelope is hosting a foreign traveller, a Cretan who claims to know many things; for Ovid's Penelope, he could be a perfect courier. But readers of Homer know who the Cretan really is, and also that after one night – cf. Penelope's *protinus*! – he will reveal his true identity to everyone. Just one more night and Penelope's long wait will be over.

Thus the first epistle of the book presents the reader with the delicate rules of a new literary game. The texts that follow must be taken as letters in a proper sense – written on a specific occasion, with a specific addressee and a specific goal. But they are strange letters nonetheless, because the reader does not expect them to have any consequence whatsoever. The third epistle is written by Briseis to Achilles. She is in the hands of Agamemnon, and the embassy to Achilles (*Iliad* 9) has failed. 'Tomorrow', Briseis has heard (*fama est* 3.57), Achilles will set sail right away ('To morrow we the fav'ring Gods implore, / Then shall you see our parting Vessels crown'd, / And hear with Oars the Hellespont resound', in the remarkable rendering by Pope). It seems to be the case that Briseis is writing at night, the crucial night between the embassy and the day of battle around the ships. At the beginning of her letter, she mentions the dangers of wandering off during the night, and we cannot object to her worries, for during the night Homer stages a dangerous exchange of espionage and night-raids. This is the only available moment, the only empty narrative space into which Briseis' epistle might be inserted. The embassy failed, and Briseis is recasting its themes in a new voice. But the next day, as Homer reassures us, will bring the resolution that Briseis seeks. In an extremely long day of battle (which leaves our school editions of the poem in a predicament, forced as they are to entitle Book 11 'the morning of the twenty-sixth day' from the beginning of the poem, and Book 18 as 'the last hours of the twenty-sixth day') Patroclus will fall, Hector will obtain the arms of Achilles, his wrath will cease, and Briseis will be allowed to return to the tent of her beloved. The conclusion will not be lacking in some bitter irony, because she will gain what she sought, but she will also lose her only friend, the gentle man who also tried to console her (cf. *Il.* 19.287ff.; *Ep.* 3.23ff.). The timeframe of the letter is but the most delicate of incisions into the sequence of the *Iliad*'s plot. Obviously the stories, whose continuities Ovid knows so well, also have discontinuities, interstices into which he may graft his texts (see Chapter 1 above).

The reader must make these incisions into a given framework that cannot be modified, such that the existence of the epistle will not have any effect upon it. Indeed this narrative context is decided elsewhere, in those literary texts (or more generically in mythologems) upon which Ovid has chosen to operate. In other words, the narrative autonomy of the letter is curiously interwoven with its pragmatic impotence, and the impotence implied by the context moves every letter into the realm of illusion. The lover is dead, gone, in love with someone else, he has left and will not return, or, if he does – in a more subtly ironic variant – it will be for some other reason, some chain of causation over which the letter has no control. The reader's narrative competence puts him or her in a state of ironic superiority compared to the limited field of vision of the first-person narrator.[4] The *Heroides* are not a mere intertextual byproduct, as is the case with so much of ancient poetry; they are also (if one accepts an almost playful definition that aims at capturing the ludic character of Ovid's *modus operandi*) real inter-texts, interstitial formations intersecting the bodies of other texts. The poet does not behave like someone who wants to fulfil his model. Such literary operations in general presuppose that one perceive within the models an empty space to be filled (whether before the fact, after, or within the very body of the story), or at least that the plot may be supplemented in one of its interrupted branches. Silius Italicus 8.50ff., for example, fills us in on what happened to Anna, Dido's loving sister, after we last saw her by the pyre in *Aeneid* 4. With Ovid it is not even the case that the narrator conceives a completely alternative plot to the traditional story line, using the latter as a 'possible world' into which new potential developments can be grafted (sometimes even with demystifying or at least ideological ends: 'if only you had spoken, Desdemona'[5]). The poetics of the *Heroides* suggest, more simply, that new windows can be opened on stories already completed. Ovid's narrative prowess is evident in the respect he shows for the traditional script. Each epistle is written in the 'blank space' of a narration already fully and densely composed, sometimes also dramatically fast-paced and action-packed. The spectacular ability of the poet has something surgical about it. It selects the most favourable point, cuts into it, then closes it back up without leaving a trace. Much is achieved by playing on the distance between the single witness, the author of the letter, on the one hand, and the wider points of view traditionally associated with a particular plot on the other. By manipulating the gap between the two, one can induce ironic side-effects in the reader's consciousness, which can, for instance, target the limitations of the witness, or even ironically undermine the values connected with the tradition, or do both at the same time. By combining these ingredients with less care, it is not difficult to arrive at a Gospel according to Judas, or a Hamlet seen from the perspective of poor old Rosencrantz and Guildenstern.

The effectiveness of this shift is guaranteed in Ovid by a fundamental narrative choice: the character who for the reader is a *witness*, when measured against his or her own intentions, is instead a *pleader*. The subjectivity of the point of view is ensured each time by the pragmatic end of the text. Even in this respect, the similarity so often invoked between the *Heroides* and dramatic monologues shows itself to be weak, episodic, and insubstantial.

II

To conquer, reconquer, or prolong love – worked into the most diverse texts and myths, the *Heroides* have these three intentions in common. This is what renders them so like one another, and so similar to a genre already consolidated before this new Ovidian *opus*: I mean, of course, Roman elegy.[6]

We know that elegy is the genre of monologue *par excellence*.[7] It is not only a question of thematic constraint – the unifying theme, as in the *Heroides*, is love – but rather of the constant effect of an individual voice drawing into itself any and every theme. Elegy could also deal with, as indeed it does, mythology, ethics, landscape, legislation, foreign policy, or trips to the seaside. What distinguishes it is its peremptory reduction of every external matter to its central focus, the persona of the poet-lover and his all-consuming purpose: the conquest and defence of love. The identifying feature of elegy is precisely this monologic reduction; as a rule, elegy has room for one voice only.

Elegy's contribution to the *Heroides* cannot be reduced (as some still do) to long lists of influences and interferences (following dull recipes of *Kreuzung der Gattungen*); in this sense even the current definition of 'lyric monologues' harbours some element of confusion. Elegy's contribution is qualitatively different from the influence of other genres, because it is not limited to subject matter and narrative techniques, nor merely to the presence of a unifying theme, love, but rather because of a unifying perspective. Elegy teaches the heroines how to 'reduce' every external reality, bringing it back to the *persona* of the lover. It teaches how to fuel a poetic discourse through resistance, the irreducibility of a personal point of view in the face of 'external' reality, while the partiality of the point of view and the pragmatic aim (the intent of the *Werbung*, or the elegiac courting ritual) reinforce one another. Ovid's choice of the love epistle ought therefore to be seen in light of this, a choice that gives the subjectivity of elegy 'institutional' form.

III

The field of study called poetics by some, narratology by others, has familiarized us with the concept that the choice of first-person narrative is a significant one, endowed with very subtle implications and variations. Without going into too much detail, I believe that the majority of scholars interested in narrative might agree on one conspicuous feature: it is typical of first-person narrative to stress the process of *subjective* reproduction of the events narrated. This narrative mode elicits from the reader a deeper participation in the 'making' of the narrative, while the hiatus between the time of the narrative and the time of its narration becomes increasingly sharp and perceptible. This readily leaves room, nonetheless, for a rich spectrum of effects ranging, for instance, from the naïve identification associated with memoir, to the complex effects of detachment and irony, stronger even and more radical than those which a heterodiegetic account is able to produce.

It is time now to consider the interaction between this homodiegetic, monologic form, and its intertextual quality noted before. It is here that a notable difference arises between elegy and 'heroid'. There is no doubt that a single elegy can project its own narrative context, by laying down the tracks for a temporal development, by taking its place in a plot already known in part, and by playing on the recurrence, throughout the book, of an 'elegiac' persona which becomes more and more defined with each successive framing. It is uncommon, however, for a text to subsume as its context a narrative sequence already known and 'quotable'. We know that in elegy the identity and the character of the speaker have great importance in shaping the meaning of the text. In occasional examples (as in the so-called *Rollengedichte*) this information can become not only supplementary but also decisive, and produce a transvaluation of the content (in some cases, even an ironic rereading of the whole). But in the *Heroides*, the whole complex of information that defines the character is, as a rule, fundamental for interpretation, even when one deals with information merely assumed and tendentiously unspoken. An epistle like Hypsipyle's, for instance, is rather dull for readers with insufficient knowledge of the myth to project a narrative frame. She wants to warn Jason by means of a tendentious reading of the story of Medea, who is seen as a barbaric and cruel witch who rejoices in shedding the blood of her kin. Hypsipyle's reading doubtless intends to sound jealous and partisan, all the more so if one recalls Apollonius Rhodius' portrayal of the young and anxious Medea. But Apollonius himself reminds us (as does in general the current mythological lore, the basic 'encyclopaedia' of myth that controls the reader's competence) that Hypsipyle, while she accuses Medea of fratricide and other plots, is famous for having conspired and led a frightful mass uxoricide. As a whole, the epistle sounds like an elegiac text (dominated by subjectivity, the presence of courting, lament and jealousy) in which the narrative context and paratextual information (identity and biography of the speaker) assume an overwhelming importance.

In the *Heroides*, Ovid has turned the monologic constraint typical of Roman elegy – restrictions of voice, thematic spheres, and ideology – into a *narrative* convention. His epistles make 'elegiac' incisions into the narrative bodies of epic, tragedy and myth. The monologic reduction of this material is but the farthest outpost of elegiac imperialism. The gap between the time of narration and the narrative time guarantees the margin for irony and reflexivity.

The other side of Ovid's enterprise is that, by proposing fifteen different elegiac subjectivities, he is able in the end to attain an objective, external gaze upon elegiac love. This cultural construction has its own natural retinue of feelings – passion, jealousy, spite, uncertainty, anxiety – and its own arsenal of tactics – threats, enticements, blackmail, self-humiliation, self-exaltation, pleas, accusations, renunciations. But to be true elegy it must be looked at from the inside. The *Heroides* pay homage to the elegiac code, a code that has the power to 'retell' – and to 'recant' – the myth only when it establishes the proper perspective. But this expansion of the code ends up distancing itself from it; it becomes a disenchanted gaze. Reproduction and seriality are generally typical of either a popular art, or of a highly self-conscious art, learned and derivative. I would say that in the *Heroides* both these strategies play a role.

These elegies cannot wholly forget the rigidity of their code. Just as before in the *Amores*, Ovid assumes that elegy is already fully crystallized *elsewhere*, and takes pains that the reader not forget this. We know that Ovid can now look at the elegiac scenario from the outside. His evolution as love poet (already completed for the most part, from what we can gather, by the time of the *Epistulae Heroidum*) led him to reformulate his heritage, the young tradition of elegy. Relativism and irony have been the guiding principles of his work, marked by the translation of passionate love into a new flirtatious code. By now he has attained a detached perspective (frequently presupposed in the *Heroides*, and dominant in the *Remedia*) from whose vantage point there now exists an 'old-fashioned' elegy. This kind of Ur-elegy is distinguished by closure, absoluteness, and the purposeful union of poetics and life-choice. It is serious, pure, and in a certain sense also ascetic. This is the main reason why Propertius is so important as a model for the *Heroides*. The procedure, consisting in rendering visible the literary and cultural code according to which one works, has curious consequences for the *Heroides*. The world represented there is no longer exactly the traditional world of elegiac poetry that we find in the *Amores*. In fact these heroines, originating in epic and drama, were not born inside and for the elegiac code, as forms and representatives of the 'elegiac Self'. They can only appropriate it with a certain dose of anachronism. Thus the appearance of Penelope in the first position of the book has already, undoubtedly, a programmatic force. Some of the procedures adopted by Ovid, as I will try to show, introduce the reader to a new literary universe, one neither old-fashioned nor modern, neither epic nor elegiac, but founded upon the hesitation between, coexistence of, and the shifting back and forth of codes and values.

IV

Penelope is not only a character from epic. She is also a paradigm for elegy, conspicuous not only for her recurrence, but also for the stability of her role as an exemplar. Her functionality is the force that transforms the myth, as it is usually said, into a paradigm.[8] When she appears in the elegiac equation, she exemplifies the value of conjugal love and fidelity at any price. Catullus closes the lengthy blessing of his epithalamium with the name of Penelope (61.130). From here springs the rhetoric of elegy: the faithful conjugal love of Penelope metaphorically figures the noblest specimen of that which the poet-lover can ask his lady. When Cynthia has proved herself inconstant and unfaithful, Propertius flings this example in her face:

> Penelope poterat bis denos salva per annos
>   vivere, tam multis femina digna procis;
> coniugium falsa poterat differre Minerva,
>   nocturno solvens texta diurna dolo;
> visura et quamvis numquam speraret Ulixem,
>   illum expectando facta remansit anus.
>
> (Prop. 2.9.3-8)

Ovid remembered these lines. The last words of Penelope's epistle allude to Propertius: *protinus ut venias, facta videbor anus* (1.116). This is how the elegiac eye looks at Penelope. But how does Penelope regard her own story?

If the whole plot could be summarized in a single symbol (admittedly hard to find in a twenty-year wait spent in women's quarters), it would be the *motif of the shroud*. Propertius himself seems to consider it exemplary. Penelope's nocturnal wiles are the symbol of her will to remain faithful at any cost, by beguiling the suitors. ('You, Cynthia,' Propertius goes on to say, 'were not able to spend one night, one day alone.') This motif is conspicuously absent from Ovid's text. Penelope's own account, a condensed, faithful, and complete retelling of the Homeric story, leaves no room for the famous trick of the shroud. As a surprised Arthur Palmer notes, 'it is strange that Ovid did not make more use of the story of Penelope's web' (n. ad 1.10). But stranger still is the use he actually makes of it.

> O utinam tum cum Lacedaemona classe petebat
>   obrutus insanis esset adulter aquis!
> non ego deserto iacuissem frigida lecto
>   non quererer tardos ire relicta dies
> nec mihi quaerenti spatiosam fallere noctem
>   lassaret viduas pendula tela manus.
>
> (vv. 7-12)

Everybody knows that her weaving is a trick: *falsa Minerva* and *nocturnus dolus* of Propertius, the *doloi* of Homer (*Od.* 19.137). The epic heroine, in so far as she is epic, is the wife of the hero of *metis*. Her ruses are the equivalent in aim and form to those of her husband Odysseus. But if he ceases to be *polyphrôn* and becomes merely her beloved, the addressee of an elegiac love epistle, Penelope likewise will no longer be the crafty heroine, weaver of lies. Thus the shroud in Ovid serves one purpose – to *beguile the time*. No objective reader faced with these lines would ever think that she is working by night to *unweave* her tapestry. But *fallere noctem* is a daring expression. It preserves more metaphorical force than does our corresponding cliché, and to be more precise, here is a question of nights – with clear erotic surplus value – not simply of time. Love's time is measured in nights. This takes us back, once again, to an elegy of Propertius:

'O utinam talis perducas, improbe, noctes
me miseram qualis semper habere iubes!
Nam modo purpureo fallebam stamine somnum,[9]
rursus et Orpheae carmine, fessa, lyrae;
interdum leviter mecum deserta querebar
externo longas saepe in amore moras!'

(Prop. 1.3.39-44)

This time Cynthia is different. This time she speaks in her own voice. She is waiting for her lover who is lingering, like Odysseus, *in externo amore* ('outside love affairs'). She finds the night to be endless (1.3.37: *nam ubi longa meae consumpsti tempora noctis* – cf. Penelope's *spatiosa nox*). She then takes refuge in the matronal activity of weaving. Cynthia is fashioning herself as a Penelope.

But Ovid's Penelope sees herself as Cynthia. Her weaving is no longer an epic trick, but only the means of beguiling the nights on which she is deprived of her rightful love. The deformation of the Homeric model betrays a subjective shift, to a point of view that 'rereads' the epic theme from an elegiac perspective. The allusion to Propertius is the clearest sign of the new codification. With a light touch Ovid teaches us that the great themes of epic can also be turned into elegy. It is enough to change the point of view and to accept the monologic constraint native to elegy.

There can be no elegiac love without rivals. Ovid discovers in Penelope the possibility for this as well. He cannot make her omniscient, but he leads her, through her feminine intuition, very close to the 'truth' (i.e. the textual objectivity of its model, the *Odyssey*).

Haec ego dum stulte metuo, quae vestra libido est,
esse peregrino captus amore potes.
Forsitan et narres, quam sit tibit rustica coniunx,
quae tantum lanas non sinat esse rudes.

(vv. 75-8)

From a symmetrical perspective, Propertius had said to Cynthia *obicitur totiens a te mihi nostra libido* (3.19.1). The reader knows that Odysseus has also given into temptation, but knows too that as soon as he was free to go (v. 80: *revertendi liber*), he preferred mortal Penelope to divine Calypso. 'I know very well that compared to you the wise Penelope has but little virtue, in form and appearance ... nevertheless, I want and long each day to see the day of my return' (*Od.* 5.215ff.). On this comparative detail hangs the language of jealousy, the erotic diction of Ovid's Penelope. *Akidnos* (cf. 5.217) means something like 'weak, of little value'. Odysseus is addressing a divine lady. But Penelope is thinking of a *foreign lover*, with all its associated connotations but with all the signs reversed. *Rudis* is someone uncultured in the games of love; *rusticus*, for Ovid, is a key word, the attribute appropriate to 'all that is opposed to the *esprit* of the city'[10] and its elegant, flirtatious culture. Spinning wool is the most obvious sign of matronly chastity. With modernizing irreverence Ovid sees in the *lanifica* ('wool-spinning') matron the type of woman who does not know how to make love. 'I hate the one who gives herself only because it is unavoidable, *siccaque de lana cogitat ipsa sua*' (*Ars* 2.685ff.). Moved by jealousy, Penelope goes so far as to perceive herself as a negative model. She establishes a dialogue with the Homeric Odysseus through the medium of light erotic poetry and its language.

V

Briseis too is a paradigm for love poetry. Her character has undoubtedly romantic features. She is the woman loved by Achilles (*Il.* 9.342ff.), and in whose name the destructive wrath began. If one were to conduct an experiment and modify the arrangement of cultural values, focusing entirely on the wounded eros of Achilles rather than on his offended pride, one could end up with an 'elegiac' *Iliad*, a great epic text inscribing itself, paradoxically, within the bounds of a 'tenuous' love story. But sometimes Roman poets prefer to stress a feature with more realistic implications. Briseis is a *slave* (*serva*: Hor. *Carm.* 2.4.3; *captiva*: Prop. 2.9.11; *ancilla*: *Am.* 2.8.11). Her relationship with Achilles is the epic projection of a theme from everyday life: an affair with a maidservant. God only knows what has been done for the love of a chambermaid![11] Ovid's epistle duly accounts for this 'sociological' situating of the paradigm. The whole movement and feeling of the letter is determined by Briseis' social position, and it may be instructive to contrast it with the tone of the noble and lawful wife, Penelope. But here too, we can detect in the narrative situation some signals implicating elegy, which already provided Ovid with a rather unusual perspective, namely, the experience of an affair with a maidservant seen from below, and not, for once, through the eyes of the free man or even the *dominus*. But what happens, in terms of the elegiac code, if a slave is loved by her master?

One is reminded of a cultural model fundamental to Roman elegy, even when it remains unspoken: the 'manservant-mistress' relationship precipitated by the bond of *obsequium* towards his lady. The elegiac Self addresses the woman he loves as his *domina*, opening up the entire semantic field that we now associate with the label *servitium amoris*. It is important for modern readers to appreciate the violent divergence of these images from social norms. In order to devise a new rapport with a woman, one calls into question the most settled of social assumptions, the distinction between free and slave, and employs it metaphorically to represent the subjection of a freeborn man to a woman, who is herself, moreover, not infrequently a freed slave. It must be remembered that in Gallus and Propertius this is not merely gallant talk, drawing upon language that might have already been widespread in Greek epigram and in Catullus' own work. It is instead a semantic field that points to the choice of a nonconformist lifestyle. The core of the *servitium amoris* is, in fact, 'the degradation implied by the process of falling in love'.[12] Indeed, this degradation can exist only if we adopt the point of view of the elegiac Self – an upper-class Roman citizen from a good family, someone in a high enough position to draw his readers' attention to his act of renunciation.

Adopting the point of view of Briseis (who speaks 'from the perspective of the harem'[13]) produces a *Verfremdungseffekt*. The topoi, by now commonplace, of Gallus, Tibullus and Propertius, are traversed from a new perspective. Her intense and literal use of *dominus* reminds us that the metaphoric realm of elegy is neither symmetrical nor bilateral. The relationship of the lover with his *domina* cannot be travelled in the opposite direction. The enamoured voice of monologue in this letter belongs to one whose social position is that of a slave (Briseis repeats this constantly), in other words, a woman who could only achieve a *higher* standing through love (she tactfully alludes to this possibility). The symbolic degradation of the lover in elegy is replaced by a literal and violent subjection: a character who speaks of herself as a *munus* (v. 20),[14] a *serva* (v. 100), and who refuses the title of *domina* (v. 101). But there are ironic novelties on the other end of the line of amorous communication as well. The choice in favour of *servitium amoris* is allied, as is well known, with the choice in favour of *militia amoris*, and the refusal to take up arms for the fatherland. Whoever takes the side of love wages war against warfare. Briseis is certainly an elegiac voice – there is hardly any other way to define the premise of her epistle, in which the subject matter is announced as a lament for and to the one she loves (in short, elegiac *querela*):

> si mihi pauca queri de te dominoque viroque
> fas est, de domino pauca viroque querar.
>
> (3.5-6)[15]

The circumstances however compel the elegiac voice to raise a cry to arms, *Arma cape, Aeacide!* (v. 87), and to condemn the degradation accompanying the *militia amoris*:

> ... tibi plectra moventur,
> te tenet in tepido mollis amica sinu.
> Si quisquam quaerit, quare pugnare recuses –
> pugna nocet, citharae noxque Venusque iuvant.
> Tutius est iacuisse toro, tenuisse puellam,
> Threiciam digitis increpuisse lyram,
> quam manibus clipeos et acutae cuspidis hastam
> et galeam pressa sustinuisse coma.
>
> (3.113-20)

She recounts, moreover, the hedonistic precept of elegiac *otium* developed in the *Amores* in nearly identical terms: *tutius est fovisse torum, legisse libellum, / Threiciam digitis increpuisse lyram* (2.11.31-2). Here we have unprecedented elegiac *querela* which rehabilitate arms and military glory and deplores otium, intimacy and playing the lyre. (Laodamia's phrase *bella gerant alii, Her.* 13.84, is less absolute by comparison.) If we look at the origin of *servitium amoris*, we have to admit that this concept had a lexical valence that was anti-conformist, libertarian, and the mark of an opposition to social conventions and constraints. But this fight against convention – in which Ovid's elegiac revisionism takes a stand – has precipitated a literary convention as well, one that has by now acquired its own weight. In so far as the *servitium* or the *militia amoris* has become a convention or an institution, one will be able to demonstrate its relativity, that partiality which the elegiac code, as a rule, ought to silence.

VI

I believe that the range of this operation depends most of all upon literary conventions and their mechanics. The question is not one of making a parody of or subverting elegy, be it in the name of poetic alternatives, or of life-styles that need support, but only of revealing some points of conventional 'weight'. Exactly the same occurs with epic. The hesitation of a Briseis or a Penelope between the epic and elegiac worlds should not be read as a parody or subversion of the epic tradition. It would be naïve to think that the amorous climate of the epistles is aggressive towards epic, intending to dissolve and subsume it under the dominion of the more 'modern' genre of elegy. It is precisely the narrative structure of the epistles – autonomous but continually threatened by the factual implications of their diegetic frames – which reminds us of how epic maintains its identity. The system of values claimed in elegy, as we have just seen, is ambiguous and relativized, just as epic too is neither nullified nor criticized, but re-explored from novel perspectives. Once again the stress falls on the power of conventions, those conventions peculiar to each genre which regulate the digestion of narrative and biographical material into the structure of the literary body. Just as is the case with the transformation of elegiac models, what is effective here is the strategy of reading in a strictly literal manner those themes that have crystallized into convention, losing touch with their concrete roots. Yet again Briseis' epistle provides us with an example.

The game of allusion between convention and experiential reality is particularly prominent in v. 52, in which the apparently 'direct' pathos and the emotional investment of the voice of monologue are most intense:

tu dominus, tu vir, tu mihi frater eras.

The success of this type of formula in love elegy is well known. Ever searching for hyperbolic expressions of everyday feelings, the poet widens the area under his *domina*'s control at the expense of any other emotional ties: *tu mihi sola domus, tu, Cynthia, sola parentes* (Prop. 1.11.23). Such catalogues of 'substitutions' all go back, more or less directly, to a famous scene in Homer: Andromache's conjugal love for Hector, made famous by the enumeration, 'you are my father, my mother, my brother, my blooming companion' (Il. 6.429-30). It is difficult, and perhaps not that important, to establish to what degree love poets are affected by the persistence of the Homeric model.[16] But it is at least legitimate to recall that this passionate and pathetic gesture was devised for a *female* figure, alone in a world of warrior heroes. It is worth noting that the lover-poet chooses Andromache's eros as his model, in spite of the fact that both the success and diffusion of the cliché serve to water down the reference, making it more generic.

But Ovid is endowed with an extremely literal poetic memory. He remembers Andromache's line as well as its Homeric context, the true original motivation for those bold words. Often the widespread occurrence of a *Pathosformel* follows a strong dose of forgetfulness, and the sublime is born from the loss of verisimilitude. In Homer, Andromache speaks as she does because she truly has no father nor mother nor brothers. War has consumed them, and her spouse Hector is literally her entire world. Beyond the possible and feared loss of Hector, Andromache glimpses total annihilation, slavery and desolation.

In the *Iliad* Andromache's fate is only tragically foreshadowed. Compared to the fears of the Trojan women, only one character appears as a concrete example anticipating their fate. This is Briseis, the prisoner of war who, like Andromache, has lost all of her loved ones in the destruction of her homeland. What is more, she has already suffered what Andromache fears: the death of her lawful husband and the reduction to slavery. In the poem's plot, in her lamentation over the corpse of Patroclus, Briseis presents the reader with a preview of Andromache's fate. After Briseis' lament, Andromache will experience another facet of this fate: she will watch her husband die. The last point of comparison – the destruction of the city, her capture and reduction to slavery – falls outside the Homeric plot, but is no less foreseeable and impending.

It seems therefore that between Briseis and Andromache there already existed a sort of natural parallelism, an easy exchange of ideas and motifs. But the transference of the pathetic formula has paradoxical implications for Ovid's text. One might see both of them mirrored in the tragic destiny of a third character certainly familiar to Ovid. I mean Tecmessa in Sophocles' *Ajax*.[17] In the heart of the tragedy, Tecmessa finds herself in a situation similar to Ovid's Briseis. She is a slave of war and a concubine, and is forced to defend her rights as a wife without actually being one, and thus to do so from a subordinate position. Hence her disheartened appeal to Ajax begins with the harsh words *o despot' Aias*, 'master'. Briseis begins

(vv. 5-6) and seals her letter (v. 154) by addressing Achilles as *dominus*. Like Ovid's Briseis, Tecmessa is frightened that her future will mirror what she has endured in the past. If Ajax should fall, a re-enactment of her past awaits her.

At this point Sophocles triggers the comparison to Andromache. Any reader of the scene in which Tecmessa appeals to Ajax will hear in the highly pathetic expression a reference to *Iliad* 6. The similarities are both meaningful and intended – Tecmessa's appeal, her anxious vision of the future, the presence of their small, frightened son – but so too are the differences. Tecmessa is not a lawful wife, and Ajax is no longer a true Homeric hero, awaiting the 'natural' destiny of the warrior. What Sophocles has *not* taken from the Homeric model is therefore also meaningful; he elicits the comparison, but stops it short before Tecmessa is allowed to utter Andromache's famous lines. The most insightful interpreters of Sophocles usually underline this 'halting' of the allusive structure: 'how could Tecmessa tell Ajax "you are my father, my mother, my brother, my husband", when the destruction of her family, even if not the very death of her father and mother, was ultimately caused by Ajax himself'? ... 'It would be inhuman for Tecmessa to so love the one responsible for the death of her parents' ... 'Sophocles is probably thereby avoiding the special horror of the idea that Tecmessa has been cohabiting with the man who killed her father'.[18] It is Sophocles' audience who must fulfil the intertextual movement, uncovering the cruel difference between Tecmessa and Andromache. The former, torn between two positions, is already living the tragic model of Andromache, but is unable to live up to it with confidence. She remains, as it were, beneath it.

Ovid closes the circle, taking his Briseis beyond the limits traced by Sophocles' dramatic tact to explore an actual 'perversion' of the Homeric model. Every single narrative given remains, as has been seen, under the explicit responsibility of Homer; it is he who tells of the brutal reality that Achilles took Briseis after killing her family. But Ovid's Briseis implores Achilles by the very sword that stabbed them. In a very similar situation, Tecmessa limited herself to supplicating Ajax by the bed that united them. By remaining perfectly faithful to Homer, Ovid discovers in the *Iliad* the key to upending the conventions. His version, however respectful, is already a perversion, precisely because the topos, an epic exemplar re-embodied as a *Pathosformel* in the elegiac tradition, now proves far too close to the concrete, real-life situation. In the same way, traditional elegiac expressions – not only 'you are my whole family', but also 'I will follow you to the end of the world', 'I am at your service', and 'you are my conqueror' – are now given new motivation and the metaphoric distance is reduced, bringing them back from sentimental hyperbole to a description of a factual state of affairs. I will move now to an analysis of what happens with the most infamous of these topoi: 'I die for love'.

VII

By now, as in the first and third epistle, the importance of the traditional status that the heroines assume is clear. They are epic characters known to elegy as *paradigms*. Elegiac poets base their work upon the 'external' provenance of the characters only then to assimilate them into the elegiac context. The paradigms have value precisely because they are summoned from 'the outside', from a different and pre-existent literary world. Ovid exploits this strategy in order to work upon the co-existence of diverse worlds. His hesitation between the codes of elegy and of epos becomes the very literary space of these epistles, and the simultaneous presence of the codes shows, at once, their power (i.e. their specific spheres of influence)[19] and their conventional, relative nature. But not all the characters of the *Heroides*, not even all the characters of epic, are willing to play this game. Dido for example is not, or at least not yet, a paradigm; rather, she is a character drawn into epic from love poetry.

By choosing a Roman model, one not yet paradigmatic and one so close in time, Ovid has risked more than usual and has paid for it – to judge from what his many critics and casual readers say – with a loss of quality. There is little doubt that Epistle 7 (in a hypothetical poll) is one of the least loved in the whole collection. One might think that the sublime Virgil of Book 4 offers, as does the great Homer, the right amount of 'resistance'. The distance between the epic and epistolary Dido does bring into play a vigorous dialectic, but the difficulty for Ovid lies elsewhere. In a certain sense the epic model has already taken an initiative that would be proper to the poetics of the *Heroides*. In short, Ovid has been pre-empted.

No doubt the rewriting needs, first of all, to diminish the points of grandeur in the Virgilian model and basically downplay its tragic features. Ovid executes this programme scrupulously. Not one of the high-pitched moments of Dido's tragic nature is preserved by Ovid, and his seventh epistle verifies *e contrario* how important it was for Virgil's heroine to become or feel (in a strictly literal and allusively precise sense) like Phaedra, Medea, Alcestis, Pentheus, Ajax, Andromache, Helen, and Evadne. Freed from these references, Dido is really a different character. But Virgil's Dido is not only an epic character with a tragic 'vocation'; she has already absorbed, to a certain degree, the specifically elegiac toxins that Ovid (as we now well know) reserves for his heroines.[20] The fact that she has already swallowed these poisons is what damages the work of assimilation. We know that for this epic love-story Virgil has pressed the boundaries of inclusiveness in his epic: tragedy, erotic lyric, epigram, Hellenistic love poetry, perhaps even comedy, and certainly Roman elegy, all contributed to its making. Nor were they merely compositional materials. Dido does not live solely in an elegiac context but (and more importantly, for the structure of the narrative) she also sometimes, intermittently, *speaks* in language that is erotic and elegiac. It is this feature

that dramatically clarifies her interior conflict and her inability to communicate with Aeneas. The large space given Dido in the epic text is more one
of self-expression than of action. It is natural that in the *Aeneid* no voice
is more 'subjective' than hers is. Correlated to this notion is the fact that
Dido, in quantitative terms, speaks a lot, a fact that is also of interest to
Ovid. In the span of her book, Dido speaks in direct dialogue for more than
180 hexameters; this corresponds in Ovid to an epistle a little over 190
verses long (an uncommon length in the *Heroides*). The near balance of
these numbers is food for thought.

Ovid's epistolary enterprise runs the risk of drowning in an excess of
stimuli. The Virgilian Dido provides practically everything he needs; often
it is simply a matter of 'declining' his model. Virgil says *uritur*, and the new
Dido *uror* (4.68; v. 25). But here the reworking of the conventions is already
an ambush. *Uror ut inducto ceratae sulphure taedae*, with its unexpected,
pyromaniacal physicality, reminds us that the fire of love is on its way to
becoming, outside the metaphor, a sad bonfire (cf. *Aen.* 4.504ff. *at regina,
pyra penetrali in sede sub auras | erecta ingenti taedis atque ilice secta* ...).
And thus the delicate, gradual progression in Virgil, from the first meta-
phors of incendiary passion up to the fatal pyre, is subsumed in an emblem
that points up its elegiac matrix.[21] Similarly, the final image (191ff.: *nec
mea nunc primum feriuntur pectora telo; | ille locus saevi vulnus amoris
habet*) condenses into an epigram the subtle progression through which,
in Virgil, the wound of love (first seen in 4.1, *saucia*) is transformed into
an actual sword fixed into Dido's breast. In this way the epistolary poetics,
which by its very nature 'compresses' the flow of narrative enunciation,
elaborates the Virgilian text by exposing its elegiac potential. Even more
often, the grand pathetic speeches in Book 4 provide models already
oriented, both grammatically and rhetorically, towards elegy. The
monologic reduction has its usual effects, by now familiar: not only is
everything seen from Dido's point of view, but we are also compelled to
participate in a process of subjective recasting imposed by the monologue
upon already known events. Compared to the structure of the *Aeneid*, the
epistle is noteworthy for its complete suppression of the all-controlling
narrator's voice, which intervenes to balance empathy and sympathy, the
voice of the character and the demands of fate.[22] But the *Aeneid* has
already familiarized us with a strong subjective voice able to produce
irreconcilable perspectives. Aeneas as impious, and his mission as point-
less and in vain – these are perspectives made sharper in the *Aeneid*
within the context provided by the narrator's voice in harmony with the
voice of fate. For this reason the uncertainty of truth that the Ovidian
monologue induces cannot attain the effects of other epistles. Virgil's 'if
only I had a child by you' overshadows, in its force and visionary autonomy,
the harshly criticized 'I could be pregnant' of Ovid.

We end up missing some of the suspense, the irony, and the playing with
conventions prominent in the 'Homeric' epistles. But there is still another

facet to explore, one connected once again with the 'time' of the epistle and that of its model.

Comparative tables of models and borrowings no longer receive good press, but a glance at the sequence in which the Virgilian models appear can still teach us a good deal. One infers from it (but it comes as no surprise) that Ovid manages to reuse not only the main points of Virgil's narrative, but also every case of Dido 'taking the stand' within the course of Book 4. The epistle's spatial continuum of discourse joins quotations, with varying degrees of exactness, from each of Dido's speeches and monologues. Needless to say, this collection of samples is redistributed within the epistle's self-contained, homogeneous and coherent monologue. We get the impression rather that the Ovidian epistle achieves a more continuous and coherent state than any of his model discourses. The psychological vacillation, the 'spiral-like' reasoning, the elegiac or dramatic ups and downs, are certainly more marked in Virgil than in Ovid. Nevertheless, for a reader mindful of Virgil the effect is paradoxical. In a single continuum we see a series of famous topoi march by – regardless of their original location and progressive disposition! – topoi we usually connect with individual contexts where the course of epic action and where psychological developments (threats and promises, hopes and suicidal despair) provided various motivations. Our first lesson in relativism.

It is good to ask ourselves also whether there exists a blank space in the model which allows for the letter's insertion (a test that proved useful for the 'Homeric' epistles). The Virgilian narrative, pressing and continuous, does not offer suitable spaces, but there is one possible point of intersection, one long since identified:[23]

> ire iterum in lacrimas, iterum temptare precando
> cogitur et supplex animos summittere amori
> ne quid inexpertum frustra moritura relinquat.
>
> (4.413-15)

Directly after this Virgil places a speech addressed to Anna, who will then often report messages (cf. 4.237ff.: *talisque miserrima fletus / fertque refertque soror*). Here an epistle becomes possible, even plausible. And it is natural to infer from this point the dominant tone of the epistle; indeed it will be supplicatory and downcast (*supplex animos summittere amori*; cf. 424: *I, soror, atque hostem supplex adfare superbum*).[24] From here derives the narrative frame as well (Aeneas has already decided to leave immediately). Moreover, the repetitions hinted at in Virgil's text (4.413: *ire ... iterum in lacrimas, iterum temptare ...*; 4.437: *fertque refertque soror*; 4.447: *adsiduis hinc atque hinc vocibus*) are certainly good justification for the persistence of Ovid's Dido. Perhaps the entire letter should be read as a clever extended commentary upon Virgil's verse (immediately before *ire ... iterum in lacrimas*), *improbe Amor, quid non mortalia pectora cogis*!

This line is a good resource for Ovid, who perhaps already anticipates, reasonably enough, that he will meet with harsh criticism for the humble submissiveness and total surrender of his Dido. In sum, the letter represents not only an intersection with Virgil's epic text, but expresses also the search for a precise elegiac 'place' within the continuity of Virgil's account. *Improbe Amor* – the reaction of the narrator, with a 'halt' sympathetically imposed upon the narrative, reveals the movement towards a liminal zone. At this critical juncture the repeated messages of love, loaded with *obsequium*, nearly brush up against the borders of the elegiac world: *temptare precando*. Anna's role as messenger of love is already a potential feature of elegy, one that the narrator, not by chance, immediately limits and reinterprets: *miserrima* is in fact a vigilant recall of the stern code of tragedy that hovers over the plot. *Miserrima ... fertque refertque soror* has a slight, but not unfelt, assonance with the stock elegiac formulas for the go-between through whom lovers keep in touch: *tabellas ... portans itque reditque* (Tib. 2.6.46), *[quaerere] quas ferat et referat sollers ancilla tabellas* (*Am.* 2.20.41). But in Virgil, *refert* does not imply a response, as in the elegiac cliché, but only unilateral repetition. True elegiac communication remains incipient and the Virgilian narrative takes another direction.

Intersection with a model is also a way to anticipate objections and emotional responses of readers. Questions of verisimilitude and, above all, indignation for the deep humiliation inflicted upon Virgil's heroine – a pejorative version of elegiac *obsequium* – have arisen in the course of the centuries. Ovid seems to insinuate that he has captured Dido having hit 'rock bottom', at the lowest possible point of her life. It is useless to protest if the queen shows very little dignity and, for example, instead of cursing Aeneas, she wishes (in the typical style of an elegiac *propempticon*) that she had not wished him to suffer shipwreck.[25] Is this a question of psychology or of situation? Is there, so to speak, another Dido, an alternative character, or is it rather the dialogue form of the epistle that prompts her strategies? The poetics of the *Heroides* implies this oscillation, but does not intend to resolve it. The consequences of the epistolary strategy cannot end here. We are not reading a new speech by Virgil's Dido after all, some sort of super-monologue that contains them all, but a letter, a communicative act that projects around itself the shadow of a situation, a strategy, and a precise purpose. We can refer in Virgil only to hints of intention, and this is moreover a rather problematic line: *ne quid inexpertum frustra moritura relinquat*.

VIII

The Ovidian epistle itself gives better indications. We can find these most of all in the opening and in the closing. The letter concludes with the *imago* of Dido writing while holding ready the Trojan sword on her lap, and it is sealed with a text-book case of poetic epitaph (v. 197: *praebuit Aeneas et causam mortis et ensem* ...).[26] It opened, moreover, with the promise of a swan song:

> sic ubi fata vocant, udis abiectus in herbis
> ad vada Maeandri concinit albus olor.[27]

The motif signals, with the utmost desirable clarity, that Dido is uttering her *ultima verba* in an atmosphere of absolute desperation. A similar usage of the motif already appears in Apollonius Rhodius, in a passage that Ovid may have had in mind, on account of certain specific similarities (the background of wet grass, the echoing riverbanks). Medea and her companions, when death seems certain, sing a death lament (*Arg.* 4.1300-3):

> ἢ ὅτε καλὰ νάοντος ἐπ' ὀφρύσι Πακτωλοῖο
> κύκνοι κινήσουσιν ἑὸν μέλος, ἀμφὶ δὲ λειμών
> ἑρσήεις βρέμεται ποταμοῖό τε καλὰ ῥέεθρα ...[28]

The conventional nature of the motif creates a slight dissonance within the epistolary framework of the *Heroides*. To be sure, if one looks to Virgil, this Dido who is ready to die is no innovation. Not only the *ultima verba* of Virgil's Dido but also, as is known, a hint contained in her first words to Aeneas, in the crisis of Book 4, head in this direction: ... *nec moritura tenet crudeli funere Dido?* (v. 307). One cannot be more Virgilian than this; *moritura* is the leitmotif for this character, and it is up to the wise reader to distinguish, in the various stages of the drama, the decreasing levels of dramatic irony. *Moritura* is first a comment by the narrator, then in a character's voice, which gradually progresses from an emotional outburst, to a dawning consciousness, to lucid desperation, and finally, to a concrete decision to kill herself. We could say then that Ovid has condensed, according to the modes of epistolary poetics, the development of a complex and volatile narrative isotope. The decision to compose the heroine's *ultima verba* as an epistle is an invitation to consider more closely the *novissima verba* of Virgil's protagonist. Dido dies (at last) saying:

> 'felix, heu nimium felix, si litora tantum
> numquam Dardaniae tetigissent nostra carinae.'
> Dixit, et os impressa toro: 'Moriemur ...'
>
> (4.667-9)

This theme of bidding farewell to life becomes, in Ovid's hands, an ironic aside within the course of a rhetorical argument the gist of which is, 'it is not true that a god is guiding you towards a prosperous future – stay here!':

> 'Sed iubet ire deus!' vellem, vetuisset adire
> Punica nec Teucris pressa fuisset humus.
>
> (7.141-2)

It would be useless to multiply examples of this sort. Every unbiased reader would admit that this letter is by no means a suicide note. On the contrary, in every detail, in every significant transformation and revision of the Virgilian model, it is an attempt to win back Aeneas.[29] (Her sense of guilt towards Sychaeus, another factor in her suicide, is played down through the symptomatic plea *da veniam culpae; decepit idoneus auctor*, v. 107.) The letter is written in that space opened up by the tenacious difference between elegy's 'dying for love' and the tragic code's *amor mortis*.

The swan song therefore turns out to be an element of illusion. Like all the other *Heroides*, this letter is endowed with an illusory aura: it is without effect, because we are able to measure it against its outcome, and it is written at the wrong time, after everything has already played out. But while the context of the myth condemns and annuls the pragmatic intention, that very intention ends up demystifying the explicit framework of the letter, which foretells her death. After the calculated uncertainty of *ne quid inexpertum frustra moritura relinquat*, the development of Virgil's narrative has Dido – in her famous *Trugrede* – mask her resolution to die with an attempt of another sort, *novis praetexere funera sacris* (4.500), the magic rites that will either dissolve, or reaffirm, her relationship with Aeneas. Ironically, Ovid has composed a letter in which the resolution to die is an ostentatious mask for the real attempt to convince and to win back Aeneas.[30] Pale with love – instead of *pallida morte futura* – the Carthaginian queen returns one last time to that elegiac world from which Virgil, by developing her tragic potential, had prematurely banished her.

So the elegiac poetics of the epistle accepts and slyly exploits the troubled subordination of elegy to epic. Yet, this is not a good reason to read the Ovidian text (as most interpreters still do) as the submissive beginning of the *aetas Vergiliana* in Latin literature. True, the swan is *abiectus*, but ancient tradition suggests that swans sing their *best* songs right before they die.

3

Voices and Narrative 'Instances' in the *Metamorphoses*

Readers of the *Metamorphoses* experience a continuous fluctuation of voices, addressees, levels, and narrative frames. But there is a growing tendency in criticism of Ovid's poem not to take this phenomenon seriously. It might be profitable (and I propose to do so in another context)[1] to undertake a comprehensive treatment of the act of narrating, of metadiegesis as fundamental to the *Metamorphoses*. But a work of this sort would be devoid of any interest if one were to accept the credo of a recent critic: 'I believe there is basically a single narrator throughout, who is Ovid himself.'[2] The goal of this chapter is to suggest that we have gone too far in this direction, and that something precious might thereby be lost.

A minor distinction is necessary. Ovid's narrative style is not truly polyphonic. The poet of the *Metamorphoses* is not concerned to characterize by stylistic means, in order to contrast the individual narrative voices he employs one with another. Thus the difference between the individual voices is to some degree neutralized. When one reasons in terms of style, the definition of 'single narrator' might be convincing. The polyphony of the *Metamorphoses* does not consist in a separation of narrative voices, but in an alternation among registers directly controlled by the single narrator's voice, according to an exhibitionary logic. This is a mimetic quality that more or less affects Ovid's entire corpus – 'our poet excels in dropping just momentarily into a given style' (Hollis [1977] 123) – but this becomes predominant in the *Metamorphoses* where the very project of the work is 'an anthology of genres' (Kenney [1986] XVIII: a very good definition, even if a bit static). More than polyphony, one should speak of *polyeideia*, of multiformity, a term that seems to be foreshadowed by the *mutatae ... formae* of *Met.* 1.1.[3]

One should not therefore expect the voices of single narrators (as is the case sometimes in Petronius) to have recognizably distinct stylistic features or even to be separable one from another. Nor should one think that a plurality of narrators might have a primarily *informative* function. Ovid, on the contrary, works hard to de-motivate his metadiegetic procedures. A flux of unstable narrative material flows through the *Metamorphoses*, a flux similar to Nature in Pythagoras' speech, and Ovid presents himself as its sole possible arbiter. The attribution of certain features of narrative to individual narrators is often arbitrary, and functionalist critics might search in vain for an explanation that would account for the interchangeability of direct and of metadiegetic narrations.

But the foregoing does not seem to me to warrant us speaking of a Single Narrator, if this implies denying the presence and the significance of the individual metadiegetic narrators. The insertion of secondary narratives into the main narrative involves for Ovid elaborate and expensive narrative frames. A certain logic of expenditure and of luxury, of conspicuous consumption, is intrinsic to Ovid's poetics. But I cannot bring myself to believe that all these narrators and narratees are brought into the narrative *only* to display their singular irrelevance. On the contrary, experience of other narrative works suggests that between frames and inserted stories mutual implications may arise, interconnections only hinted at, but integral to the creation of meaning. For example, an internal audience's reception of a story can suggest to the reader a model of interpretation (which in turn may be adopted or dismissed). In other cases, the identity of the narrator can have an implicit relation to a theme, or even to the style of the narrative entrusted to him or her.[4] These are general guidelines to be kept in mind, even if our discussion will focus almost entirely upon specific examples.

A river as narrator

The stories narrated at a banquet that Achelous the river-god hosts, with Theseus and other heroes as his guests, occupy the central portion of the poem (the second part of Book 8 and the beginning of Book 9). Lelex, a hero with an archaizing name, tells the story of Baucis and Philemon (8.618-724). Achelous responds with the tale of impious Erysichthon's punishment (8.728-878), and with the autobiographical account of his duel with Heracles (8.879-9.88). Two recent observations shed some light on the connection between these stories and the narrative situation that frames them.

On the literary level, *Baucis and Philemon* and *Erysichthon* have a certain affinity: taken together, they are the most outstanding 'nest' of Callimachean influence in Ovid's works (and for that matter, in any other Latin poet known to us). The principal model for *Baucis and Philemon* is the short poem *Hecale* (the fragments of this work, however limited, still offer remarkable potential for comparison), and *Erysichthon* echoes the central nucleus of Callimachus' *Hymn* VI.[5] Incidentally, we have here two Callimachean models in hexameters – that is, technically speaking, epic, like the *Metamorphoses*. Let us turn now to the narrative frame in Ovid.[6] The first story is narrated by Theseus' maternal uncle, and Ovid points out that among the listeners Theseus is the most impressed:

Desierat, cunctosque et res et moverat auctor
Thesea praecipue;

(8.725-6)

Theseus' reaction, as Kenney observes, must have a subtle metaliterary
motivation: the story so strikes him because Theseus himself is the hero
of the Callimachean model for this account. The simple hospitality of
Baucis and Philemon corresponds perfectly to the humble welcoming of
the old Hecale that so moves the hero in Callimachus' *Hecale*.[7] There is
also somewhat of a contrastive implication: in the narrative frame a god
hosts mortals, whereas in the metadiegesis gods are hosted in a human
abode.

But as Hinds has observed ([1987b] 19), the character of Achelous, the
master of the house and narrator of the *Erysichthon*, also merits consideration. In reality he is a very peculiar figure, since he is at once a god and
a river in flood. An interesting coincidence: in the poem's endless variety
of narrators, the very one who offers the setting and the voice for Callimachean narrations is a wide river laden with debris – a most blatant
negative symbol according to the poetics of Callimachus.

This suggestion deserves further amplification. The narrative situation
of the banquet begins with Achelous' introduction of himself:

Clausit iter fecitque moras Achelous eunti
imbre tumens. 'Succede meis' ait 'inclite, tectis
Cecropida, nec te committe rapacibus undis!
Ferre trabes solidas obliquaque volvere magno
murmure saxa solent. Vidi contermina ripae
cum gregibus stabula alta trahi, nec fortibus illic
profuit armentis nec equis velocibus esse.
Multa quoque hic torrens nivibus de monte solutis
corpora turbineo iuvenalia vertice mersit.
Tutior est requies, solito dum flumina currant
limite, dum tenues capiat suus alveus undas.'

(8.549-59)

It is good to stay put, he tells them, and wait for the waves to become
tenues once again – a common theme both in *recusationes* (cf. Prop. 3.3.24;
3.9.36) and in literary theory (cf. Hor. *Ars* 28).

The swell of the river (853: *intumui*) continues until the end of the
narrative situation:

Discedunt iuvenes: neque enim, dum flumina pacem
et placidos habeant lapsus totaeque resident
opperiuntur aquae.

(9.94-6ff.)

A great river, *tumens* ('swollen'), roaring and laden with debris, is an image bearing a curious resemblance to the great Assyrian river in Callimachus' *Hymn to Apollo* (2.108-9), for generations of poets a symbol of the 'grand' poetry to be rejected. Achelous' violent sweeping force is also reminiscent of an important predecessor of Callimachus' Euphrates: Cratinus the poet is in Aristophanes figured as a torrent that swept away every obstacle and carried away logs and boulders in its path (Ar. *Eq.* 526ff.). From this perspective, the figure of Achelous operates somewhat as an emblem. The great river, while he describes himself, 'speaks' a lofty style: his first words are epicisms, such as the vocative *inclite ... Cecropida*, and his descriptive style itself is accordingly tumid and overflowing. His account of the destructive effects of his flood resembles well-known similes proper to epic. The river's high tide, the occasion for the narrative, also influences his style.

The story narrated by Achelous is in a certain sense coherent with these premises. Comparisons between Ovid's and Callimachus' *Erysichthon* have all agreed on one point: Ovid rewrites his model by exaggerating its style.[8] Many humorous and realistic bourgeois features of the original are lost. To make up for this, Erysichthon takes on a sinister and superhuman stature. The divine apparatus grows overpowering, and the demonic personification of Hunger (*Fames*) towers over the account. Ovid's transcription 'epicizes' Callimachus, and the 'tumid' identity of the narrator Achelous is, in the end, the signal of this awareness. Greedy and insatiable, Erysichthon is an excessive hero, fitting for the context. His hunger is a self-propelling force, it grows *inattenuata* (8.844). This unusual epithet (a *hapax* in Latin) seems to play upon a literary register: *attenuatus* is a technical term of literary criticism for a 'slender' and reduced style, as opposed to an exuberant *redundantia*.[9] Unable to curb his hunger, Erysichthon greedily consumes any available resource until he consumes himself. Meanwhile, by imitating Callimachus in terms that suggest an inflation and crisis of the Callimachean programme, Ovid dilates the style of his model and creates a field of contradictiory tensions.[10] A similar field of tensions (as is now commonly thought) affects the very proem of the *Metamorphoses*, where opposing connotations are conjoined in an almost provocative manner: *deducere* a *carmen perpetuum* is, in Callimachean terms, an undeniable contradiction.[11]

To claim that Achelous ought to be viewed in light of the Euphrates in Callimachus, a point on which my whole analysis rests, might seem unwarranted. But it is hard to overstate the importance of this symbol of 'tumidity' in Roman poetry. Ovid's river can be added to a list that includes the Euphrates (not only in Callimachus, but also in Propertius 2.10.13), the Simois and Scamander (Prop. 3.1.26-7), and the Rhine, both muddy (Hor. *Sat.* 1.10.37, 62) and polluted with blood (Prop. 3.3.45).[12] The Achelous is the largest and most ancient of the rivers in Greece, and figures as a symbol of the kind of elevated and grandiose poetry one should reject (linked to the poetry of Antimachus?)[13] in the first 'Callimachean' elegy of Propertius:

> tu satius memorem Musis imitere Philitan
> et non inflati somnia Callimachi.
> Nam rursus licet Aetoli referas Acheloi,
> fluxerit ut magno fractus amore liquor ...
>
> (2.34.31-4)

The myth that Propertius evokes, the defeat of Achelous in the battle with Heracles, is narrated by Ovid's Achelous at the beginning of Book 9, directly after the story of Erysichthon.

Before we leave this insidious terrain, I would like to mention two other possible applications of this image to narrative contexts; I mean certain sequences of narrative in which the image of a muddy river, certainly coherent and motivated by the context, might retain some literary-critical connotation.

We know that the *Fasti* is a work pervaded by an anxious question.[14] This text, while it develops according to the implicit norms of elegiac narrative, also confronts the limits of these norms and delimits its own territory in a dynamic confrontation with other poetic genres. The poem is written in the meter of elegy, and on the horizon can be glimpsed the competition of 'light' love-poetry composed in couplets. On the other hand, the narrative themes of the *Fasti* are often a bit higher, or heavier, than the elegiac form can bear. So too with respect to epic, there is a problem of contiguity and of trespassing. In order to guarantee its own autonomy, the *Fasti* avoid some themes belonging quintessentially to heroic epos (and which instead are more suitable to the *Met.*). It is significant, for example, that Ovid abstains from battle scenes.

This rule is confirmed by a single exception, well noted by Heinze ([1960] 339): 'Wenn Ovid Schlachtberichte ... vermied, so ist der Grund gewiss der, dass die elegische Dichtung prinzipiell solche Schilderungen ablehnt ... *Eine* [Heinze's italics] Ausnahme nur macht Ovid ....' The reference is to the battle of the Fabii along the river Cremera (*Fast.* 2.195-241). In this scene, which according to Heinze ought to be viewed as the extreme point of 'epic' excursion granted to the *Fasti*, a great emphasis is placed upon a flooding river. The Cremera impedes the march of the Fabii and sets the stage for the battle:

> ut celeri passu Cremeram tetigere rapacem
> (turbidus hibernis ille fluebat aquis) ...
>
> (*Fast.* 2.205ff.)

Without a doubt this scenario is well suited for the most epic scene in the *Fasti*. The description of the bloody battle includes three epic similes, one of which is the image of a rushing torrent (it overflows its usual banks and

invades everything, 2.219-22), concluding with an echo of a famous line of
Ennius (v. 242 = Enn. *Ann.* 370 V.2). The detail of the swollen river is
absent from historical sources (as far as we know) and I suspect that in
Ovid it plays a precise role. The Fabii halt at the edge of a river, *rapax* and
turbidus, as if to mark the farthest point of extension of the world of the
Fasti with respect to epic grandeur, the limit beyond which the elegiac
Ovid of the *Fasti* would be a trespasser.

Something similar might be observed in a 'pure' elegiac text, antipodal
to epic, such as *Amores* 3.6. This elegy is a long appeal addressed to an
obstinate little stream obstructing Ovid's path to his love. The erotic
situation lies completely in the background, abstract and vague; Ovid
turns his whole attention to the obstacle and to the strategies aimed at
overcoming it. The river is described in essentially 'anti-Callimachean'
terms: it has muddy banks (3.6.1), abundant and even filthy waters (v. 8:
et turpi crassas gurgite volvis aquas). These features accord well with the
narrative function of the stream that obstructs the amorous quest of the
elegiac poet. But what is intriguing are the arguments Ovid uses to
appease the flood. To honour the unnamed stream, the poet lists lofty
examples of great rivers which have felt the power of love (among whom
are Achelous with his horn broken during his duel with Heracles, v. 35ff.).
He then goes on to develop a long narrative example, the story of a river
in love, but, significantly, the story is of *epic* provenance: Mars' rape of Ilia,
who afterward was offered consolation by the Anio. The entire story, not
only the meeting with Mars but also the final union with the Anio,
appeared in a prominent position at the beginning of Ennius' *Annales*.[15]
This episode, though transcribed by Ovid in his own manner and in the
style of elegy, is indeed an unforeseen guest in a poem of the *Amores*. The
outcome of Ovid's effort is rather ironic when seen in this light. While the
poet speaks, that is, as he retells the Ennian epic, rather than being
calmed, the river swells even more:

> dum loquor, increvit latis spatiosus in undis,
>   nec capit admissas alveus altus aquas.
> quid mecum, furiose, tibi? quid mutua differs
>   gaudia, quid coeptum, rustice, rumpis iter?
>
> (3.6.85-8)

Once all hope has been lost, Ovid upbraids the river with appropriate
epithets: *lutulentus* (95), *non candide* (105). The elegy as a whole is much
more amusing if a specific part of Ovid's audience, namely the small circle
familiar with debates concerning poetics, recognized the reciprocal relevance of several narrative features: the rustic, sullen and untamed character of the muddy river, its opposition to love, the overflowing effect of the
allusion to Ennius.[16]

Many of the observations made so far must remain conjectural. After all, there are not many perspectives from which to describe a flooding river, and the Callimachean symbolism, though well known in Ovid's time and even a bit commonplace, did not have exclusive copyright on the image.[17] I think, however, that it may be healthy to keep open this connotative dimension. The literary public of late Augustan Rome, a significant portion of it at least, was certainly able to appreciate manipulations of concepts and literary symbols of this sort. But this is a secondary level in the *Metamorphoses* (luckily for it) and the poem is perfectly enjoyable and interesting even for those who do not ask of it such questions. But even so, we are not obliged to ignore, while reading the poem, the presence of individual narrators and particular narrative settings. The hypothesis that between metadiegetic 'voices', stories, narrative settings, and narratees, implications may arise, reciprocal references in the text, deserves in each case at least our serious consideration. All the more so, since from now on we will not move from an allusive dimension – admittedly always conjectural and secondary – but will concern ourselves with concrete problems of interpretation, cases in which the identity of the narrating voice and its relevance to the narrative poses difficulties, suggesting not only poetic implications, but also differences of meaning.

Orpheus and Ovid

By ignoring the spectrum of narrative levels in the *Metamorphoses*, many Ovidian critics tend to flatten out internal narrators and conflate their voices with the voice of the primary narrator. The characters who narrate thus become transparent functions and fail to grab our attention. This habit of 'transparent' reading has some justification. In the *Metamorphoses*, the act of narration is constantly a spectacle, and the audience's attention is at each moment focused upon the virtuosity of the conductor. The primary narrator's voice is omnipresent and it will have the privilege of rounding out the lengthy narrative with the word *VIVAM*. No other poet (before Ariosto in the Renaissance) is able to maintain such an uninterrupted perception of a 'central' narrative voice against which the whole is measured. We are a bit like Orpheus' audience, the *theatrum* surrounding, and held mesmerized by, the magnetic singer.

But if Orpheus somewhat resembles Ovid, perhaps he too ought to be taken seriously. Among all the poem's narrators, he is the one who most evidently presents himself as a poet. The other, more esteemed practitioners of poetry in the poem are gods, Apollo and Calliope (incidentally, the parents of Orpheus). More so than a usual narrator, as a poet Orpheus has the right to open his stories with proemial formulas:

> Ab Iove, Musa parens – cedunt Iovis omnia regno –,
> carmina nostra move ...
>
> (10.147-8)

Dira canam: procul hinc natae, procul este parentes,
aut, mea si vestras mulcebant carmina mentes,
desit in hac mihi parte fides, nec credite factum ...

(10.301-3)

These two introductions correspond to two separate story sequences: the pederastic loves of the gods (10.152-3), and the criminal passions of maidens (10.153-4). The first of these two overtures leaves no room for controversy. Only an absent-minded reading (still found however in some commentators) can separate the proem from Orpheus' personality and from the themes of the song it introduces. It is clearly not enough simply to recall the formula *ek Dios arkhomestha / Ab Iove principium*.[18] Orpheus is not merely reciting a stock phrase (like those who say, 'let us begin from Jupiter,' only to move immediately to another topic). Orpheus begins from Jupiter *because* he is going to speak about Jupiter. The god will be the first protagonist of the new song that consists of a catalogue of divine loves for human boys, and Orpheus rightly puts in the first line the most important god of all. The trite traditional motif is taken in a literal sense – a characteristically Ovidian move – and becomes, at the same time, mercilessly blasphemous. Given that Orpheus is about to sing how Jupiter overcame Ganymede, a very ambiguous light is cast on the traditional attribution of omnipotence (*cedunt Iovis omnia regno*). He thus shows how it is possible to rewrite an old repertoire of hymnological formulas into the unexpected register of *Mousa paidikê*.[19]

This is indeed Orpheus' new Muse, not his mother Calliope formally invoked at line 148 – Calliope, as we know from the hymn to Ceres at 5.341ff., is a god-fearing and unsuitably traditional poetess. Orpheus, on the contrary, is innovating here. His new poetics is dictated by a personal choice, caused by the loss of his wife Eurydice:

ille etiam Thracum populis fuit auctor, amorem
in teneros transferre mares, citraque iuventam
aetatis breve ver et primos carpere flores.

(10.82-4)

The idea of associating Orpheus with pederastic love comes directly from a famous passage of Phanocles, a fragment of a long poem dedicated to the Muse of pretty boys. Ovid's Orpheus is viewing himself in the mirror of this model of homoerotic poetry:

... Πρῶτος ἔδειξεν ἐνὶ Θρήκεσσιν ἔρωτας
ἄρρενας οὐδὲ πόθους ᾔνεσε θηλυτέρων

(Phan. fr. 1.9-10 Powell)

The connection between the two themes sung by Ovid's Orpheus, ephebic love affairs and the illicit passions of women, has been much discussed.

The logical connection – praise for male love, denunciation of female perversion (cf. 10.152ff.) – is fairly clear, and as in Phanocles it is well harmonized with the Maenad's revenge (cf. fr. 1.7ff. Powell, with *Met.* 10.7). Homoerotic love is described as a *diligere*; that of women for men as lust (cf. 10.153ff.). It might also be the case that Ovid has been inspired by the passage of Phanocles, pressing and altering its meaning a bit: *pothous theluteron* clearly signifies 'desire *for* women' (*theluteron* being simply an elegant variation on the adjectival construction *arrenas*), but in theory it could be interpreted as a subjective genitive (the lusts *of* women).

We thus have Orpheus as a singer of *paidika*, deriving from the model of Phanocles and, at the same time, composing poetry *in the style* of Phanocles.[20] The *Amores* of Phanocles were, according to the available evidence, in catalogue form, a point-by-point homosexual version of Hesiod's *Catalogue of Women*, perfectly comparable to Orpheus' song on the gods' love for ephebes. Orpheus' homoerotic mission needs to be read within the context not only of Ovid's Alexandrian culture and his interest in lesser-known poetic genres, but also in the context of Augustan culture. The most authoritative manifesto of Augustan poetics had chosen Orpheus as exemplar for the *civilizing vates* ('poet-seer'). According to Horace, Orpheus had established the prestige of poetry through a constructive program of legislation: his Orpheus taught lawful and civil love, and corrected wild and promiscuous sexuality:

> silvestris homines sacer interpresque deorum
> caedibus et victu foedo deterruit Orpheus ...
> ... Fuit haec sapientia quondam,
> publica privatis secernere, sacra profanis,
> concubitu prohibere vago, dare iura maritis.
>
> (Hor. *Ars* 391-8)

This edifying Orpheus had fought in favour of marriage and against a primitive sexuality, performed (as Horace explains in a parallel passage, *Sat.* 1.3.109) *more ferarum*. Now we meet him again singing of frivolous loves for boys and, in an aggressive reversal, women with incestuous and bestial passions. Myrrha argues with herself and justifies her incest with the argument that the animals do it too (10.324: *coeunt animalia nullo / cetera dilectu ...*).

Given this, the second 'proem' quoted above also appears problematic and ambiguous, or at least it should. Still, modern interpreters of Ovid are accustomed to ironing out the difficulty with a simple interpretive move: *dira canam*, and what follows, is a direct intrusion of the primary narrator, or better yet, of Ovid himself, since here the author, more than the primary narrator, has more to fear should his text come across as too immoral. In other words, we ought to forget for a while the voice of Orpheus. In this case the *Metamorphoses*' intrusive primary narrator is bending the rules of the game a bit. But modern critics know how to account for his intrusion.

The immorality of Myrrha's story, they say, is truly excessive, even for the libertine Ovid, and this makes the author's precaution necessary in order to limit his liability. (But would it not have been easier to insinuate, as Callimachus had, that 'this myth is not mine, it belongs to someone else?' After all, Cinna's *Zmyrna* had been around for a couple of generations, with a retinue of admirers and even professional commentators, and to Ovid's tastes it had already become passé).[21]

It is natural to turn, by analogy, to the story of Byblis, the other narration on incest in the poem. There, as the primary narrator, Ovid expresses a direct caveat on the scandalous content of the story about to begin:

> Byblis in exemplo est, ut ament concessa puellae;
>
> (9.454)

But before becoming a negative example, Byblis takes pains to provide herself with the best examples in an opposite sense, that is, those exhorting *towards* incest: Saturnus, Oceanus, Jove, the children of Aeolus (9.498ff.), with the amusing addition, *unde sed hos novi? cur haec exempla paravi?* The entire story of Byblis is developed in a paradoxical mode, as a salacious contrast between the amorality of the ends and a cool-headed technical analysis of the means. The problem of incest, exorcised by the poet with a single verse, dissolves into questions of seductive techniques, highly concrete problems of amorous strategy. The heroine behaves as if she were an ideal reader of the *Ars amatoria*. I would agree, in general, with Kenney ([1986] 429ff.): Ovid broadcasts his morals very 'tongue in cheek'.

The case of Orpheus is made peculiar by the presence of an intermediary narrator, whose prerogatives we would be forced to violate if we overlook his presence. Almost all critics agree that Ovid 'is peeking through the figure of Orpheus' (Solodow [1988] 40), and by this is meant, surprisingly, that the moralizing proem should be taken seriously. The uneasiness that makes this solution attractive has various causes. Some (Galinsky [1975] 90), in order to save the role and the voice of Orpheus, appeal to the contrast between the pure and idealized love for his wife Eurydice, on the one hand, and the sinister transgression of Myrrha, on the other. But the shifting of Orpheus to free homosexual love makes this dichotomy rather doubtful. To this some have objected (Solodow [ib.]) that Orpheus' puritanism would be too hypocritical: the discrepancy is an invitation for the reader to hear the 'authorial' voice. Others (Haupt-Korn-Ehwald-von Albrecht [1966] ad loc.; Fränkel [1945] 220 n. 70) do not accept that the mythical singer is contrasting the luxury and redolence of the Orient with his native Thrace, in terms clearly alluding to traditional praise of Italy. Rather than admitting an Orpheus who speaks like Virgil in the *Georgics*, they prefer to think that the metadiegetic narrator is for a while eclipsed. In this way, for those who accept that the voice of the proem is Ovid's own, any difficulty and contradiction is thus resolved.

But all the ironic effects of the situation are lost by this move. I will turn now to examine these point by point.

> Dira canam: procul hinc natae, procul este parentes!
>
> (10.301)

The implications here are very similar to those of *Ab Iove principium*, the only difference being that here the pious formula is not denaturalized but inverted. The true poet-seer should avoid impure persons, and it is indeed a traditional feature of Orphism to begin singing with a solemn expulsion of the uninitiated. 'I will speak to whom it is allowed to speak: shut the doors, profane ones!' is the typical beginning of an Orphic *hieros logos*, from which derives Horace's *arceo* (*Carm.* 3.1.1).[22] Instead of continuing with a *virginibus puerisque canto*, Ovid's Orpheus, who announces *dira* and not *sacra*, has to exclude from his audience parents and daughters. The conventional formula of chasing away is already present as an ironically inverted subtext in Ovidian passages such as *Amores* 2.1.3: *procul hinc, procul este severae!*; *Ars* 1.31: *este procul, vittae tenues, insigne pudoris* (cf. Verg. *Aen.* 6.258: *procul, o procul este, profani*). But another important aspect will appear, as we will see shortly, if we take into account the real audience of Orpheus' song:

> aut, mea si vestras mulcebunt carmina mentes,
> desit in hac mihi parte fides, nec credite factum;
> vel si credetis, facti quoque credite poenam.
> Si tamen admissum sinit hoc natura videri ...
>
> (10.302-5)

These lines clearly assume the narrative voice of Orpheus. The soothing power typical of his poetry (*mulcebunt*) has now become a danger against which he has to warn his audience, and it is therefore emphasized in this context.[23] The tone of the warning is once again ironic. Orpheus asks his audience either not to believe in the reality of the incest, or to believe the crime *and* its necessary punishment. The division between the two events, transgression and punishment, is in no way innocent. The punishment itself, the seal of divine justice for Myrrha's story, is clearly the least plausible element in the story. The transformation of the pregnant Myrrha into a perfumed tree, one able nonetheless to give birth to a child, is a typical example of a 'metamorphosis not to be believed'. In strictly Ovidian terms, we have here a case of *in non credendos corpora versa modos* (as the *Met.* is defined in *Trist.* 2.64). The transgression is realistic, the expiation pure fantasy. The suspension of disbelief asked of the reader applies not to the moral nucleus of the story, but to the concluding moral – or at least the two themes are coupled in an ambiguous light:

gentibus Ismariis et nostro gratulor orbi
gratulor huic terrae, quod abest regionibus illis
quae tantum genuere nefas.

(10.305-7)

The contrast with faraway lands of the East, rich in spices and incense, but marked by other disadvantages, is central to the ideology of Virgilian *laudes Italiae*:

Sed neque Medorum silvae, ditissima terra,
nec pulcher Ganges atque auro turbidus Hermus
laudibus Italiae certent, non Bactra neque Indi
totaque turiferis Panchaia pinguis harenis.

(*Geo.* 2.136-9; cf. also v. 117)

This correspondence is the source of irony.[24] Orpheus is obviously not speaking about Italy; but he shows that it is possible to compose, with conventional rhetorical material, highly improbable *laudes Thraciae*. The situation bears some similarity to the episode of Baucis and Philemon (8.618ff.), where the description of country life, simple and idealized, intentionally recalls the classic praise of country life found in Virgil and Horace. Reading these passages one feels transported into the traditional world of the Italian countryside, as seen through the nostalgic and austere eyes of the first generation of the Augustan period. But the concrete localization of the ideal peasants produces a slight dissonance. Baucis and Philemon live *collibus in Phrygiis* (8.621), and thus belong to a people associated mostly with luxury and vice, a distillation of oriental delicacy. The effect is to relativize the ideological restrictions and nationalistic conventions on which the *laudes vitae agrestis* are based.[25] As far as concerns the story's narrator, might it not be significant that while he tells about a frugal meal he is enjoying a luxurious banquet (cf. 8.573 with 8.678ff. and Verg. *Geo.* 2.506)?

In our passage, Orpheus contrasts the Thracians with the East, full of perfumes but also of aberrant passions – which together form an indivisible unity, since Myrrha will become an Oriental perfume, an imported luxury. In this framework the choice of *Ismariis* is noteworthy, and very peculiar if Ovid was interested in having us forget the narrative setting, and wanted instead to project us into the familiar dimension of praise for Italy. The Thracian emphasis is embarrassing for more than one reason. Orpheus, as we have seen, is busy disseminating pederasty among the Thracians. *Ismariis* is an epithet that makes one think of wine and Bacchic cults much more than of moderation and simplicity of habits. Very soon, Orpheus will become the victim of a bloody bacchanal unleashed by his disdain for female orgies. Certainly the Thracians do not produce perfumes and ointments, but is it also the case that they are unfamiliar with criminal desires and passions? Common sense, well represented by Cornelius Nepos, revolts against this idea: *Thraecas, homines vinolentos rebusque veneriis deditos* (*Alc.* 11.4). The main episode of the *Metamorphoses* staged in Thrace, the tragedy of Tereus and Philomela, explains the shameful passion of Tereus for his sister-in-law as a typical Thracian phenomenon, linked to the libidinous nature of the entire race:

> Sed et hunc innata libido
> exstimulat, pronumque genus regionibus illis
> in Venerem est; flagrat vitio gentisque suoque.
>
> (6.458-60)

The raped Philomela will afterwards say to Tereus, *omnia turbasti* (6.537), a standard reproach for incest, suitable to the enormity of the crime. The echo of *regionibus illis* (10.306 with 6.459) undermines the nationalistic emphasis of Orpheus.[26]

One last point remains, valuable for our analysis. The entire context invites us to take Orpheus seriously as the speaker of the 'proem'; this is the only way the text becomes coherent with its implications, i.e., ironical. We often find Ovid dull and superficial because we do not take him literally enough. We should also think seriously about the presence of an audience.[27] There is no longer any reason to believe that 'go away, daughters, go away, fathers', ought to refer to Ovid's audience. But of whom is Orpheus' audience composed? We find basically three categories, well known from the mythical tradition: (a) walking trees (10.88ff.); (b) animated rocks (11.2); (c) mesmerized animals.[28] Trees and rocks are clearly in no great danger of being led down the path to incest. The case of animals is even more symptomatic. In accordance with a known philosophical *topos*, Myrrha will soon make it clear that incest is the most natural of practices among beasts and birds:

> coeunt animalia nullo
> cetera dilectu, nec habetur turpe iuvencae
> ferre patrem tergo: fit equo sua filia coniunx,
> quasque creavit init pecudes caper; ipsaque, cuius
> semine concepta est, ex illo concipit ales.
> Felices, quibus ista licent!
>
> (10.324-9)[29]

Natae and *parentes* are out of the picture here; Orpheus is preaching against incest to an exceptional audience (the only one imaginable with these prerequisites) for whom incest is a natural and legitimate practice. The civilizing mission to which Horace devoted Orpheus – barring human beings from promiscuity and intercourse *more ferarum* – has been displaced by a relentless parody. Orpheus sings to his audience of animals a theme which *to them* cannot possibly be of any harm. (In the very same way, Ovid points out that the *Ars amatoria* is innocuous and beyond reproach: it is addressed to those who already practise free love, certainly not to upright matrons.)

Pythagoras and Ovid

The example of Orpheus has shown that it is dangerous to neglect the individuality of narratees and internal narrators as well as the specific circumstances attending each narrative act. Before posing questions about the narrating voice of the author, or Single Narrator, one should take seriously, and also very literally, the narrative instance, or level, in which the metadiegetic narrators are positioned. In a poet like Ovid, one should never lose sight of the potential for irony, and the metadiegetic structure is precisely the most fitting site, as we have been observing, for these ironic 'dub-overs' of the primary narrator's voice.

This perspective is difficult to reach, however, for those inclined to view internal narrators as possible mouthpieces of the author. A real contradiction exists between an ironic reading, like the one developed here, and the temptation to read 'through' subordinate narrators in search of a genuine authorial voice. I believe a discussion of the episode of Pythagoras (*Met*. 15.60-480) can shed some light on this dichotomy, even if some digression is required in order to discuss it, as well as a slight bending of terminology. After all, Pythagoras is not a narrator, strictly speaking, even if he is in fact an internal narrative voice and, for that matter, among the most important and most fully developed. I am led to choose this field of analysis because Kenney – an important reader of Ovid close to my own point of view, and very interested in the ironic depths of Ovidian narration – selects Pythagoras as the most plausible candidate for the role of direct authorial voice. Pythagoras is the only truly historical character in a poem which otherwise stars gods, demigods, gods 'in waiting' (Aeneas, Romulus, Caesar and Augustus himself), heroes and legendary characters, or personalities insubstantial to say the least, such as Numa, or the uncanny praetor Cipus with his horns displayed. The content of Pythagoras' doctrine – metempsychosis and the eternal flux of souls – seems to have a definite connection with the main theme of the poem, transformation. The precise modalities of this connection are heavily debated, and rightly so, since the *Metamorphoses* do not seem to me to display a clear integration between mythical and scientific levels, between the realm of transformation tales and that of Pythagorean doctrine. The identity of the speaker and the content of the episode are nonetheless an appealing argument for those who think Pythagoras is voicing Ovid's most deeply held beliefs (Kenney [1986] 460), or even a universal theodicy.

It is also true that Pythagoras could reinforce his role as a mouthpiece, or 'voice-over', since he has a certain aura of being a teacher of truth. Still, the experience we have had with the 'civilizing' Orpheus problematizes this type of credential, to say the least. Moreover, in antiquity – and in

Roman culture in particular – Pythagoras' status as a teacher is a highly resisted one. Hence, for example, one of the most visible features of Pythagorean doctrine, namely vegetarianism, in Ovid's time rarely failed to elicit ironic responses. This example is significant, since Ovid's Pythagoras delivers a discourse – although its attendant themes are multiform and often grandiose – written entirely to advance a rather limited and surprisingly modest proposal: 'don't eat meat'. It has been noted, with a certain amount of radicalism, that Pythagoras offers Ovid's readers an eloquent speech *de rerum natura* framed by the precept 'strive for five!'[30] This dietary precept, a subordinate element of the Pythagorean tradition deriving from the desire for radical reform of life, sees its rank and function changed; it becomes the source, end, and didactic goal of *physiologia*. This shift of level might hide an agenda. Those who find in the discourse of Pythagoras the 'deep convictions' of the author do not think, obviously, that Ovid was a fanatical vegetarian. Instead, the fascinating nucleus of Pythagoras' revelation is his image of nature as a universal flux, as well as the instability and transformation that marks both the entire digression and its style of exposition. But these interpreters pay a high price: in order to bring the author's voice to the surface they are forced to disregard the context, and sharply divide the doctrinal nucleus from its bizarre 'vegetarian' framework.

This brings us back to a familiar problem. The search for an authorial voice conflicts with the specific features of the context and with the qualities of the metadiegetic voice. It is fitting again to begin from the narrative context and the problems it poses. Ovid reaches Pythagoras through Numa. It is Numa, his disciple, who introduces us to the world of Croton and Pythagorean doctrine. This connection had been historically discredited in Augustan Age culture, and it is impossible that Ovid was not aware of this fact. On the basis of the chronology that most ancient historians adopt, the disciple Numa was almost two hundred years older than his teacher: 'four generations', as Dionysius of Halicarnassus says, who together with Cicero and Livy is one of the harshest critics of the belief that Numa and Pythagoras were contemporaries.[31] But Ovid makes no attempt to overcome the obstacle; on the contrary, the narrative bridge uniting Numa and Pythagoras is constructed in such a way as to highlight the contradiction. Numa arrives in Croton and asks an old man about the *aition* of the city. He receives a rather intricate answer: the city has an eponymous hero, a guardian hero, and an 'historical' founder. While a guest in ancient Croton, Heracles had foretold the founding of the city; then, in a following, but still ancient, era (cf. 15.20: *illius ... aevi*), he compelled a certain Myscelus to cross the sea and colonize that land. Thus, the city's remote history already had many layers by the time of Numa. But Dionysius is particularly sceptical on this point, since in Numa's time Croton did not even exist and its founder Myscelus is connected with a later period. In Ovid, therefore, Numa arrives in a non-existent city and asks about the achievements of someone yet to be born.

This is the framework for Pythagoras' teachings. Numa is temporarily out of the picture, but implicitly present as an auditor, such that at the end of the episode he leaves Croton full of wisdom (15.479ff.: *talibus atque aliis instructum pectora dictis / in patriam remeasse ferunt ...*). Meanwhile, the introduction to the didactic discourse offers at least a couple points of critical tension. Here is how the audience of disciples is described:

> coetusque silentum
> dictaque mirantum magni primordia mundi
> et rerum causas et, quid natura, docebat.
>
> (15.66-8)

An attentive and admiring audience is naturally an important accessory for any didactic text. The Pythagoreans, moreover, are famed for the stress they place upon listening ('acusmatic' is one of their current labels), upon silence taken as a rule, and upon unconditional reverence ('as the Master said'). *Coetusque silentum*, placed at the end of the line, draws immediate attention to itself. It is important for the pupils to pay attention in hushed silence, but the use of *silentes* as a noun (as when in general *silentum* falls at the end of the hexameter) occurs elsewhere in Latin only with the metaphorical meaning 'the deceased'.[32] We catch a glimpse of the absurd image of Pythagoras holding class for a gathering of the dead – and indeed, as we have seen, one of the disciples ought to have been dead for generations.

A second element of surprise arises in the final line of the introduction:

> primus quoque talibus ora
> docta quidem solvit, sed non et credita, verbis:
> 'Parcite, mortales, dapibus temerare nefandis ... '
>
> (15.73-5)

The framework for didactic communication has very precise, but simple, rules: one needs only an addressee, and an attempt to persuade him or her. Didactic texts nurture and control the figure of the recipients, goad them to attention, guide them, anticipate objections and counter resistances. The focal point of the discourse, as Lucretius shows, rests on its credibility, on the capacity of the didactic voice to make itself understood and to induce belief. I am not referring to an abstract ideal. Ovid stylizes the entire speech of Pythagoras as a didactic text, or better yet, with its extreme density of the stylistic markers for this genre, as a hyper-didactic exhibition (see below). Such a text focuses on the figure of the addressee and the issue of credibility. We have seen that Pythagoras has a proper audience (even if there is room for ambiguity, on which more later). But Ovid points out, at the last possible moment before ceding the floor to the teacher, that all his effort will be in vain: granted, Pythagoras has a *learned* voice, but he is not *believed*. The didactic rules are invoked only to signal their inefficacy and failure.

The notion that Pythagoras' teaching may not work could seem like a merely casual ironic jab, but it is not hard to imagine what is lurking behind the scenes. Lucretius, the great conceptual and stylistic model influencing the whole episode, is a textbook case of 'disbelieved' poetry. The *doctus Lucretius* lavished treasures of science and eloquence without being able to leave a lasting impression on either Memmius or the Roman audience whom Memmius represented. The case of Pythagoras is similar in outcome and style, but antipodal in content. Like Lucretius, Pythagoras too fights against the fear of death, but with opposite arguments. The former's dictum 'the soul is mortal, matter transforms', becomes 'the soul transmigrates and is immortal, all else perishes'. From this point of view, the solemn apostrophes *mortales* (15.75), *genus o mortale* (139 [*genus immortale*, Lachmann!]) sound out of place, if abstinence from meat depends on the idea that *morte carent animae* and *nihil interit*.[33] The concept of fluid universal change is brusquely shifted from matter to spirit. The effectiveness of the new message depends on one's point of view. Many readers of the third book of Lucretius feel that the mortality of the soul is, after all, not a very good antidote for the fear of death. Pythagoras, coming from the opposite direction, can play his hand: it might be that reincarnation is much more effective on this score than Epicurean materialism. On the other hand, Ovid and his readers know that they do not live in a Pythagorean culture; Pythagoras' great efforts, like those of Lucretius, have produced only marginal results and have lost the great battle for a receptive audience.

But there is a pivotal point that still eludes us. The struggle against the fear of death is only a secondary element in the message Ovid relates. The text hammers obstinately – and probably with a loss of seriousness – upon a completely different and much more limited theme. Animals should not be killed for any reason. They should not be eaten nor sacrificed. Even here, naturally enough, Pythagoras' mission anticipates its own failure: Roman society is not a world of vegetarians. But we have lost sight of Numa, whom Ovid presents as the main addressee for the Pythagorean doctrine. Is it possible that Pythagoras' failure affects him too?

We know that Numa, chosen king of Rome, leaves in search of new knowledge; his Sabine heritage was not enough for him (cf. 15.4ff.). He later leaves Croton suffused with doctrine, returns home and fulfills his mission as a wise and peaceful civilizing king:

> coniuge qui felix nympha ducibusque Camenis
> sacrificos docuit ritus gentemque feroci
> adsuetam bello pacis traduxit ad artes.

>   (15.482-4)

According to the didactic model that Ovid presupposes, Numa has gone from being student to teacher, by putting into practice the teaching he received. One can observe that the mention of Egeria and the Camenae sounds a slightly dissonant note, since in the antiquarian tradition such local influences connected with the lore of archaic Latium are for the most part *alternatives* to the claim for Pythagorean origins. If Numa has been schooled by the nymphs, perhaps there is no need to connect him with Pythagoras; or has there maybe been a fusion of the two cultures? Ovid does not say, but in what Numa does at Rome we find a specific answer: *sacrificos docuit ritus*. This is a solid and incontestable tradition. Numa founded practically all the sacerdotal colleges upon which Roman state religion was based. Without Numa there would be no Flaminii or Salii, no Vestal Virgins and no Pontifex, no rites of the Argei, no *Agonalia*, no *Fordicidia*, and so on: all the auguries, colleges, rites, and annual festivals bound to and connected with the art of sacrifice that unfolds (like a crimson thread of blood) from the age of kings down to Ovid's own time. In sum, Numa is responsible for the fact that the backbone of Roman religion is animal sacrifice. In *Fasti* 4.629, we see the king at work. He asks, while slitting the throat of two ewes, how to stop a famine, and in thanks for the answer he founds the annual rite of *Fordicidia*. Thirty pregnant cows must be slaughtered each year, drenching the curia in blood, and their foetuses are to be extracted by the priests and burned by a Vestal. Ennius' *Annales* provide a good witness for this practice: the first merit of Numa, mentioned in fr. 114 Skutsch, is *mensas constituit*: 'he instituted the tables of sacrifice'.

Sacrifice is the culmination of Numa's activity as king, but it was also, as we have suggested, the focal point of Pythagorean doctrine as staged by Ovid. The prohibition against killing animals and eating meat culminates in a ban on slaughter for religious and sacral purposes:

> Longius inde nefas abiit, et prima putatur
> hostia sus meruisse mori ...
>
> (15.111-12)

> quid meruistis, oves ...
> quid meruere boves? ...
> immemor est demum nec frugum munere dignus,
> qui potuit ...
> ruricolam mactare suum ...
> nec satis est, quod tale nefas committitur: ipsos
> inscripsere deos sceleri numenque supernum
> caede laboriferi credunt gaudere iuvenci!
> Victima labe carens et praestantissima forma
> (nam placuisse nocet) vittis insignis et auro
> sistitur ante aras auditque ignara precantem
> imponique suae videt inter cornua fronti,
> quas coluit, fruges, percussaque sanguine cultros
> inficit in liquida praevisos forsitan unda.

Protinus ereptas viventi pectore fibras
inspiciunt mentesque deum scrutantur in illis.
Unde (fames homini vetitorum tanta ciborum est!)
audetis vesci, genus o mortale! quod, oro,
ne facite et monitis animos advertite nostris ...

(15.116-42; cf. 463-9)

Ovid gives the impression of having done his research on the Pythagoreans.[34] To give but one example, consider the winged words with which Pythagoras introduces his cosmological revelation:

sequar ora moventem
rite deum Delphosque meos ipsumque recludam
aethera et augustae reserabo oracula mentis ...

(15.143-5)

These lines contain a subtle reference to the etymology of the name Pythagoras, from '*puthios*' (the Sybil at the Delphic oracle), and '*agoreuein*' ('to proclaim'; cf. *recludam, reserabo*) attested by Aristippus in Diog. Laert. 8.21 (cf. also Lucr. 1.734ff.; 5.110ff.). One can thus infer that the choice of this line of argument is a conscious restriction, indeed, one which Ovid states explicitly: *talibus atque aliis ... dictis* (15.479). As usual, the narrator of the *Metamorphoses* does not hide the fact that the actual narration is the result of a process of selection: his act of storytelling is also an act of suppressing some narrative material.[35]

The result is paradoxical, and it should be appreciated not so much on the level of philosophical implications (as a battle 'for' or 'against' Pythagoreanism), as on the level of communicative form. As already noted above, Pythagoras' speech presents itself as a hyper-didactic text. It contains an unprecedented density of appeals to the reader – *animos advertite* (140), *animos adhibete* (238), *mihi credite* (254)[36] – and a varied series of five imperatives and five hortatory subjunctives that emphatically close the entire sequence (473-8). It is marked by typically didactic formulas, such as *nonne vides* (361 & 382),[37] by topics and images used as expository transitions – such as the flight of mind (146ff.: *magna ... canam ...*), lifting sails to the wind (176ff.), horses and the turning-post (453ff.) – and by metalinguistic formulas that direct the discourse within the constraints of didactic communication (172 *doceo*; 174 *vaticinor*, 238 *docebo*). All of the above, together with the insistent usage of the second person, assure the connection not only to a communicative function, but also to the tradition of a literary genre. It is only natural that in this connection Lucretius is given the leading role. The will to overturn the ideology of the *De Rerum Natura* is evident in both the philosophical theme (the immortality of the soul) and in the programmatic choice of the *mirum*. When Pythagoras pursues and catalogues *mirabilia* and *paradoxa*, in the spirit of Pliny the Elder, it is hard not to think that the attitude of Lucretius is diametrically opposed to his own. 'Don't be amazed that', and 'what is so strange about?' are the ligaments of thought and the appeals to the addressee that oppose Lucretian science to eclectic curiosity and dilettante polymathy.[38] With his ideology and mentality overturned, Lucretius is represented solely as a formal constraint and generic model.

On this point, one should understand and interpret the problematic relationship between Pythagoras and Numa as a sudden degeneration of the didactic genre. The lack of real communication between teacher and student undermines the basis of didactic discourse. After having sat in that proverbially attentive audience, Numa returns home and does the exact opposite of the precepts he has received. The leading 'didactic' hero of Roman poetry, Aristaeus in the *Georgics*, was a model of respectful compliance. His obedience to the sacrificial precepts constituted a clear model of successful didactic communication. His willingness to learn, and to translate learning into action, confirmed *sub specie narrationis* the didactic status of the entire Virgilian poem.[39] To this confirmation Ovid's didactic model opposes an image of frustrated expectation and failure.

We can also offer an exact precedent for the idea of Pythagoras being 'learned but still not believed'. In Callimachus' *Iamb.* I, the narrator Hipponax tells of Thales, who uses geometric figures 'invented by the Phrygian Euphorbus' (fr. 191.59ff. Pf.). The context is highly ironic. Hipponax and Thales himself are a little older than Pythagoras, but the difficulty of chronology can be ironed out – with a wink – given that Pythagoras himself claimed to have already lived once, about six hundred years before, as the Trojan hero Euphorbus. Simply call him 'Euphorbus' and Pythagoras can now be the teacher of his predecessors. The discrepancy in time recalls the chronological difficulties involved in the link between Pythagoras and Numa. But Callimachus focuses his attention on the vegetarian message and on its inefficacy:

$$\text{Κἠδίδαξε νηστεύειν}$$
$$\text{τῶν ἐμπνεόντων· οἱ δ' ἄρ' οὐχ ὑπήκουσαν ...}$$
(vv. 61-2)

Even if only by the working of an adverse *daimon*, people did not obey him: just like Ovid's Numa who becomes a wise and peaceful king, but also a slaughterer of animals.

Our discussion of Pythagoras and his addressees might end here, but there is still more to be drawn from that episode of Petronius' *Satyricon* which too is set in Croton. According to Porphyry (*VP* 18, cf. Dicaearchus fr. 33 Wehrli), as soon as Pythagoras arrives in Croton he is appreciated for his experience and natural talents. His eloquence gains him the sympathy of the elders and he takes an active part in the education of the youth. The elders are pleased that the young converse with him (Isocr. *Busir.* 28). His 'conquest' of Croton finds an interesting counterpart in the analogous successes of Eumolpus in the *Satyricon*. Eumolpus (who has a portentous name, that of the founder of the Eleusinian Mysteries) acquires a reputation for being wise and concerns himself, for personal advantage, with the education of youths. Pythagoras' conquest culminated, as we know, in the victory of precepts such as the immortality of the soul and its corollary, abstinence from meat and from killing animals. Eumolpus, on the contrary, promulgates a will that becomes an invitation to cannibalism. The Crotonians take him seriously, and display their eloquence in demonstrating that anthropophagy is right. Their leader, Gorgias, bears the name of a sophist also renowned for his Pythagorean affiliations. Between these two narratives, one could say, there is a relationship of parodic inversion. But our analysis suggests that in a certain sense Ovid's irony paves the way for Petronius' parody.

The clues collected so far undermine somewhat the traditional idea that Pythagoras is principally a mouthpiece for the author. But we have so far avoided the deepest level of Pythagoras' discourse: that in which the universal principle of change is revealed (15.420ff.: *sic omnia verti / cernimus*). This principle impinges upon the entire world of the *Metamorphoses* and in some sense the narrative style of the poem as well. Perhaps we have encountered, at last, an 'unmediated' voice. The idea that things are in flux is pure Ovid, it is the ideological basis of the poem and the source of the perpetual motion of its style and subject matter. We can grant that here more than elsewhere the figure of Pythagoras becomes transparent, a thin veil between the reader and the subject dearest to the poet. All the more so, since in this eulogy of change and disorder Ovid has nested his grandest prophecy of Roman greatness. The urgency of this theme can explain, according to some scholars, even the genesis of the character of Pythagoras: he is a wise man and a singer of truth introduced at the right moment to combine prophetically the origin of Rome and the triumph of Augustan order.

The Augustan voice: the prophecy

Thanks to Pythagoras, the *Metamorphoses* crosses paths with Rome as *domina rerum* and the Julian dynasty, and reaches, at last, the telos towards which a grand Augustan poem should tend if it wants to be a worthy companion of the *Aeneid*. The notion of a prophetic bridge between remote antiquity and the Augustan present is certainly to be measured against Virgil. Prophecy (through Jove, Anchises, and the shield of Vulcan) is the device by which the epic poet is able to break through into the present. This is also true for Ovid, but with a difference in motivation. The *Metamorphoses* is not bound, like the *Aeneid*, to a chronicle of events more than ten centuries in the past, and its programme (from the origin of the cosmos down to modern times) does not need to resort to prophecy as a *strictly necessary* device. We will return to this problem later on.

Pythagoras, with his universal knowledge and his Delphic connections, might seem the ideal candidate to be mediator of past and future. His chronological situation, more or less halfway between Troy and Rome, is a detail worth bearing in mind. But Ovid's original move is to present Pythagoras' prophecy as an act not of foretelling but of *memory*. The old man from Samos has already heard, as is likely, news about the rise of Rome, but his prophecy is based upon a gaze into the past. He remembers what he has heard said centuries before, in a previous life:

> quantumque recordor,
> dixerat Aeneae, cum res Troiana labaret,
> Priamides Helenos flenti dubioque salutis ...
>
> (15.436-8)

Quantumque recordor is a poignant detail: what makes Pythagoras exceptional in ancient tradition is his prodigious memory, reaching back to previous reincarnations. The name of his father, Mnesarchus (the one who 'remembers his own beginning'), must fit in here somewhere. The best known avatar of Pythagoras is his existence as the Trojan warrior Euphorbus ('Good Food'?).[40] Callimachus, as we have seen, has already toyed a little with the potential for this exchange between different ages. As a former Trojan, Pythagoras is favourable to Rome. His extraordinary memory (160: *nam memini*) gives him access to the era of the Trojan War, and would allow him to remember valuable details. Lucian portrays a cock who, having been Euphorbus (via Pythagoras), transmits previously unpublished details about the Trojan War. But Ovid's Pythagoras possesses a memory that one could call intertextual. His recollection of the war (15.161ff.) coincides very literally with a scene in the *Iliad* (the death of Euphorbus, *Il*. 17.43ff.). His punctilious *memini* can be compared with the *memini* of Ariadne in Catullus 64, and with the *memoro* of Mars who recalls Ennius' *Annales*:[41] these are, in the true sense of the word, textual memories.

The prophecy on the future of Rome has an even more sophisticated background. Euphorbus recalls a prophecy that the prophet Helenus had given to Aeneas when the fortunes of Troy were in decline. The memory takes us back to the intersection between the *Iliad* and the *Aeneid*. Euphorbus is a Homeric character, Helenus and Aeneas are carried over into the *Aeneid*, and the prophecy resembles something that Helenus tells Aeneas in *Aeneid* Book 3 (starting from the exordium *nate dea* ..., 15.439 = *Aen*. 3.374). The nexus between Euphorbus and Helenus is implicitly but very carefully prepared: Helenus is the greatest Trojan augur and a character strictly connected both to Apollo and with Delphi. Euphorbus has very similar affinities, not only through Pythagoras' 'Pythian voice', but also as the son of Panthus, the Trojan priest of Apollo who has Delphic connections.[42] The link has ironic consequences with respect to the *Aeneid*.

If the prophecy can be given so early, we are led to think that Virgil might have dispensed with the entire toilsome quest, with its ambiguous prophecies, misleading clues, and its deferrals from one site to another. Already before the fall of Troy, Aeneas would have known all that he needed and could have taken solace beforehand in the promise of a great kingdom overseas.[43] There follows then a more general ironic inference. If Pythagoras' prophetic knowledge turns out to be bookish expertise (accessible to any reader of Homer and Virgil), would one not be allowed to think that every prophecy, almost by definition, is pronounced *after the fact*?

But Pythagoras' historical knowledge is not limited to Troy and Rome. Before he announces the rise of Rome, he has to record the decline of illustrious Greek cities:

> Clara fuit Sparte; magnae viguere Mycenae;
> nec non et Cecropis, nec non Amphionis arces:
> vile solum Sparte est, altae cecidere Mycenae.
> Oedipodioniae quid sunt, nisi fabula, Thebae?
> quid Pandioniae restant, nisi nomen, Athenae?
> Nunc quoque Dardaniam fama est consurgere Romam ...
> (15.426-31)

The whole passage, up to the first signs of Rome's greatness, has been since the time of Heinsius highly suspect and considered worthy of deletion,[44] the reason being that one gets the sense of a blatant anachronism which clashes with the 'voice' of Pythagoras. The decadence of Greek cities is a typical theme of late-Republican and Augustan sensibilities. In a letter of Sulpicius to Cicero (*Fam.* 4.5.4) one hears the romantic emotions of a Roman traveller on his Grand Tour. His gaze embraces names of flourishing cities of the past, Aegina, Megara, the Piraeus, Corinth; today the educated traveller sees (with some understandable exaggeration) mere ruins. The contrast between extinct grandeur and present ruins is a noble and sober theme of Augustan poetry. Take for example Propertius (naturally in his own voice): *omnia vertuntur ... et Thebae steterant altaque Troia fuit* (2.8.7-10). But can we allow this point of view in the ancient Pythagoras? If one wants to salvage these lines, not suspect on the matter of style, one should accept the idea of intentional anachronism. Pythagoras, while illustrating the theme of transience, lets himself be carried away, and when he reaches the theme of Rome and Augustus, he speaks in the voice of Ovid.[45] (Two other possible alternatives – namely that Pythagoras in his omniscience might be indifferent to chronology, or that Ovid himself is – seem to me hardly worth consideration.)

But Augustan poetry knows how to regard the theme of transience from more complex, less linear, perspectives. A fine example occurs in Anchises' revelation in *Aeneid* Book 6. His is a vision of the future, like that of

Pythagoras, culminating with the destiny of Rome. But before this point it touches upon the greatness of the cities of Latium:

> hi tibi Nomentum et Gabios urbemque Fidenam,
> hi Collatinas imponent montibus arces,
> Pometios Castrumque Inui Bolamque Coramque.
> Haec tum nomina erunt, nunc sunt sine nomine terrae.
>
> (*Aen.* 6.773-6)

At first sight, Anchises is merely foreseeing a development that anticipates the expansion of Rome and paves the way for it. Now – about four centuries before the founding of Rome, according to the chronology accepted and made famous by Virgil – these cities are still to come, they are lands without names. Anchises foretells the names they will have (*haec tum nomina erunt*). But Virgil and his readers already know these names, and they connect them with contemporary reality. Now – in the age of Virgil and Augustus (or of Horace, Strabo, and Lucan)[46] – the cities of Latium in this catalogue are ghost towns, extinct, depopulated, or regressed to countryside, quite often countryside infested with malaria. Speaking of a place of this sort, Horace describes it as more depopulated than Gabii or Fidenae (*Sat.* 1.11.7ff.). The line of development that Anchises announces is shadowed by the spectre of impermanence. In the readers' own time these cities yet to be named will be *nothing but* names and ancient ruins (*nomina erunt*; cf. *Aen.* 7.412: *nunc magnum manet Ardea nomen*).

This perspective can enrich our understanding of Pythagoras' speech. Paradoxically, Pythagoras more than Anchises has some chronological uncertainties. It is unclear whether Ovid wishes to anchor him to the time of Numa or to the philosopher's own traditional floruit. But for our purposes, a difference of a century or two should not cause us too much worry. In this span of time, Rome is growing, we are told, and this is true; and Sparta, Athens, etc., are pure names, ruins, literary topoi. If we read these accounts in context, and not as an aside of the author, a problem arises. Many readers rebel against the idea that Athens, Sparta, and even Thebes, are presented as archaeology. What would Pericles or Epaminondas think of this? But the names of Ovid's characters are very different: Cecrops and Amphion, the remotest founders; Oedipus and Pandion, lords and leaders of Thebes and Athens in mythology and tragedy. These are all characters whom the poem's chronology have long since left behind. The temporal distance is emphasized by heavy epithets like *Oedipodioniae*, *Pandioniae* (both *hapax legomena* in Ovid's works), their resonance evoking *magni duces* or *tyranni* of the past (to return to Propertius 2.8.9). Pythagoras is speaking, with every right, about the original flourishing of these cities, the only one he could know in accordance with the chronology. The grandeur of Athens under its founding kings goes back a long way in time – back to Book 2 of the *Metamorphoses*, in fact, for those who follow Ovid:

Tritonida conspicit arcem
ingeniis opibusque et festa pace virentem.

(2.794-5)

As any cultured Roman knew, a dark and decadent middle age falls between the Greek origins, exalted in myth and literature, and the florescence begun during the Persian wars. In this intervening void (Pythagoras speaks in the golden age of Ionia and Magna Graecia), Athens and the other cities are at the nadir of their fortunes. Thus Pythagoras speaks exactly as a contemporary of Ovid would, unaware that a new cycle of ascent and decline will bring these places to the acme of historical and cultural importance, and then again to the verge of nonentity. His theory of universal flux is truer than he himself could show; it is not liable to verification even by its author.

If we allow the discourse on Greek cities to be joined to the voice of Pythagoras, an interesting consequence emerges concerning Rome.[47] Let us assume that the prophecy of Rome's ascent is only what it claims to be, namely, an extrapolation by Pythagoras, and not an intrusion of Ovid the omnipresent narrator:

nunc quoque Dardaniam fama est consurgere Romam ...

(15.431)

Pythagoras contemplates the decadence of Athens without being able to presage Pericles or Euripides. He foresees (through Homer and Virgil, as we have seen) Rome's trajectory of ascent up to Caesar and Augustus. But then what? How can we be sure? The poet has taught us that prophecies, in as much as they are given *ex eventu*, are always inseparable from their end-point. In *Fast.* 1.509-36, Ovid ventures into the most interminable prophetic glimpse that any Roman poet ever dared sketch (cf. *Aen.* 8.340ff.). Carmenta the soothsayer sets foot with Evander upon the soil of the future Rome, and immediately, well before Aeneas in the *Aeneid*, she foretells all that will happen up to the furthest point foreseeable by Ovid. Augustus' successor, son and grandson of a god, will come into power, and Livia (whom Carmenta sees as her heir) will ascend to heaven. Ovid, with a touch of cruelty, remarks that from this point on Carmenta can say no more:

talibus ut dictis nostros descendit in annos
substitit in medios praescia lingua sonos.

(*Fast.* 1.537-8)

This is truly a sore point for epic prophecy. Poets are able to motivate the prophetic point of departure well enough. Virgil's Jupiter, for example, when forced to address the anxieties of Venus, also takes pains to justify the extraordinary span of his foresight: *fabor enim, quando haec te cura remordet, / longius, et volvens fatorum arcana movebo* (*Aen.* 1.261ff.). But this careful narrative justification conceals an inevitable inconsistency: the prophecy has its goal already fixed, and it moves from the narrative present to reach, with a rather suspicious degree of exactness, the present of the author and his text.

The future of Rome beyond Augustus is still a mystery, and the poet of *cuncta fluunt* (15.177) takes no chances on the crucial point of Rome's *eternity*. After Pythagoras has declared that change rules the world, there can be no confidence on this score. Now at last it is the author's turn to speak. At the end of the poem Ovid finally has a direct word, in the voice of the author, and connects, like a well-mannered official poet, the success of his poetry to the greatness of Rome:

> quaque patet domitis Romana potentia terris,
> ore legar populi, perque omnia saecula fama,
> siquid habent veri vatum praesagia, vivam.
>
> (15.877-9)

The poet expects for himself eternal life and immortal fame – vast fame, because it will be as wide as the universal confines of the Empire. It has been noted, however, that Rome offers only a spatial, geographic measure. Perhaps trained by Pythagoras, Ovid does not link his immortality to the destiny of empires; he does not conflate the dimensions of space and time, nor does he weave together the endurance *per saecula* of his *carmen* with the durability of Rome. He tactfully marks out his difference from the author of the *Carmen Saeculare*, who had identified his own literary glory with the glorious perseverance of Rome.[48]

What Ovid has to say about the imperium of Augustus had already been exhausted a little before this point. As in the first book of the *Aeneid*, Jupiter calms Venus in her anxieties with a prophecy about the destiny of the Julian line culminating in the peaceful rule of Augustus. The coincidence has a contrastive effect that deserves emphasis. Through Jupiter's prophecy the *Aeneid*, which narrates a brief span of time during an age already a millennium in the past, is able to reach out and touch the Augustan present. This use of prophecy is clearly a guarantee for Augustus: a story of the distant past which the narrator contorts so as to include the glorification of the present. But the structure of the *Metamorphoses* is diametrically opposed to this point of view. The plan of the poem unfolds from the origin of things down to modern times. Employing Jupiter's prophecy in this programme is a little arbitrary. It is not motivated by the narrative structure out of a lack of other means. The *Metamorphoses* come to a sudden halt with the death of Caesar, and the prophecy, instead of guaranteeing Augustus an otherwise unthinkable presence, ends up rather underlining his *absence* from the poem. The temporal span of the prophecy is in tune with this choice. In the *Aeneid*, Venus hears about the outcome of a millenarian history. But Ovid's Jupiter exerts much less effort: if Venus could be patient for just a couple more years, there would be no need for the prophecy. If the poet had not resolved to end precisely here, a narration of the glory and successes of the Princeps would be unavoidable.

In the *Tristia* (2.560), Ovid chose to represent his poem as a work culminating with Augustus:

> in tua deduxi tempora, Caesar, opus.

The obvious echo of *Met.* 1.4 reminds us most of all that the proem speaks in a slightly different way: *ad mea ... deducite tempora carmen*. This is a bold move, highly egocentric, which not all translators of the *Metamorphoses* give proper force.[49] When he addresses the Princeps, Ovid describes the plan of his work as 'from origins to Caesar Augustus'. But to his own audience he had already clearly said 'down to *my* times'. Depending on the circumstances, he might have also claimed that Augustus' empire, among all the ages of the universe, is given the *least* consideration in the poem. It is true that the latest event the poem recounts, the death of Caesar (15 March 44 BCE) with his transformation into a star and apotheosis (after July 44 BCE), is an obvious eulogizing concession to Augustus. Ovid could have said, 'from the origins down to your coming' – but he did not do so, and the chronology plays clever tricks. Since he was born on 20 March 43 BCE, Ovid has succeeded in the egotistical endeavour of telling a story from the creation of the world down to his own conception.

In perfect coherence with the poem's thematic system, the concluding event is viewed as a catasterism. The continuous and repetitive structure gives the reader an impression of duplication and seriality. The weight of the authorial voice announcing this new miracle cannot be separated from the work's overall narrative context. This is still the same voice that has led the readers from chaotic beginnings, and the metamorphosis of Caesar cannot be separated from the fabulous fabric of preceding metamorphoses. It is the last and closest, certainly, but the principle regulating it is no different than what transformed the Minyeiades into bats or the Cercopes into monkeys. The aura of incredibility that suffuses the entire poem seems to envelop this final miracle as well. The only difference being that this time, as Ovid warns his readers, at the last moment but firmly, things are a bit different – *we must believe*:

> Ne foret hic igitur mortali semine cretus
> ille deus faciendus erat.
>
> (15.761-2)

Caesar's transformation into a god in fact conceals a final movement, a metamorphosis not to be told, more serious and terrifying than any other: that which makes Octavian the first being of a species never seen before.

These lines seem to me of the utmost importance for our discussion of the *Metamorphoses*' Augustanism. In fact, a large part of our discussion rests on highly controversial allusions, which moreover will probably remain controversial forever. We are dealing with cases in which Ovid, according to 'anti-Augustan' critics, sends out signals while remaining, so to speak, below deck. These are ironic allusions, disenchanted and defeatist, critical, blasphemous or even subversive, smuggled beneath the fabric of an impeccable courtier's discourse. Supporters of Augustanism observe that these allusions are not necessary for our comprehension of the text, or that Ovid was in no position to afford them. Or even (depending upon their personal attitudes towards Augustus) these critics object that Augustus' power was neither repressive nor totalitarian, and that Ovid had no need to adopt a secret code if he wanted to lead some sort of literary opposition. Interpreters from the opposite camp counter this by objecting that the audience of the time was not monolithic, and that Ovid – under the authoritarian and repressive rule of Augustus – had no choice but to proceed by means of 'a rhetoric of ambiguity and innuendo' (Hinds [1987b] 25ff.). 'Augustans' ask the other side for proof, unambiguous expressions to this effect, and receive the answer that the nature of the phenomenon is such that it does not allow for readings that are not ambiguous. The truth is that the question so posed only allows for solutions that are too subjective, both depending on our image of Ovid and, even more, on our image of Augustus and his regime. We are coming dangerously close to the 'circular' controversies opened up by the allusions to the Emperor in Senecan tragedy or, better yet, to the praise of Nero in the *Pharsalia*. Personally, I have tried to read with the eyes of a partisan such verses as Lucan 1.40-2:

> ultima funesta concurrant proelia Munda.
> his, Caesar, Perusina fames Mutinaque labores
> accedant fatis ...

If we take into account the fact that classical poetry places importance on the position of the vocative in its context, the effect here is striking. It is hard to avoid the impression that Caesar, that is Nero, is one of the disasters listed by the poet, a deadly catastrophe like Munda, Perugia and Modena. But the effect works only if we look from the start with the eyes of an anti-Neronian partisan. Lucan's own position and the internal history of the *Pharsalia* continue to be uncertain data on which to ground our interpretation.

The phenomenon that we are discussing in Ovid is different. The authorial voice is not sending out encrypted messages or subterranean allusions. There is no subversive sense running between the lines. We would like, on the contrary, to apply to Ovid's voice the prerequisite that has been important in our reading thus far: every narrative expression is to be viewed in context, taking into account the audience, the speaker, and the temporal frame set up by the text.

Ovid is clearly stating – with an extreme clarity that no other Augustan author possesses – a blatantly evident truth. Caesar had to be made a god because Octavian *could not be a mortal* (or even 'for fear that' he was a mortal). This hindsight motivation for Caesar's deification is by no means as absurd as it seems to some modern critics.[50] In the terms imposed by Augustan propaganda, Caesar is precisely the projection of his son. His apotheosis comes from the future, not from the origin, as was the case in the obvious parallels of Heracles and Romulus (cf. *Fast.* 2.144). Augustus moulds Caesar into a 'double' of himself. The two characters are mirror images: they bear the same name (a fact obscured by our modern habits of onomastics, and a source of problems for Virgilian critics), and they are modelled upon one another in official iconography (at first the young upon the old, but then vice versa).[51] Let us imagine a modern historian called upon to re-evaluate Caesar's position in Augustan ideology and literature. It is likely that her analysis, disenchanted, distanced, endowed with complex tools, would arrive at one crucial point: Caesar is important (and continues to be so) as the father of Octavian Augustus. His role as model for the Principate can be, for various reasons, problematic or exposed to winds of hostility, but his function is essential and permanent. The main reason for this delicate function is among the simplest, and has more to do with biology than with ideology: *Augustus too will die someday*. If he does not want his power to be revocable, it has to rest upon some form of continuity, and only the continuity of a family can ensure the permanence of the regime. In this sense, the idea that Augustus is the first and only example of a new species has its own dangers. The key to this continuity, in religious and ideological terms, is the expectation of Augustus' apotheosis. But this is an expectation that must be prepared for, cultivated even with a kind of pedagogy. Augustus' chosen mode for this preparation is to exploit the exemplary role of an analogous past event. The apotheosis of Caesar, the sign of Octavian's victory in the Civil Wars, is the symbolic threshold for the transfer of power, but also – a very significant point – the pledge and anticipatory reflex of what awaits the Romans when Augustus begins to wane.[52] Our modern historian could not but agree with Ovid: Caesar has been made a god because Augustus cannot be mortal.

This is why it is not correct to interpret Caesar's apotheosis as a relic of the early Augustan Age, an outworn legacy left to Ovid by Virgil and Horace. Too many Ovidian scholars view the end of the *Metamorphoses* as a triumph of rhetoric, of courtier language severed from all reality.[53] In particular, it is easy to put one's finger on certain themes that seem to 'show up late', because our literary-historical categories associate them

with other seasons and other situations. Caesar's apotheosis feels more
natural in the context of the difficult years between the rise of Octavian
and the battle of Actium. What then was a symbol of crisis, unrest within
a void of power, and with messianic expectations, appears now as an empty
compliment. But things are not exactly this simple. Around 8 CE, the
problem of what happens when a leader dies is more urgent than ever.
Similarly, the wish that the Princeps will not tire of the earth,

> tarda sit illa dies et nostro serior aevo,
> qua caput Augustum, quem temperat, orbe relicto
> accedat caelo faveatque precantibus absens!
>> (15.868-70)

– to many this sounds empty and rhetorical. It seems particularly so in
comparison with Virgil's *Georgics*, and with Horace in his first civil lyrics:

> serus in caelum redeas diuque
> laetus intersis populo Quirini ...
>> (*Carm*. 1.2.45ff.)

> tuque adeo, quem mox quae sint habitura deorum
> concilia incertum est ...
>> (*Georg*. 1.24-5)

> hunc saltem everso iuvenem succurrere saeclo
> ne prohibete! ...
>> (ib. 1.500ff.)

> iam pridem nobis caeli te regia, Caesar,
> invidet ...
>> (ib. 1.503-4)

But the confrontation is unavoidable, and Ovid himself has anticipated it.
Many years have passed, and the fashion of calling the Princeps *iuvenis*
would now sound ridiculous. Horace's lyrics and Virgil's *Georgics* were
addressing their passionate appeal 'don't leave us!' to a leader in his early
thirties. The *Metamorphoses*, on the other hand, is written for an audience
familiar with these poets, but who can also not ignore the fact that
Augustus is now over seventy.[54] For this audience, the civil rhetoric of the
first Augustan poets posed an insidious question. Before taking his leave,
Ovid reminds us that a new transformation is inevitable, and it too will
have to be faced.

4

Teaching Augustus through Allusion

'Le style c'est l'homme même', répète-t-on sans y voir de malice ... Le style c'est l'homme, en rallierons-nous la formule, à seulement la rallonger: l'homme à qui l'on s'addresse?

(Jacques Lacan)

Of the Roman poetry composed during the lifetime of the first emperor, two texts merit the title of 'Letter to Augustus'. The modern habit of calling the older one 'Hor. *Ep.* 2.1' and the more recent 'Ov. *Trist.* 2' does not assist comparative readings of these two texts, just as it risks obscuring the autonomy of each text in the book of which it forms a part – the so-called book 2 of the *Epistles*, and the *Tristia*, where the second book has little in common with its brethren.[1] The reflections I offer here will suggest the importance of a comparative analysis, and will centre on the crucial presence of a didactic addressee by the name of 'Caesar Augustus'. The first appearance of this paper in a collection devoted to the topic of the *didactic addressee* influences the aims of this study and the method it uses; but it does not imply the presupposition that these texts are generally considered didactic.

Two premises

First of all, I will treat both poems as didactic texts. In doing so, I intend to conduct an experimental reading, and not to assign Horace's hexameters and Ovid's couplets to a category at once historical and atemporal that might be labelled 'didactic poetry'. Hence, I propose a reading, admittedly partial and tendentious, of two texts, which no present literary historian, at any rate, has been willing to categorize with precision.[2] In general, even when dealing with 'pure' didactic poetry, I am not in favour of marking out the territory too strictly. I consider that the basic requirement which any text, or part thereof, must meet to be identified as didactic is the presence, at any level of the literary structure, of an addressee, and the intent to instruct him or her. Thus I accept as didactic those texts in which the instruction is 'serious', 'less than serious', or openly parodic, as well as

texts where the figure of addressee is located on (or moves through) a wide
spectrum of levels (including patrons, dedicatees, Implicit Readers, Model
Readers, or the work's general public). Experience teaches that rigorous
applications of the concepts 'instruction' and addressee, 'intentionality'
and 'poetics of the author', end up throwing out with the bath water not
only the baby – but the bathtub too.[3] Focusing on how a text 'constructs a
didactic addressee' has at least two important advantages. First, it allows
one to regard the addressee as someone whom the reception of the text can
– or should – modify. Secondly, it sheds light on the relationship of power
implicated in the process by which poetry creates meaning. The narrator's
authority, the control exercised by the author and the addressee on the
textual message and its interpretation, the relation between these textual
instances and political power – these are all questions that we will
encounter in the following pages, where the central issue will be the
relationship between poetics and power.

   Secondly, I will not accept a preliminary separation between politics and
aesthetics, between social function and literary function. To treat *Ep*. 2.1
as a text solely about poetics simply because its main theme is the current
state of letters can lead to a reductive vision of the role Caesar Augustus
plays in that text. The simple presence of that extremely peculiar addressee, I would argue, is enough to make the reading of the epistle
potentially binary. What Horace has to say about poetry also affects the
political image of Augustus, just as the decision to address Augustus
makes *Ep*. 2.1 a special or unique text about poetics. It is not by chance
that the epistle reaches its climax of tension when the matter in question
is 'how to represent the Princeps'. So too, to treat *Tristia* 2 as a political
statement just because Ovid is an exile writing to the master of his fate,
means losing sight of the fact that a great part of the epistle is a lesson in
literary history. The text's political dimension can be recuperated only by
coming to terms with its nature as a literary-critical commentary, not by
overlooking it or treating it as an incidental expedient. This does not mean
reading the two poems as projections of political intentions and programmes – for instance, by interpreting Horace's letter as a text of
'integration' and Ovid's as one of 'opposition'. Indeed, this is the mistake I
want to avoid. Our reading of Horace will show that one of the letter's
fundamental themes is the difficulty of speaking about Augustus in poetry.
Ovid, on his part, assumes a much more subordinate position. His entire
portrait of Augustus is drawn from the values and stereotypes of imperial
propaganda. With the sources at our disposal, we can hardly even imagine
what it meant to be 'against Augustus'. We have to resist the temptation
to place Horace and Ovid on two different points along a political arc, to
deduce from this their authorial intentions, and then finally to deduce the
meaning of their messages for Augustus. As Ovid says in *Tristia* 2 (in
reference to something else) 'a book is not proof of personal conviction' (v.
357).

I hope that these premises allow us to examine the didactic structure of these two epistles. This will enable us, first of all, to highlight what they have to say about their theme, in both cases literature – 'what is the position of modern poetry in Roman culture?', 'how should one read the erotic poetry that is now being indicted?' It will also allow us to hold in view the links between knowledge and power, a relationship no student of didactic poetry ought to ignore. Calling upon an addressee nicknamed the 'augustus' could not have been an act free from political implications – but in general neither is didactic poetry.

Teaching Augustus to the Romans

The peculiar complexity of *Ep.* 2.1 can be ascribed to a basic tension: here Augustus is both student and teacher. The text teaches Augustus – and *a fortiori* Rome's literary public – the basis for a new literature: severance from the past (archaic, neoteric) and reform of literary institutions. The text in turn learns from Augustus, since the political model of the Principate influences the form of the new poetry for the new times. The division of labour made between politics and literature allows Horace to teach the Princeps, but this division is continually transgressed, since the poets need to learn how to speak to and of Augustus, and to do so they have to learn from him. The urgent task of devising a poetics for the Principate awaits the poets, but general readers too need to acquire sufficient knowledge. The reality of the Principate does not allow for univocal or easy definitions.

Historians of the Augustan Age have long since accustomed us to the difficulty of pinning a stable definition upon Augustus' Principate. More recently, a different point of view is gaining ground, which suggests that the very indeterminacy of Augustus played a decisive role in constructing his power (e.g. his wavering between the roles of citizen and ruler, man and god, conservative and revolutionary, etc.). It was in the construction of 'Augustus' that the necessary answer to the crisis of the Roman State appeared, a crisis of which Augustus himself was an essential component.[4] Students of Augustan poetry ought to be receptive to this point of view. All the structural analyses of *Ep.* 2.1 agree on one important point: the addressee of the letter is a shifting figure, one that changes shape as we read. Augustus is implicated in Horace's poem within the diverse images of man-god, ruler, consumer of literature, patron for poets, and a potential subject for literary works. It is evident that the present multiplicity demands an eye for nuance and for overall structure. As a whole, the letter offers a *summa* of the 'several personages that here appear under the name Augustus',[5] but in its individual phases of development, the poetic discourse only activates here and there particular relevant features. For a long stretch of the letter Augustus fades out, to the point of dissolving into a generic didactic addressee. In other parts, mainly the beginning and the end, the addressee is singled out for his uniqueness, by his attributes of power, his responsibilities, his personal preferences. Ovid will demolish this mediating and distributive rhetoric when, in the turn of a single couplet, he appeals to Augustus calling him 'god' and 'man':

> iuro
> per te praesentem conspicuumque deum,
> hunc animum favisse tibi, vir maxime ...
>
> (*Trist*. 2.53-5)

To be sure, the trope of swearing 'by the god' of the character to whom the letter is addressed comes straight from Horace:

> praesenti tibi maturos largimur honores
> iurandasque tuum per numen ponimus aras.
>
> (*Ep*. 2.1.15-16)

But in Ovid respect for the differences and even the nuances of Augustus' image has disappeared. The addressee of *Tristia* 2 is a monolith, that of *Epistles* 2.1 a kind of prism.

This is why Horace's letter to Augustus is also a didactics and a poetics for the Principate. The Romans have a lot to learn, and Horace's poetry, with its peculiar sense of decorum, can help them. Augustus is, by turns, a protective god, a ruler who watches over the fate of literature, a man who prefers some cultural commodities to others,[6] a patron, and a worthy object for encomiastic literature. The success of an argument depends on the ability to select the right stress and appropriate features of the interlocutor. Eduard Fraenkel shows that Horace in his letter has a winning strategy:

> Horace is indeed turning to Augustus (cf. *Ep*. 2.1.214ff.); he also makes it plain that for the purpose of his present discussion it is Augustus' reaction to poetry that matters the most. But at the same time he is exceedingly careful not to isolate the Princeps from the rest of the reading public by placing him on a pedestal of his own. Augustus is to appear as one, though the most distinguished, of the educated Romans interested in poetry. ([1957] 395).

We will return to this problem of 'not isolating the Princeps from the rest of the reading public' when we deal with *Tristia* 2. For now I would like to question whether Fraenkel's reading is able to maintain the distinction between what we think about Augustus and what Horace teaches us about Augustus, and also whether he distinguishes sufficiently between the effect of Horace's strategy and the resistance that gives it its reason to be as well as its form (a more difficult line to draw). Right after the passage quoted above, Fraenkel calls upon historians of the Principate to ask themselves whether such a letter could have been written for Louis XIV. The comparison is intriguing. Fraenkel was certainly aware that the relationship between Augustus and the literati functioned indeed as the model for the cultural politics of the Sun King.[7] But the difference between Augustus and French absolutism is one of those points where historicism implodes, and its approach to the past ends up losing sight of its own origins. The project of the noble and tormented book of Fraenkel was influenced by an absolutism less remote in time; his reading of Horace turns back the clock, since it both returns to the great prewar philology, and because politically it obscures the use of the Augustan model employed in a more recent period of German culture.[8] Starting from these premises, Fraenkel overlooks the fact that the effect of 'civilized conversation' in *Ep.* 2.1 is a construction, a projection of the literary text. The point is not that 'Augustus did not let the literati treat him like the Sun King', but rather that 'this poet is shaping a relationship of power purposely different, in terms of flattery, from absolute power'. Somewhere behind the negation 'Augustus was no Louis XIV' one can sense a stronger denial: 'Augustus was not like a twentieth-century dictator'. Beyond this denial we glimpse the genesis of a work so conflicted: a reconstruction of Horace that is also a reconstruction of the method of Leo and Wilamowitz, and the obliteration of a recent past – with its atavistic and regressive politics – which could never be despised enough. It is no easy task to consider ourselves as outside this debate, nor would we be more clear-minded when reckoning with our own cultural roots.

As an alternative, one can propose a reading of *Ep.* 2.1 that takes account of both the results – the image of Augustus that Horace projects – and the contradictions that the poet poses and confronts. This will be a reading produced by the sum of the effects *plus* the detection of resistances and contradictions. If all of the above sounds abstract, we can return to interpreting a specific point of text.

Towards a poetics of the Principate

> nec sermones ego mallem
> repentes per humum, quam res componere gestas ...
> et formidatam Parthis te principe Romam,
> si quantum cuperem possem quoque ...
> (*Ep.* 2.1.250-1; 256-7)

Horace puts a new spin on the standard *recusatio*. The poet is not only, as usual, unable (i.e. reluctant) to undertake a celebratory epos; the real problem is that the potential result, a bad poem, might harm Augustus, ending up literally defacing his image. Many have already noted that line 256 ought to be seen as a recasting of a famous, and infamous, line of Cicero:

> o fortunatam natam me consule Romam!
> (*Poet.* 8 Courtney = 17 M.)[9]

Recognizing this allusion, or denying it, opens up an interesting alternative. Fraenkel, who chooses the second avenue, reads v. 256 as the climax of an effective example of panegyric: 'the choice of the words, their arrangement, and the heavy rhythm all seem to suggest the *gravitas* and power of Rome and of her leader' ([1957] 398).

But what happens if we try the first hypothesis? The entire closing of the letter (of which the panegyric of 251-6 is merely a subordinate gesture) is dominated by the idea that bad poetry does disservice to its dedicatees. Authors of encomiastic epic 'stain' – as ink stains – the deeds which they sing (235-7). Alexander paid in hard cash for the *ridiculum poema* of Choerilus (237-8);[10] still, he had forbidden the reproduction of his image by painters and sculptors other than Apelles and Lysippus. Virgil and Varius do not betray (245; *dedecorant*) the trust of their patron Augustus. The zeal of the inept damages the object itself (260), especially when it turns to rhythm and poetry (261), since what is ridiculous then sticks in the memory and becomes proverbial:

> discit enim citius meminitque libentius illud
> quod quis deridet, quam quod probat et veneratur.
> (262-3)

'I, Horace, would not want to be disfigured in public by a portrait that makes me ugly, nor do I want to be embellished by ill-executed lines' (264-6).

Cicero's line had become proverbial for the rare combination of two negative elements, both of interest to Horace: shoddy workmanship and encomiastic intent. We could not hope for a more perfect example; excessive praise has produced a ridiculous poetic text that will be forever remembered for its rhythm and verbal malformation.[11] Horace's line is at once the reformation and the recollection of the false step taken by Latin literature. Horace cancels out certain memorable defects, at the same time bringing into view the traces of a disliked model. The result, I would argue, is to transform the art of allusion into a political gesture. The avoidance of the infamous jingle *-natam natam* shows that a new good taste has become active in panegyric. The isometric substitution of *te principe* for *me consule* insinuates that the new 'good taste' is interwoven with a new discourse of power. A new poetics of the Principate, measured and well-mannered, is coming into being. The Principate, with its classical sense of measure, acts as a sense of decorum opposing the excesses – political and poetical – of the late Republic. That age had witnessed a period of frantic competition and excesses. It was a time when a Cicero, along with many other consuls, could feel like the *pater patriae* and be tempted into rising to the level of an Alexander. Augustus, on the other hand, who remains unchallenged on that level, ought to refuse immoderate praise, just as the Princeps should refuse to be a monarch. Similarly, Horace refuses the task, just as he defuses – simply by mentioning it – the petard by which Cicero had hoist himself.

The true enemies in the epistle to Augustus are not, as it might seem, archaic and archaizing poets, but rather yesterday's masters, the neoterics and the entire culture of the late Republic. Horace eschews celebratory epic – that typical of the age of Cicero, Pompey, Volusius, and Archias – but distances himself no less from its critics of Callimachean persuasion. What worries him most is remaining prisoner to an old dichotomy between fruitless celebration and the poetry of and for overly refined, rootless vagabonds. The epistle comes to a close with the image of a failed celebratory poem being used as wrapping paper in the market:

> in vicum vendentem tus et odores
> et piper et quidquid chartis amicitur ineptis.
>
> (2.1.269-70)

There is a clear echo of the destiny Catullus promised to the poetaster Volusius, the author of a celebratory epic: wrapping mackerel (95.8). Catullus opposed to Volusius' fate the triumph of a lasting neoteric masterpiece about Smyrna, i.e. 'myrrh' (95.1-6); hence, perhaps, the deeper irony of *tus et odores*?

To speak of such things in the presence of Augustus has its price. When at the end the tone becomes more sarcastic, Horace must take the place of the Princeps and offer himself as the victim of ridicule: '*I* do not want to be the butt of jokes, ridiculed along with the one who sings my praise, brought to market in a grotesque funeral as recycled paper'. Augustus, if he wishes, can disregard the potential criticism contained in the allusion to Cicero, and read the panegyric at face value without worrying about the thin line between praise and blame. Certainly the addressee of the letter is not directly exposed to caustic effects. At a healthy distance from the closing, the letter has already offered Augustus an institutional and collective praise that goes far beyond the most daring ambitions of Cicero:

> nil oriturum alias, nil ortum tale fatentes.
>
> (2.1.17)

But Roman readers who know the language of allusive art have room to ponder upon the difficulties and contradictions that arise when a poet finds himself speaking to and about Augustus.

Tristia 2 and the paranoid reader

A tendency in recent criticism, frequently associated with the name Umberto Eco, offers to our detached gaze some examples of deviant reading: paranoid readings – suffering from a persecution complex, secret conspiracies, police investigations – shameless appropriations of texts that believe their intentionality violated. It is against this deviant background that one might reasonably claim that some 'limits' ought to be placed on interpretation.

But there can be cases more subversive, more liminal, with respect to the limit-cases that Eco usually chooses. (1) What happens if the text is 'inside' – or projects around itself – a maniacal climate of persecution and obsessive suspicion? Would it not then be the case that even the act of fixing 'limits of interpretation' could be negotiated and contested? (2) The appearance of deep fracture lines between the various functions of the addressee and the public is not irrelevant. (3) What happens when 'how to interpret a poem' is not only a problem that the text places on the table (as any poetic text does) but is the very *content* and *problematics* posed by the poem? *Tristia* 2 fits this peculiar profile because, (1) treachery, suspicion, persecution, self-accusation and self-defence are continuously evoked as points of reference; (2) the text is intended for a peculiar addressee, Augustus, who can hardly be considered part of the 'normal' audience to which the publication of the work appeals; the more this audience is distanced from the addressee, the more a road opens up for a subversive reading; (3) the entire argument of this long letter is a response to an explicit hermeneutical problem concerning the meaning of a poetic text. *Tristia* 2 deals with how another poetic text, the *Art of Love*, should be interpreted – and how it has been interpreted.

From Horace to Ovid

Ovid starts out by showing that poetry can have an important didactic function in Roman society. As examples he selects two rare cases of poetry that Augustus had commissioned for public functions: songs in honour of Demeter (23-4) and songs in honour of Apollo (25-6). This latter reference is important not only because it touches upon (by necessary implication) Horace's *Carmen Saeculare*, but also because it re-enacts the self-reflexive move of *Ep.* 2.1.134-8, where Horace, as an example of poetry shaping a people's civilization, offers a summary of one of his own public poems, the *Carmen Saeculare* in fact (*poscit opem chorus et praesentia numina sentit ...*). Imperial patronage is a powerful guarantee for Horace, who involves the authority of his own poetic voice in this system of power, and it is exactly this relation of direct patronage that is of interest to Ovid (2.24-5: *dicere iussit Opi: / iusserat et Phoebo dici ...*). The Princeps' *iussa* show that in its own way poetry counts too.[12] Later on, Ovid takes up again a standard theme of Horace's literary epistles, the social utility (*prodesse*) of poetry (2.263-76), but he is constrained to do so from the weak side of theory. The poetry of the *Ars* will not be harmful – as long as it is read *recta mente* (2.275). Even the theme of 'how to celebrate Augustus', an unexpected guest in *Tristia* 2, shows that Ovid is looking to *Ep.* 2.1 as his model

and contrastive background. In the manner of Horace (see above), Ovid
argues that he does not lack the will, but the strength, for a celebratory
song:

> et tamen ausus eram. Sed detrectare videbar,
> quodque nefas, damno viribus esse tuis.
>
> (2.337-8)

The idea that a poorly written panegyric does more damage than no
panegyric at all puts in a nutshell the complex of problems dealt with in
the closing of *Ep.* 2.1. The corresponding theme of remuneration, however,
is developed in reverse:

> acceptum refero versibus esse nocens.
> Hoc pretium curae vigilatorumque laborum
> cepimus ...
>
> (2.10-11)

Ovid reckons in the balance (*acceptum refero*) the bitter price the emperor
has paid in full for his poetry. In the same language, Horace had described
the ample proceeds for court poetry in honour of Alexander (*incultis qui
versibus et male natis / rettulit acceptos ... Philippos*: *Ep.* 2.1.234-5).[13]

Augustus' *iussa* prove to readers of *Ep.* 2.1 that Horace's poetry appeals
to the highest of collective interests. The support of the Princeps is
essential, since the letter is written by a poet ill at ease in his relationship
with the public. The Romans love Augustus more than their political past,
but they do not welcome modern poetry: *sed tuus hic populus ... fastidit et
odit* (2.1.18-22). Ovid's situation in *Tristia* 2 lies at the opposite pole – the
imperial indictment has cut short the career of a poet certain of his readers'
favour:

> quo [sc. *ingenio*] videar quamvis nimium iuvenaliter usus
> grande tamen toto nomen ab orbe fero;
> turbaque doctorum Nasonem[14] novit et audet
> non fastiditis adnumerare viris.
>
> (2.117-20)

The solidarity of his reading public takes the place of the Princeps. At this
point Ovid can rewrite, but also vary, the famous appeal that opens and
dedicates *Ep.* 2.1 to Augustus:

> Cum tot sustineas et tanta negotia solus
> res Italas armis tuteris, moribus ornes,
> legibus emendes, in publica commoda peccem
> si longo sermone morer tua tempora, Caesar.
>
> (vv. 1-4)

Horace was teaching how one should speak to Caesar; the Princeps is engaged in the reading of an epistle that deserves his attention for the very reason that it is addressed to Him, someone who only has time for serious matters. The letter will be more serious than usual, and will respect the Princeps' priorities. This *sermo* must reach a compromise between Horace's traditional levity and humility, and the solemnity required when writing to, and about, Great Men.[15] Ovid, who is presenting the Princeps with a much longer text (578 lines vs. Horace's 270), and on much lighter, and more private, themes, recuperates Horace's move:

> Scilicet imperii princeps *statione* relicta
>   *imparibus* legeres carmina facta modis?
> Non ea te *moles* Romani nominis *urget*,
>   inque tuis umeris tam leve fertur onus,
> lusibus ut possis advertere numen ineptis,
>   *excutiasque oculis otia nostra tuis.*
> Nunc tibi Pannonia est, nuc Illyris ora domanda,
>   Raetica nunc praebent Thraciaque arma metum,
> nunc petit Armenius pacem, nunc porrigit arcus[16]
>   Parthus eques timida captaque signa manu,
> nunc te prole tua *iuvenem* Germania sentit,
>   bellaque pro magno Caesare Caesar obit.
> Denique ut in tanto, quantum non exstitit umquam,
>   corpore pars nulla est, *quae labet*, imperii
> urbs quoque te et legum *lassat tutela* tuarum
>   et *morum*, similes quos cupis esse tuis.
>
>   (219-34)

For purposes of brevity I italicize what seem to me the key points in Ovid's rewriting of Horace. Two general aims are operative in this passage: (1) to 'update' the socio-political picture from the Rome of twenty-five (?) years before, to that of 9 CE; (2) to intensify the rhetoric needed to represent the Principate. I am not alone in perceiving signs of tension and of stress.[17] Ovid is showing how the language of panegyric can be adapted by elegy, a genre no less humble than Horatian *sermo*, but with a different structure. The result is a poetic discourse asymmetrical and irregular – *imparibus* in v. 220 conflicts with *statione* in v. 219. The 'unbalanced' elegiac couplet is set against the mythic stability of the Emperor-World-Guardian. With a true *coup de théâtre* Ovid devises a rhetoric in which the hierarchy of the Principate is mirrored on the level of form. The structure of the couplet formalizes a relation of power: serious vs. (and above) frivolous, moral vs. immoral, control vs. licence, public vs. private, just as in the metric form peculiar to this genre, hexameter vs. pentameter:

> fas ergo est aliqua *caelestia* pectora falli
>   et sunt notitia multa *minora* tua;
> utque deos caelumque simul *sublime* tuenti
>   non vacat *exiguis* rebus adesse Iovi,

de te pendentem sic dum circumspicis *orbem*,
  effugiunt curas *inferiora* tuas.
scilicet imperii *princeps* statione relicta
  imparibus legeres carmina facta modis?

(213-20)

On the side of normalization, *caelestia, sublime, orbem*, and *princeps* look down, from the height and solemnity of the hexameter, at the pentameter's descending movement towards elegiac weakness: *minora, exiguis, inferiora, imparibus modis*. The sense of these lines comments upon their own decomposition into contrasting metrical unities that counterpoint one another on alternating levels. But recuperating elegy into the discourse of power comes at a price for Augustus. The Princeps is reading an elegy that explains to him how he does not have the time either to read or fully to understand this poetic genre. What for Horace was a form of courtesy ('Engaged as you are in working for our good, it would be wrong, and not very patriotic, to waste your time with poetic distractions ...') now becomes a subtle defensive move. If Augustus does not pay too much attention to the formal and hierarchical praise, he might detect an argument running like 'distracted as you are by matters of state, how have you found time to read frivolous erotic verse – and *to condemn me for it*?' After all, to insist so strongly on the fact that Augustus has no time to be a good reader might be a way to mobilize Ovid's traditional readers. There are still readers who, unlike Augustus, know how to appreciate and to participate in the lesser, inferior, and odd world of elegy. In such a case, they will relish the fact that in its own way *Tristia* 2 is elegy as well.[18]

This brings us back to the parallel between vv. 219-34 and Horace. *Tristia* 2 was published in a period marked by a crisis concerning the grain supply, heavy military engagements, and private scandals. 'Private' is a rather inadequate description, since the meaning of these scandals is precisely that of opening up, in the private sphere of the individual, spaces where the central power might intervene. We can now see clearly the double edge of Ovid's rhetorical escalation. Augustus is no longer merely engaged by his duties as in Horace (*tot sustineas et tanta negotia solus ... tuteris*); he is now exhausted by a workload of titanic proportions (*tuis humeris ... onus ... lassat tutela ... bella ... inrequieta*: 222, 233, 236). It might come to mind, even if the theme is unappreciated by official propaganda, that the Princeps is in his seventies. Ovid notes that Germany perceives Augustus as 'young through his offspring' (2.229), which is a respectful way of insinuating his age. His sacrifice for the common good (235) seems now to require greater expenditure when compared to the time of *Ep.* 2.1. The Princeps, already in the time of Horace, improves Roman morals: *res Italas ... moribus ornes, / legibus emendes*. The allusion is to the laws concerning marriage and his censorial activities. But neither Horace nor Ovid, after so many years, offers a key to the mysteries

of the written and unwritten constitution, of the *cura morum et legum*
undertaken or given up, literal or metaphoric.[19] Both Horace and Ovid are
instead a key to understanding that the essence of Augustus' role lies in
the impossibility of defining it with any stability. But Ovid shifts the accent
not a little when he writes:

> urbs quoque te et legum lassat tutela tuarum
> et morum, similes quos cupis esse tuis.
>
> (2.233-4)

The alliteration underlines a new labour, and maybe a tension as well, a
crisis of consensus. Enforcing the laws on marriage and on sexual behaviour 'belabours' the Guardian of Public Morals. The *mores* of Italy seem
reluctant to abide by those of Augustus, and among those *mores* not 'up to
standard' contemporary readers could number some thorny examples
drawn from the house of Caesar. Fully consumed by this mission, the
Princeps *has had no chance to read* light verse (*nostros evoluisse iocos*,
2.238). This is the point that most interests me. If he has not read *Ars
amatoria* (which he has indeed punished!) the Princeps would not be in the
best position to interpret *Tristia* 2. The first addressee of *Tristia* 2 is a
reader who is not a good judge of *ioci*. First there is one obvious implication: Augustus did not know how to read the *Ars*. But there is also a second,
and more biting, one: among the possible readers of *Tristia* 2, Augustus is
the most disadvantaged.[20] The lesson in literary history that is about to
begin employs as addressee a man who can read 213ff. as serious panegyric – and thus miss the re-emergence of the *ioci* filtering through imperial
repression. It is not so much a question of asking to what extent the
particular expressions of panegyric can be read as ironic digs, or as
innuendo of uncomfortable references, or as anti-conformist nuances.[21]
The real problem is that these lines construct Augustus as a reader of
poetry. On this playground, come what may, the Princeps will have to learn
the rules of a new game: how to interpret an elegiac text that becomes ever
more self-referential.

How to read the *Ars* in(to) the *Tristia*

The language of oversight and incomprehension weighs heavily upon the
reception of the *Ars amatoria* (213, *falli*; 214, *sunt notitia multa minora
tua*; 216, *non vacat ... adesse*; 217, *effugiunt ... inferiora*; 219-20, *scilicet ...
legeres?*; 223, *ut possis advertere*; 238, *numquam ... evoluisse*; 239, *vacuum
tibi forte fuisset*; 245, *neve ... possis dubitare*). But such an insistence might
also involve the reception of *Tristia* 2. A text so deeply entangled in the
difficulties of reading another text is perhaps not the most useful medium
for putting forward a proof of one's innocence.

The distraction of the Princeps prompts Ovid's rereading of the *Ars*:[22]

at si, quod mallem, vacuum tibi forte fuisset,
   nullum legisses crimen in Arte mea ...
neve, quibus scribam, possis dubitare, libellos,
   quattuor hos versus e tribus unus habet:
'este procul, vittae tenues, insigne pudoris,
   quaeque tegis medios instita longa pedes!
Nil nisi legitimum concessaque furta canemus,
   inque meo nullum carmine crimen erit.'
(2.239-40; 245-50)

If Augustus has not been an attentive reader of the *Ars*, he will not remember that the lines between 247 and 250 repeat *Ars* 1.31-4 with an exactness spoiled by but one infidelity:

nos Venerem tutam concessaque furta canemus.
(1.33)[23]

Generations of readers have doubted, and will continue to doubt, whether the *Ars* draws a sharp distinction between 'safe' and 'illicit' sex, but this is not what matters most here. The interpolation *nil nisi legitimum* shows that one can never be safe enough. The *Ars* was protecting itself against accusation, but it was condemned. Now the author rereads parts of his poem for Augustus: there is no *crimen* in the *carmen*, even if the two words share an uncanny assonance. But *Ars* 250, the line inserted in the *Tristia*, picks up line 240, a verse written instead for *Tristia* 2, and the sequence becomes so circular that it begs the question:

'nullum' legisses 'crimen' in Arte mea

'you would have read the words "no crime" in my *Ars*', meaning: 'that text is not culpable because it clearly states "I am not a culpable text" '.

The return to *Ars amatoria* 1 in *Tristia* 2 does not end here. A few verses later Ovid develops by analogy the case for his defence. If the *Ars* persuaded, unintentionally, some matrons to sin, it makes no sense to punish the work on this account. It would be just as absurd to do away with the places that might provide occasion for immorality, such as theatres, the Campus Martius, the Circus, porticoes, and temples of the gods (279-88). The parallel is stimulating, given that in the Rome of 9 CE nearly all of these public works derive more or less directly from the Princeps and his household. Ovid, author of the *Ars*, corresponds to Augustus, author of Rome; both are beyond any suspicion. But there is a problem: loitering around public works for amorous encounters is precisely the theme of the first didactic section of *Ars* 1.67-100.[24] The literal quotation of *Ars* 1.31-4, the proem, is a strong signal and an invitation to carry on the comparison. Among the public works recommended for propositioning that figure in the *Ars* one finds the porticoes bearing the irreproachable names of Livia and

Octavia. The poet of *Tristia* 2 now explains that the *Ars* is as innocent as the imperial monuments – as long as we forget that the *Ars* had *recommended* lecherous loitering around theatres, circuses, porticoes, temples, etc. If someone has sentenced the *Ars amatoria*, how can *Tristia* 2 be innocent? The poet of the *Tristia* displays all his eloquence to demonstrate that erotic poetry of the past is fictional and false:

> magnaque pars mendax operum et ficta meorum.
> (2.355)[25]

But who has the authority to decide which of Ovid's works are sincere, and which are included in the indeterminate *magna pars* made up of lies? This is not a very prudent choice of words for a poet who has recently taken up imperial panegyric and judicial self-defence. 'I have always been mostly a liar' is a curious preface for a text acting as a deposition *pro veritate* and a defensive appeal *pro domo sua*.

Augustus learns to read the poets

The advantage of this point of view is that it helps to make sense of one of the more embarrassing features of *Tristia* 2: the long, grievous catalogue of poets, both erotic and non-erotic, and of other more or less important literary genres spread out over a span of nearly 200 lines. The perspective adopted here helps us understand how Ovid might have compelled his Muse to perform the tedious and long-winded task of inserting a small literary encyclopaedia into an apology to the emperor. How did it happen that the most self-conscious artist of his time chose to speak like one of the least original grammarians? This systematic approach to literature – one that Horace, for example, had also avoided in the *Epistle to the Pisones*[26] – is not, as it might seem, empty filler that removes more pressing themes from the stage. For all of this didactic material is the premise necessary to achieve the effect we are dealing with here, namely, the figuring of Augustus as a novice to be initiated into the reading of poets. A didactic addressee cannot take shape unless the text assumes the right posture of instruction.

But to say 'posture' is reductive, since *Tristia* 2 has much to teach about poetry even to readers who are not Caesars. Let us consider for a moment what the poem tells us about Ennius:

> sumpserit Annales (nihil est hirsutius illis)
> facta sit unde parens Ilia, nempe leget.
> (2.259-60)

Hence, if a reader is predisposed to malice and vice, she will do well to avoid also the good old-fashioned *Annals* of Ennius, a poem that exhibits

– practically in the exordium – a story of illicit sex between Mars and a Vestal Virgin.[27] A little further on, Ovid seems to retract this suggested reading. There are light texts – beginning with Catullus, Calvus, and Cinna – and more serious texts, like Ennius' *Annals*:

> utque suo Martem cecinit gravis Ennius ore,
> Ennius ingenio maximus, arte rudis ...
>
> (2.423-4)

Evidently Ennius is a safe text, solemn and serious, with room only for Mars, as is fitting for the purest of epics. It is a pity that 'Mars' is also the answer to the question that the perverse matron asks in 2.260, 'who has made Ilia a mother?', and that the nearness of *Martem* and *gravis* echoes a famous Virgilian line, an epic verse in which the original and originating scandal of Roman history is seen in full light:

> Marte gravis geminam partu dabit Ilia prolem ...
>
> (*A.* 1.274)

The reader who recognizes these hints has a clearer view than Augustus: there are texts that have escaped his persecuting zeal. Without a violated Vestal, there would have been no history of Rome and no beginning of Roman epic. Even worse, Augustus might have been wrong about the *Aeneid* too:

> et tamen ille tuae felix Aeneidos auctor
> contulit in Tyrios arma virumque toros,
> nec legitur pars ulla magis de corpore toto,
> quam non legitimo foedere iunctus amor.
>
> (2.532-6)

I have argued elsewhere that these lines are a tendentious, but also meticulous, reading of the *Aeneid*;[28] *arma virumque* at once recalls both the proem – and hence, the epic poem in general – and the scene in which the hero and his arms are physically framed in Dido's bedroom (cf. *A.* 4.495: *arma viri, thalamo* ...). A tendentious reading perhaps, but Ovid was not the last reader of Virgil to argue that Dido's story represents an opening of epic towards love poetry, and that many love the *Aeneid* more for Dido than for Aeneas. This intertextual precision suggests that Ovid is bringing the *Aeneid* to the Princeps' attention, so that the Princeps, before the eyes of common readers, will have to put 'His' poem on trial. Virgil too has succumbed to elegy, and Augustus did not notice it. Maybe Augustus has already been duped by another elegiac poet, Propertius, who had announced the *Aeneid* in the following terms:

ut regnem mixtas inter conviva puellas
   hoc ego, quo tibi nunc elevor, ingenio!
me iuvet externis positum languere corollis
   quem tetigit iactu certus ad ossa deus;
Actia Vergilium custodis litora Phoebi,
   Caesaris et fortis dicere posse ratis,
qui nunc Aeneae Troiani suscitat arma
   iactaque Lavinis moenia litoribus.
Cedite Romani scriptores, cedite Grai!
   nescio quid maius nascitur Iliade.

                        (2.34.57-67)

Just like Propertius, Ovid joins in one single movement (a) the refusal of epic, (b) a description of his own *ingenium* as a light poet, (c) the representation of the *Aeneid* in two tight couplets, and finally, (d) a re-evocation of Virgil's bucolic poetics.[29] Propertius had created an implicit contrast between the announcement of the *Aeneid* and the frame: the love poet, wounded by passion, lies languidly on a bed of unwound garlands after a night of banqueting, while Virgil 'sets in motion/wakes up' the arms of Aeneas. Propertius' *suscitat arma* is the subtext for Ovid's 'he led the arms and the hero into the Phoenician bed'. Thus Aeneas finds himself more or less within the soft elegiac nest from which Propertius observed the hero's deeds from a distance. Ovid has picked up the Propertian opposition between elegy and epic, collapsing the boundaries between them. Propertius had delegated to Virgil epic and celebration of Augustus; Ovid unmasks Virgil to find an erotic poet outside of imperial control. After the announcement of the *Aeneid*, Propertius had offered a sympathetic summary of the *Eclogues*. The effect was to detach from the project of the *Aeneid* Virgil's youthful poetry, viewed in terms of an eroticism related to elegy. Ovid takes this a step further:

Phyllidis hic idem teneraeque Amaryllidis ignes
   bucolicis iuvenis luserat ante modis.
Nos quoque iam pridem scripto peccavimus isto ...
                    (2.537-9)

By rewriting Propertius, who in turn rewrote Virgil in an elegiac key, Ovid goes so far as to name him as an accomplice. *Iuvenis* sounds a bit different from *audaxque iuventa* (Verg. *G.* 4.565). The *Eclogues* are now poetry of youth in the same sense as the *Ars* – they are erotic poetry. In the end, to accuse the *Ars* is to accuse Virgil as well.[30] Propertius had shown, in 2.34, how distinct genres could regard one another with respect. Ovid foists upon his master a poetics of impurity and border crossing.

'Naming names': intertextuality and delation in the case of Tibullus

> Credere iuranti durum putat esse Tibullus,
>   sic etiam de se quod neget illa viro;[31]
> fallere custodes idem docuisse fatetur,[32]
>   seque sua miserum nunc ait arte premi.[33]
> Saepe, velut gemmam dominae signumve probaret,
>   per causam meminit se tetigisse manum,[34]
> utque refert, digitis saepe est nutuque locutus,
>   et tacitam mensae duxit in orbe notam;[35]
> et quibus e sucis abeat de corpore livor,
>   impresso fieri qui solet ore, docet:[36]
> denique ab incauto nimium petit ille marito,[37]
>   se quoque uti servet, peccet ut illa minus.
> Scit, cui latretur, cum solus obambulet,[38] ipsas
>   cui totiens clausas excreet ante fores,[39]
> multaque dat furti talis praecepta docetque
>   qua nuptae possint fallere ab arte viros.
> Non fuit hoc illi fraudi, legiturque Tibullus
>   et placet, et iam te principe notus erat.

                                        (2.446-64)

This passage is unparalleled in Augustan poetry. It would be difficult to find another sequence of this length (18 lines) which not only alludes with high precision to a series of places in a predecessor's work (recombined in what appears very much like a *cento*), but also continually reminds us that the text is recalling that other text *verbatim*. It is more a summons than an allusion – and more a calling of a witness than of a text – since here indeed Ovid is exploring a new frontier of poetic memory: judicial intertextuality. This citation, unprecedented in extent and for its literalness, can be explained only as a naming of an accessory. It demonstrates how Tibullus is no less dangerous than the *Ars amatoria*. Ovid accentuates the didactic status of his text; the amount of citations, such that only a didactic manual in prose could afford, turns *Tristia* 2 into a true textbook on Roman elegy. The plagiarized poem, in its turn, is a true didactic text, since Tibullus' elegies, when anthologized in this way, turn out to be an archetype for erotic didactics. The group of samples that I have gathered in notes 31-9 serves to anticipate by two millennia the patient work of philologists who have traced the amatory system of the *Ars* back to its many Tibullan sources.

If all of this gains Augustus' trust, there is a trap waiting for him at the end. An inexperienced reader of elegy might actually believe that Tibullus had created, before Ovid and without imperial retaliation, an *ars* for deceiving husbands: *qua nuptae possint fallere ab arte viros* (462). Those who know Tibullus raise their eyebrows; 'in all of Tibullus' elegies we never find either *nubeo* or *nupta'* they will say[40] – and this is something Ovid would really like to say about the *Ars amatoria* too. Ovid reveals, in the body of evidence provided by Tibullus, an old trick of elegiac poets. These poems about real love affairs are constantly playing a game of marginality and reticence. The *puella* is a free woman, maybe married, or perhaps a courtesan; the *vir* is sometimes the fiancé, other times the panderer, still others the husband. If the *Ars* is under accusation, so too is the entire elegiac tradition from which the *Ars* has learned (well before the Julian laws) to play with fire without being burned. Literary allusion, at this point, is no longer a game without consequences. If writing has become a socially dangerous activity, quotation is a practice under fire as well, and poetic memory can be conflated with naming names. The history of Roman poetry, to which *Tristia* 2 provides a decisive contribution, is from the beginning based on informing and delation, and on turning over its books to the auditing authority of its didactic addressee. A question remains, most important for modern students of Propertius, Catullus, and Ovid, but surely not irrelevant for the judicial edge of the *Tristia*: what relation connects these fluctuating poetic codifications with so-called real life?

Vita verecunda, Musa iocosa

> Crede mihi, distant mores a carmine nostro
> (vita verecunda est, Musa iocosa mea).
>
> (2.353-4)

For faithful readers of Ovid, this exculpation is not new; it comes from the central part of the *Remedia amoris*:

> si mea materiae respondet Musa iocosae,
> vicimus, et falsi criminis acta rea est.
>
> (*Rem*. 387-8)

The entire section, lines 361-98, is of great interest. Students of *Tristia* 2 sometimes neglect it, since it is a programmatic apology written under very different conditions, without the pressure of exile and with no intention of answering the Princeps. In effect, the lesson of the *Remedia* – which is, we should not forget, a didactic poem at all levels – is not identical, but rather complements that of *Tristia* 2 by inverting it. In the *Remedia*, Ovid was responding to literary-critical charges, and the result seems like his personal version of Callimachus' Prologue against the Telchines (cf. *Rem*. 397: *hactenus invidiae respondimus*). He is accused of writing too daringly (362: *Musa proterva*), so in his defence he outlines the first principles of literary criticism. There are light genres and solemn genres. Homer leaves no room for the *deliciae*, while the elegiac meter wants only wantonness. Thais, the character who serves as a symbol for the *Ars*, could not start playing the role of Andromache.[41] Ovid's Muse cannot be censured because she follows the rules of the *prepon*: the proper matter for elegiac couplets is frivolous and flirtatious. Ten years later, facing much more serious charges, Ovid rearranges the cards on the table: 'You want the truth? Read in a certain way, even Homer and Virgil will turn out immoral. My Muse corresponds to the literary genre I have chosen, but my life is impeccable.'

The sharp line commonly drawn between the apology of the *Remedia* and the apology from exile has two drawbacks. The first is that it assumes a neat separation between poetics and politics (an attitude I have criticized in the second of my opening premises). The *Remedia* tackles a literary problem, *Tristia* 2 is faced with a political trial, and this, the reasoning goes, accounts for the entire difference. The second drawback is that it obfuscates almost completely the context of the *Remedia*. It is usually assumed that *Rem.* 361-98 is a response to criticism stirred up by the publication of the *Ars*. This is all very well, and goes hand in hand with the 'curative' poetics of the work: a cure for love, an antidote for malignant critics. If this assumption reinforces the parallel with *Tristia* 2, it also produces a negative effect. One is led to forget the role the apology plays in the structure of the new poem and in the context of the *Remedia amoris*, as though lines 361-98 were a detachable insert that could be pulled out and put back into the preceding poem.

On the contrary, the context is of great interest. In the lines preceding the apology, Ovid deals with repulsive odours (356: *stomacho nausea facta meo est*) and says he will give advice on how to fall out of love during copulation (357). The line in which the didactic action resumes after the digression (399) begins with the suggestive words *ergo ubi concubitus*, and describes a number of erotic positions in which one's lover will seem appalling. Clearly, the self-defence is not placed at random in the structure of the poem; it interrupts a passage where the *Remedia* displays the same irreverence as its antecedent, the *Ars*. The poet is relapsing into his old ways. True, he shows some modesty (359: *pudor est mihi dicere*), but the last line before the apology, *ingenio verbis concipe plura meis* (360), undermines the entire self-defence. The poet wilfully provokes readers' malice, and invites them to imagine more than what is really said. This is to say that Ovid's didactics, whether the author is chaste or not, is concerned to construct a lascivious *reader* – the same character that according to *Tristia* 2 has 'misinterpreted' Ovid's erotic works against the author's intention.

Furthermore, I am not so sure that the text of the *Remedia* is sealed airtight against political implications. The apostrophe to detractors is figured as a response to a *censure* (362: *quorum censura Musa proterva mea est*) – in short, an attack. But in the late Augustan Age, the word *censura* is not so easily separable from the power to control morality monopolized by the Princeps. The apostrophe itself is set up in such a way that the anonymity of the enemy borders on the grandiose image of *Iovis ira*, the most common signifier of Augustan repression:

summa petunt dextra fulmina missa Iovis.
at tu, quicumque es, quem nostra licentia laedit ...
(370-1)[42]

In conclusion, while the general tone remains literary-critical and Calli-machean (372: *ad numeros exige quidque suos*), it is hard to avoid the idea that these new Telchines are not simply malevolent reviewers – they are censors and moralists.

In *Tristia* 2, Ovid offers the enemy what he should have granted him long before. He no longer argues in defence, 'I do what my literary genre requires of me' but 'how I write is not how I live'. This is no small concession. The erotic verse of Ovid, Tibullus and Propertius had accus-tomed the reader of elegy to equating life and writing. The *Ars amatoria* had exploited this presupposition more than any other work, making of it its divine inspiration.[43] In his palinode, Ovid almost discovers the notion of 'elegiac persona' that many critics of this century boast about. The author and the subject of erotic experience can and must be separated.

But the opposition between author and persona, at any given moment, is liable to deconstruction.[44] The verse in the *Remedia*, 'use your imagina-tion to fantasize more than my words are saying', still has some validity. The tendency to read love poetry as part of an autobiographical web is not solely the error of critics of the preceding generation (the so-called 'bio-graphical fallacy'); it is a feature of the text and is part of the erotic poet's strategy who anticipates the horizon of expectations. Without curious readers, identification, and furtive glances, elegy does not work, and the notion of the elegiac persona continually turns into its opposite, the poet-lover. This letter to Augustus is presenting him with the mirage that elegy and real-life can be separated, an illusion not so much because elegy is life, but because readers of elegy cannot stop the process that fertilizes their imaginations.[45]

On the other hand, the pale excuse 'my life is not like my work' is already traditional before it reaches Martial; if Augustus has read Catullus, he would know that that brave love poet had introduced this theme into Roman literature:

nam castum esse decet pium poetam
ipsum, versiculos nihil necesse est.
(16.5-6)

Before we dismiss the parallel with the concept of an 'apologetic topos', we might pause to reflect on it for a moment. If *Tristia* 2 is a letter on how to read poetry, it is not a given that allusion play a marginal role in the text. No Roman poet, and Ovid in particular, had ever neglected the resources of allusive art, and the time has come to deploy these resources so that Augustus may gain the experience of an attentive reader.

One of the main problems in handling allusion is the difficulty of knowing where to stop. A text alluded to already had its own context, and it is not always clear whether, and to what degree, this first context should fade into the background, or whether it might be pertinent to remember it in its new context. A good reader and a good poet know that intertextuality can unleash a real struggle for power by which the poetic act proliferates indeterminate meanings. The echo in *Tristia* 2.353-4 of Catullus 16 is an instructive case. One might choose to treat it as merely a topos, and the corollary would be that Catullus' statement then becomes – a paradox, etymologically speaking – *atopic*, when set free from its original context and put in the service of Ovid's rhetorical strategy. Ovid would be saying, in effect, 'unlike my Muse, I am a *verecundus* poet; Catullus has already said this, as is known, remember? "My *versiculi* are *parum pudici* (16.8), but I am chaste (16.5)" '. But what if the original context of Catullus 16 refuses to disappear? What interpretive authority can guarantee that Ovid is not inviting his reader to 'localize' the intertext and to perceive the resulting effect?

The allusion is engaging, since Catullus 16 seems to many readers a strange example of apology. This poem's assertion of purity is hard to swallow for those familiar with Catullus' polymetric verse, and it would be dangerous to take seriously verses so 'designedly incongruous'[46] with both the context of Catullus 16 and that of Catullus' book in general. Furius and Aurelius have drawn from Catullus' *versiculi ... molliculi* and *parum pudici* conclusions about the poet's *mollitia*. Is this not a procedure analogous to that of the Princeps, who convicted Ovid of immorality on the basis of poetic *lascivia* (2.345) and for *deliciae* and *mollia carmina* (2.349)? But if they still insist that the work is the man, Furius and Aurelius will find themselves exposed to a nasty surprise. If they read Catullus 16 in this spirit – and this, I fancy, might be the real jab of the poem – it will turn them into a *pathicus* and a *cinaedus*. If the poems are in some way true, these disingenuous and 'biographizing' readers cannot help but to actualize Catullus 16 too, and they will thus have both orifices sexually violated by the poetry Catullus offers them:

> 'Pedicabo ego vos et irrumabo
> pedicabo ego vos et irrumabo'

They are forced to read this line at the beginning of the poem – and to repeat it when the poem comes to a close. There is an obvious paradox in the fact that a poem responding to charging of licentiousness contains words like *pedicare* and *irrumare*. A less obvious paradox exists in that Catullus can write, simultaneously, with the logic of metaliterary *mise en abyme* and with that of the most trivial graffiti ('If you can read this, Furius and Aurelius, you're down on your knees!'). I am not saying that all of this is operative in *Tristia* 2; I am only saying that no interpretive authority (not even Augustus) can decide where to stop the process set in motion by an allusion to a text such as Catullus 16. The context in Ovid resembles that in Catullus not only since each text discusses similarities and differences between life and work, but also because Furius and Aurelius read Catullus in the same way that Augustus has shown that he reads Ovid (cf. 2.7-9). They all believe that poetry can be read in the concrete terms of real life. If he follows the traces of allusion, Augustus will find himself on a slippery slope. If he ignores them, he will once again be a duped reader, a didactic addressee exposed to the ironic superiority of an audience possessing better interpretive abilities.

Crime and literary allusion

I have one final step to take, and it is the least pleasant. I have so far tried to avoid the pressing questions of historical reference posed by *Tristia* 2: 'the mystery of Ovid's exile', to use a familiar formulation. My reading of *Tristia* 2 as a didactic text – one that teaches how to read, and to misread, poets – has allowed me to steer clear of the dark line dividing this text from its historical occasion, that is, what Ovid had done, his *carmen et error*. I have to admit that I do not find this question irrelevant to the reading of *Tristia* 2. Not because Ovid here offers us a key to solving the mystery, or because the text is a plausible representation of the judicial process that relegated the poet (outside of any official procedure) to the Black Sea. But rather, because no one, I am afraid, can read this apology without feeling curious about what went on behind the stage. The more Ovid talks about his *carmen*, the more we wonder about his *error*. It seems to me plausible that this drive to fill in the blanks was even more pronounced in the audience for whom Ovid originally wrote – people who knew more than we do, but not enough, and who were deeply curious about the isolated world of the Court. Perhaps Ovid foresaw a particularly patient audience for *Tristia* 2, ready to read through almost six hundred lines of apology in search of some indiscretion that never arrives. We may object to later efforts to reconstruct plots and events on the basis of slender and perhaps misleading clues disseminated by the artist in his works *ex ponto*. We may laugh about modern philologists who work like old-fashioned private eyes. But every time we reread these hundreds of lines, we hear at length of Anacreon, about treatises on the uses of the top, about eroticism in Attic tragedy, and we grow ever more frustrated. We find no answer for our suspicions, nor can we simply drop them, and we feel taken in by the strategy of an author who, in turn, is a victim of imperial power.

Consider the famous lines in which Ovid pushes his reader's curiosity to the limit, only to frustrate it:

> cur aliquid vidi? cur noxia lumina feci?
> cur imprudenti cognita culpa mihi?
> inscius Actaeon vidit sine veste Dianam …

illa nostra die, qua me malus abstulit error,
parva quidem periit, sed sine labe domus ...
(2.103-5; 109-10)

Let us hear for a moment what a historian might say who has explored in depth 'the mystery of Ovid's exile'. A brief diagnosis from his pen might read: 'a text, namely the *Ars*, was used as circumstantial evidence in a political-sexual scandal (more sexual on the surface, more political at the core).[47] The scandal might be connected with the mishap of the younger Julia (8 CE), granddaughter of the Princeps, an event that in turn reopened the wound from the scandal of the elder Julia, daughter of the Princeps, and mother of the younger Julia (2 BCE).'

Luckily, we are not searching Ovid's text for clues to this political-familial plot. If we read the lines on the *error* as a normal poetic text, the first reaction might be to identify their model. Ovid is speaking in the voice of Damon (*vidi ... me malus abstulit error ... perii[t]*), who committed suicide for love in Virgil's eighth *Eclogue*:

ut vidi, ut perii, ut me malus abstulit error!
(8.41)

Like Damon, the poet is not guilty, only unfortunate. The beginning of the end for Damon had come during an innocent scene:

Saepibus in nostris parvam te roscida mala
(dux ego vester eram) vidi cum matre legentem ...
Ut vidi, ut perii ...
(8.39-41)

I have two conclusions to draw, one reasonable, the other arbitrary. The latter presupposes (1) a reader of manic suspicion (the Princeps, used to conspiracies?), and (2) a curious reader, who knows how Ovid cannot speak openly without provoking the reader in (1). Damon's downfall is caused by something he sees: a mother and a daughter engaged in innocent activities in a garden (they are collecting *roscida mala*).[48] If the poet is here trying to point out the nature of his *error* to us, we might gather he has seen something relating to a mother and a daughter together. My inference is no doubt arbitrary. But it would be even stranger to imagine a contemporary reader able to keep under control his or her own reading of a text that is both reticent and allusive.

The second conclusion expels all speculation on the nature of the *error*. We take now a saner reader, interested in Ovid as a poet and in his poetic models. Once again the result is stimulating. The poet has been punished for an unnamable *error* and for a *carmen* universally known, a poem about love. But how does he choose to represent his error? In the erotic language of one of the most famous love scenes in Roman poetry, the eighth *Eclogue*.

When we recall that *Tristia* 2 is, officially, a palinode of erotic elegy, Ovid's persistence is impressive. Augustus-the-reader, if he understands allusive art, is sent from Ovid's punishment back to the source of erotic inspiration that constitutes the principal charge of guilt.

Horace is not the only Roman poet who lectures Augustus about poetry. *Tristia* 2, if Augustus knows how to listen, is above all a lesson on one important aspect of poetry, its instability of meaning. Attempting to control the meaning of *Tristia* 2 leads to a collapse of the interpretation already given to erotic works by the interpretive community of Roman readers. Rereading erotic works undermines the judicial structure of *Tristia* 2. The intertextuality connecting *Tristia* 2 to erotic poets like Catullus, the bucolic Virgil and Tibullus maps out a genealogy of poets who have eluded political powers and the control of imperial police.

Augustus, Perses, and 'Kings'

Above all, *Tristia* 2 is a real and serious didactic poem. Like every true didactic poet, Ovid discovers an addressee-function suited to his message, different from those of his antecedents, but also linked to those past experiments. The glorious Memmius and the idiotic Perses are still active in the Princeps as pupil. This latter most of all, and the *Works and Days*, need to be recalled because their didactic thrust has fallen out of fashion. Hesiod (the founder of didactic discourse to which every new poet defers) had kept Perses quiet with the authority of high-thundering Zeus (v. 8). But now the didactic addressee is Jupiter Tonans himself, or at least his earthly double. Now Dike turns out to be an even harder theme than it might have appeared to Hesiod. 'Crazy is he who is willing to fight against the stronger' (*WD* 210) perhaps contains now an even more poignant truth, now that it does not comment on the parable of the hawk, but speaks directly in the voice of the nightingale gripped in the claws of his master the King.

> ῏Ω βασιλῆς, ὑμεῖς δὲ καταφράζεσθε καὶ αὐτοί
> τήνδε δίκην· ἐγγὺς γὰρ ἐν ἀνθρώποισιν ἐόντες
> ἀθάνατοι φράζονται ὅσοι σκολιῇσι δίκῃσιν
> ἀλλήλους τρίβουσιν θεῶν ὄπιν οὐκ ἀλέγοντες.
> τρὶς γὰρ μύριοί εἰσιν ἐπὶ χθονὶ πουλυβοτείρῃ
> ἀθάνατοι Ζηνὸς φύλακες θνητῶν ἀνθρώπων,
> οἵ ῥα φυλάσσουσίν τε δίκας καὶ σχέτλια ἔργα
> ἠέρα ἑσσάμενοι, πάντῃ φοιτῶντες ἐπ᾽ αἶαν.
>
> (Hes. *WD* 248-55)

The thirty thousand guards stationed round the globe, enforcing Justice and keeping watch over the deeds of men, were strong allies of the didactic poet, who balanced with the 'eye of Zeus' the dangerous authority of the 'kings'. The prosecuting of the *Ars* demonstrated that gods less attentive to the claims of Justice could exercise these forces of absolute power.[49] Still, not even the thirty thousand invisible can impose a final reading on *Tristia* 2 and rescue the addressee from the dangers of learning.

5

Future Reflexive: Two Modes of Allusion and the *Heroides*

In recognizing an allusion the reader moves backwards in time from the text she is reading towards an earlier tradition, already familiar: but I would say that there is a particular fascination in this process because it repeats and – simultaneously – reverses the original direction of the stream of literary 'creation'. Where the writer has worked from the old towards the new, the reader finds his way by means of clues that send him back from the new towards the old. In other words, allusion and literary self-consciousness are not easily detachable entities. In some texts, often narrative or dramatic works, this use of allusion has certain self-referential characteristics that enhance its effect on the reader.

If the text is asked to provide an analogy for its intertextual origins, one could say that the *past* is the most natural site for any form of intertextual recall. When Aeneas recognizes his own past in the temple at Carthage, and the reader recognizes the Epic Cycle in these images, a feeling of analogy, of natural following-on, is created: the reader, the character who is the focus of the action, and the Roman poet, are all in the same line, and together acknowledge the epic tradition as the background against which the new narrative has to be visualized. (What reader, character and poet have in common is also that they need, each in his own way, to break free from this tradition. The inclusion of epic memories in the temple of Carthage discharges a debt and prefaces a way out from the epic past.) But this is a 'smooth' kind of effect, which comes about so naturally that at times it can be noticeable without being intentional. Any reader who also knows the *Iliad* can hardly read the *Odyssey* without being conscious of references to the story's glorious antecedents, and it is extremely difficult to make a distinction between what is remembered by the characters of the *Odyssey* and what might be deliberate allusions to the *Iliad* as a literary text.

But what happens when the older tradition enters a new text as a view of the *future*? The idea that the characters can have a future that has already been written down is much less natural, and calls for constant negotiation between author and reader. A certain alignment is now broken. The literary tradition – a source of power, control and anxiety, a perfect analogy for the past in everyone's life – is now displaced, and a potential for irony opens up. Unless the characters are gifted with second sight, the effect approaches what we usually call dramatic irony: the information that the author shares with the audience tends to create a sort of complicity between them directed against the characters. This is the starting point of my analysis; but I want to keep an eye also on the issue of 'reflexivity', literary self-consciousness. A combination of these two ways of reading has, or at least ought to have, a strong influence on our way of interpreting certain Alexandrian and Augustan poets.

Readers of Theocritus' Cyclops can remember the feeling of delicate irony that arises from seeing through the eyes of that strange young lover:

> νῦν μάν, ὦ κόριον, νῦν αὐτόγα νεῖν μεμαθεῦμαι
> αἴ κά τις σὺν ναῒ πλέων ξένος ὧδ᾽ ἀφίκηται
> ὡς εἰδῶ τί ποθ᾽ ἁδὺ κατοικῆν τὸν βυθὸν ὕμμιν.
>
> (11.60-2)

'Now in truth, my girl, now I should really like to learn to swim: somebody might arrive here in a ship, a stranger, to teach me how sweet it is to live in your deep-sea dwelling.' The Cyclops' ingenuousness is in dramatic contrast with what the reader already knows: that a Stranger will really come from the sea, one day, but that he will not be Somebody (*tis*) but Nobody (*outis*) and that he will not teach the Cyclops to swim.[1] This knowledge of the future, from the *Odyssey*, is an obvious source of irony; but it also forces the reader to enter into discussion with the text she is reading: who is this new young Cyclops, and how is his idyllic setting related to the desert island that the earlier epic has made familiar? Are concepts such as 'genre' and 'fiction' relevant and brought into play? Our concept of literature as a logically cohesive continuum of texts undergoes an identity crisis, caused by the fact that traditional characters are to be seen in a new light: this lovable young Cyclops comes 'before' Homer's solitary monster, but at the same time hints at the prospect of a parallel world, still open to different possibilities and deaf to the claims of the tradition. Many other displacements could be relevant to this strategy: young and infant heroes, some infant gods in Callimachus, the Argonauts travelling 'before' the *Odyssey* with Medea 'before' her tragedy .... The Alexandrians have a preference for children and young people, which is often discussed in terms of realism, or of anti-heroism, but could be seen also in this light: the characters are caught in the process of becoming 'themselves', of becoming traditional; their innocence provokes a reading which is absolutely not innocent. Readers of Apollonius, for instance, experience a recurring bifurcation: are we reading a new version of the traditional construct 'Medea', or the early biography (and aetiology) of Euripides' *Medea*? When this strategy is successful, the narrator is free to combine independence and allusivity.

Writing is dangerous

We are frequently struck by a feeling of foreknowledge while reading Ovid's *Heroides*, and modern analyses often seem to undervalue this dimension. The missing element may or may not be of great importance, and our first case study is fairly innocuous. Penelope concludes the first letter in the collection with a sad forecast:

> protinus ut venias, facta videbor anus.
>
> (1.116)

in which she sees herself as an elegiac poet would have described her. This is not just a vague impression, since the line is actually a clear allusion to Propertius' Penelope:

> illum exspectando facta remansit anus.
>
> (2.9.8)

Ovid masterfully turns two slow spondees (*illum exspectando*) into quick dactyls (*protinus ut venias*), as endurance yields to impatience. This allusion has something of the manifesto about it, and is highly suitable for the opening of a collection of letters in which elegy rewrites traditional characters. We see, precisely, a Homeric situation through elegiac spectacles. But the first epistle (as Duncan Kennedy has shown in a brilliant study)[2] also carries a further type of implication: the situation in which Penelope is writing is richly ironic because, according to the model of the *Odyssey* and its internal time-scheme, at this very moment – while she writes, and wonders where he is – a stranger is already knocking at the gates of her house. If we look at this verse from the Homeric point of view – so different from that of the elegiac poets – our vision of it becomes bifocal. Penelope and her husband are certainly about to see each other again but – inside the epic world – she isn't the one who will look old. It is Odysseus, on the contrary, who returns home in the guise of an 'old, old man' (*Od.* 13.432) and will even be compared to a *graus* (18.27), an *anus*.

This method of conjugating an allusion in the future tense, if recognized, can also offer some more significant results, not least in the field of textual criticism. Briseis writes to Achilles: 'ill fortune never releases the unlucky',

> nec venit inceptis mollior hora meis?
>
> (3.44)

Recent editors have found no difficulties in this line, which comes down to us without textual variants, and interpret Briseis' meaning as 'a sweeter time for my plans does not arrive'. But Planudes' translation indicates that some lost witness read *inceptis ...malis*, and *malis* in the place of *meis* was also independently conjectured by Karl Lehrs and approved of by Housman. Both are silent about their motives, but if they were objecting to the use of *incepta* as a noun in this context, I agree: Briseis has no 'plans' or 'enterprises' to be frustrated by destiny, she is nothing but a victim. Torn from her native land and family, widow, slave, slave to love, property of Achilles carried off by Agamemnon, what Briseis intends to say is 'there has been no sweeter hour for me, since my ills began'. Ovid's heroine has a single hope left for the future, the friendship of Patroclus, who has always treated her with kindness and tried to comfort her. After the letter has been written, her future in the *Iliad* is the death of Patroclus: 'for me an evil always follows an evil' she will complain once more, *kakon ek kakou aei* she will lament again (Hom. *Il.* 19.290). *Kakon ek kakou* is a cruel motivation for reading *malis* in her previous, Ovidian lament.[3]

The next letter opens in softly seductive tones as Phaedra invites Hippolytus to read her wooing missive:

> Perlege, quodcumque est. Quid epistula lecta nocebit?
> (4.3)

'Read it all, for what it is worth: what harm can come from reading a letter?' Commentators do not speak of this lightly-suggested topos of invitation to the reader, which may be addressed not only to Hippolytus but also to the 'hesitating purchasers' of the *Heroides*. But the readers of Euripides are invited to connect, and indeed dub, this innocent invitation with Theseus' inhuman, rending cry on reading another letter by Phaedra, her letter to him:

> Βοᾷ βοᾷ δέλτος ἄλαστα ...
> οἷον οἷον εἶδον ἐν γραφαῖς μέλος
> φθεγγόμενον τλάμων
> (Eur. *Hipp.* 877-80)

The handwriting of this harmless love letter is the vehicle of a powerful weapon that can also kill: the trustful Theseus had said 'Come, let us open the seal, let us see what this message wants to tell me'.[4] If Ovid's readers continue to look out for danger signals, his Phaedra frustrates them.[5] The elegy runs its course, deliberately avoiding any reference to the tragic code, until, in the very last line, another apparently innocent touch reminds us that yes, after all Phaedra is a product of the tragic stage:

> Verba precantis
> qui legis, et lacrimas finge videre meas!
> (4.175-6)

If Hippolytus, the reader, follows her suggestion literally, and pictures to himself the heroine in tears, he will find himself sharing the exact viewpoint (*finge videre*) of a spectator of the Euripidean tragedy – his own tragedy, which could still be commuted if he allows himself to be seduced 'out' of the tragic world. Late in the tragedy Hippolytus will utter the impossible wish to become a spectator (1078f.), to look at his own tears from the outside.

Intertextual irony depends on the play between different codes of reference, which give rise to contradictory expectations. The nymph Oenone writes to Paris to regain his love, and, at the same time, to remove him from the dangers of the Trojan war. By returning to Oenone and abandoning the dangerous Helen, Paris will be safe:

> Non ego cum Danais arma cruenta fero.
>
> (5.156)

Commentators have little interest in this emphatic negation, and some translator even misunderstands *cum* – 'I do not bear arms *against the* Greeks', perhaps because a Phrygian nymph should be on the Trojan side anyway. A heroine who speaks in this way to a Trojan hero is no novelty in Roman poetry: the first hemistich en bloc, with the general idea, comes down in direct line from Dido's negation when she tries to regain Aeneas' love:

> Non ego cum Danais Troianam exscindere gentem
> Aulide iuravi classemve ad Pergama misi.
>
> (4.425-6)

The reader who recognizes this model can feel reassured, just as the addressee of this letter should: Dido did not take the part of the Greeks against Troy, therefore Paris has no dangers to fear from Oenone. But Oenone's life history does not end with this letter: our sources,[6] which draw material from the Trojan cycle and surely also from more recent poetry, tell us that Oenone will give important assistance to the Greek invaders in revenge for being abandoned. So, even with a bare outline of the main sources for this letter, we are in a position to understand that Paris' future is written in reverse in Ovid's Virgilian model.

Sometimes the future implies a new reading of past experiences. The letter written by Dido contains a dire prediction: if Aeneas abandons her, she will come back to haunt him as a wretched ghost (7.69ff.). His prediction of the future tallies nicely with its Virgilian model: Virgil's Dido had also said, in a more tragic and threatening tone, *omnibus umbra locis adero* (*Aen.* 4.386). What Ovid's text invites us to notice is a simple echo, an alignment. But his exact choice of words – *coniunx, ante oculos*, and *imago* – the new words which he introduces as a variation on the Virgilian model, produces a supplementary effect which is somewhat disturbing. In the second book of the *Aeneid* Aeneas has narrated (and to Dido herself) the sad story of Creusa: *coniunx ... erepta Creusa* (2.738); *visa mihi ante oculos et nota maior imago* (2.773). The future that Dido envisages is not so different from the past. What is in store for Aeneas is an unbearable replay, a *second* encounter with *another* pitiful ghost of a lost bride.[7] He could even have problems in distinguishing the two revenants.

Deianira writes to Heracles (*Her.* 9) because rumour has brought bad news: her husband is in love with the captive Iole. This is an apt beginning for a letter which is centred on acts of communication and on impediments and interferences in communication. Deianira receives vague *news* about her husband, then writes a *letter*, but a new *rumour* informs her (by means of a messenger) that Heracles is dying because of Nessus' tunic: her letter to Heracles thus becomes the *announcement* of a suicide. In fact, even the tunic that Deianira sends to her husband is a message, and an ambiguous one at that: she sees it as love magic, but the Centaur had programmed it as a death philtre. Thus far it is clear that the letter is an intriguing meditation on a leading theme of Sophocles' *Trachiniae*.[8]

There is strong dissent on the authenticity of *Her.* 9, and scholars tend to neglect its ironical effects even when they are well in evidence. (As is well known, authenticity can be best proved through small details, formal patterns which escape the full consciousness of an artist: since I will be busy with narrative structure and intertextuality, that is not my province. On a different tack, I tend to show that the epistle is much more clever, ironical, and implicated with its Sophoclean model than it is often thought: as a consequence, those who think that the imitator is always an inferior poet should, in my view, accept Ovidian paternity.) Some critics find it absurd that a large part of the letter should be given over to the re-evocation of Heracles' love-affairs with Iole, and earlier with Omphale: a piece of erotic padding which clashes with the end of the letter and only serves to reiterate the trite elegiac motif of the 'conqueror conquered': even invincible heroes are captured by a woman. (Of course, this long erotic section accounts for the inclusion of *Her.* 9 in the collection: a very incompetent move, if that is the only function which is perceived by readers.) Yet it is this very topos, however trite – and the fact that it is very elegiac and very trite adds piquancy to the Ovidian context – that Sophocles' Heracles uses to describe his own downfall. The hero who has overcome so many monsters has now been destroyed by a woman (*Trach.* 1058ff.). This time the victorious woman is Deianira herself: it is she, and not Omphale or Iole, who is the real dark lady of the piece, with that embarrassing name of hers ('destroy the male', glossed in 9.144 *virum ... perire*).

The critical handling of a line such as 141

semivir occubuit in letifero Eveno

in lernifero(que) veneno: in lorifero eveneno: lernei tabe veneni: in lotifero Eveno *Bentley*: in lentifero Eveno *Madvig*: tibi letiferoque veneno *Lehrs* shows that low estimation of this text can even creep into the domains of textual criticism. Modern conjectures are purely decorative and dilute the significance of the line: the 'lotus-producing' and even the 'lentil-producing' Evenus. Some ancient variants, even if impossible, are suggestive and point in the right direction: *in lernifero veneno, lernei tabe veneni.* The name of the river, the Evenus, should be restored, and combined with the epithet *letifero.* A precious metrical effect (spondaic hexameter with hiatus) and a striking metrical anomaly (the final syllable of *occubuit* used as a *longum*) are not wasted if one pauses to think about the *narrative* effect of this line. It is important to notice that the couplet 141-2 is immediately followed (in line 143) by the arrival of the news of the tunic's deadly message for Heracles. In a sense, writing *letifero Eveno* brings about Heracles' doom: *scribenti nuntia venit / fama* ... (143f.). This is not only tragic irony: this is tragic irony laid bare, a self-conscious exaggeration. Mention of the deadly river sets the stage for the hero's death: Deianira unconsciously 'writes' his death. Nessus' death in the river Evenus is, unknown to Deianira, the cause of this disaster, and her words play on the edge of this hidden truth. *Letifer* in Ovid often has the meaning not only of 'lethal, deadly' (the place of Nessus' death) but also of 'poisoned': the tunic smeared with poison is called *letiferam ... vestem* in *Met.* 9.166. In the waters of the river Evenus, in fact, the blood of the dying Centaur had formed a lethal mixture with the venom of the Lernean Hydra (*Trach.* 717). So the Centaur's blood has not only stained, but infected the Evenus (the two meanings are simultaneous in *infecit sanguis equinus aquas,* 142). The very name of the river is in tension with the key-word *veneno,* which is deferred to line 163 when the truth becomes clear: *illita Nesseo misi tibi texta veneno.* After her casual mention of the death of a *semivir* – 'half-man', i.e. the Centaur[9] – Deianira will discover that this far-off event is the reason while she is losing her own *vir*: the Centaur had promised her a charm possessing *vires amoris* (162) but it is actually a deadly poison, a *virus.* The same dangerous alchemy of puns is in the parallel version of the *Metamorphoses*: 9.155 *vires*; 157 *viro*; 158 *virus*; 161 *vis*, an intertwining of virility and poison.

A major puzzle in this letter is emphasized by the line which is repeated four times, as a sort of refrain:

> impia quid dubitas Deianira mori?
> (9.146 = 152 = 158 = 164)

Why should Deianira continue writing what had begun as a letter to her husband? After all, we are quite sure that she is going to kill herself – if for no other reason than because we have read *The Women of Trachis.* The letter now looks like a dramatic monologue, and the author is indifferent, to say the least, to reconciling his strategy with the poetics of the collection. Some critics have seen this hybridization as evidence that the letter

is spurious. In effect, the repetition of this gloomy line puts us in mind of
a tragic lament; more exactly, of a tragic *form* of lament, *ephymnion*.[10]
Tragedy enters this text with a powerful marker: after a hyperbole of tragic
irony, we discover that the tragic model has become form, not just material,
for the content of this epistle.

The formal irruption of tragedy into the elegiac texture directs us to the
Sophoclean model – only to discover that the Deianira of *The Women of
Trachis* utters no lament, either for Heracles or for herself. In an exceptional dramatic solution, she vanishes wordlessly (*Trach.* 813) from the
scene and immediately kills herself on the marriage bed. Ovid has his
Deianira speaking in this blank of the Sophoclean model. The Ovidian
refrain 'What is keeping you from dying, Deianira' sounds like an implicit
self-reproach – not only because she is crushed by shame and guilt, but
because by her delay she is swerving from the path laid down by the official
model for this letter, the *Trachiniae*.[11] Once again we see, and I shall come
back to this later, how intertextual irony could be linked to a kind of
self-referentiality. The text sees its future reflected in the mirror of its
model, and at the same time sends its reader backwards to that model. Her
repeated lament identifies Deianira as a character born for the tragic
scene, opens a play of difference with the elegiac medium, and finally
sends her back to a kind of intertextual order of things.

A brief consideration of Medea's letter (*Her.* 12) is rewarding in the same
perspective. The authenticity is, again, controversial, but for my limited
purpose it would be enough to show that the letter is very rich in literary
self-consciousness. Some of the main facts have been neatly established by
Peter Knox: the letter starts with a dramatic stylization, 'which derives
from tragic monologue'; the end 'looks suspiciously like a preliminary to
further action'; the structure entails 'a powerful influence exerted on the
author of this epistle by a dramatic representation of Medea'.[12] Indeed, the
final threat in aposiopesis, *quos equidem actutum* ... (12.219), stops on a
word which clearly derives from Roman tragic lexis, *actutum*.[13] Medea is
passing from letter-writing to action – to scenic action (*actus*). She feels a
divine possession (213 *viderit ista deus, qui nunc mea pectora versat*),
highly suitable for tragic characters and for tragic poets as well: perhaps
the same force which propels Medea in the Ovidian tragedy (fr. 2 Owen,
feror huc illuc ut plena deo).[14] Yet we are still reading a letter, a text poised
below the tragic level:

> *nunc animis* audi verba *minora* meis
> (12.186).[15]

A disputed line from Euripides, *thumos de kreissôn tôn emôn bouleumatôn*
(1079) exhibits an increased tension between *animus* and arguments. The
Euripidean tragedy starts when someone notices that Medea is preparing

'something new': *dedoika d'autên mê ti bouleusêi neon* (37) and the Ovidian Medea, probably *entheos*, ends with a powerful preface to action:

nescio quid certe mens mea *maius* agit.

(12.214)

There is a hint of a complicity between tragic persona, frenzied to *nefas*, and the demoniac inspiration necessary to a tragic poet. (Readers of Seneca's tragedies should notice this anticipation.) Medea has a *mens* which could conceive unspeakable plans; this potential is inscribed in her name, because Apollonius already connects his *Mêdeia* with *noon kai mêdea kourês*.[16] Realizing her *mens* and her plans, Medea is now becoming herself – an idea which will prove attractive to Seneca. The main point is that she speaks not only as a self-conscious character, but also (by implication) as a self-conscious author:

nescio quid certe mens mea *maius* agit.

There is a tradition of tragic characters moving to greater deeds: *maior mihi moles, maius miscendumst malum* (Atreus in Acc. 200 R.[2]); *maiusque ... aliquid cupio* (Oedipus, Sen. *Phoen.* 353-4, wants real tragic action: not just civil war, but mutual fratricide and the suicide of a mother). And there is also a tradition of *maius* used as a poetical prooemium or promise. Eumolpus enters the *Satyricon* as a man *exercitati vultus et qui videretur nescio quid magnum promittere* (Petron. 83.7). *Maius opus* is for Virgil the announcement of a higher epic, with kings, battles and *animi* (*Aen.* 7.41-5); *maius opus* describes the *Metamorphoses* seen from the angle of Ovid's humble elegiacs (*Trist.* 2.63). More importantly, the constellation *nescio quid ... maius* is found nowhere else in Augustan poetry[17] except in a famous passage of literary criticism, Propertius 2.34.66:

nescio quid maius nascitur Iliade.

In other words, Medea is suggesting that a new poetic kind is called for: she could not write a letter about her 'greater' actions, and this material, unspeakable for elegiacs, is reserved to the heights of a *cothurnata*. A poor version of this line of thought would be a dry 'see my (and Ovid's) tragedy', but there is more than that. Medea implicates her readers in a difficult question: in a different setting, she could be different. Drama and elegy have different and conflicting codes, and literary consciousness diffracts the identity of mythical personae. It is difficult to say how far this Medea – seen through Apollonius and Euripides, Ovid's tragedy and Ovid's elegiacs – is still *one*.[18]

The example of Deianira enables us to make a distinction which is of vital importance to our argument. Here we have a model, Sophocles, which is already a powerful source of dramatic irony. (Ovid, as we have seen, comments on the device, lays bare the mechanism.) Deianira introduces the action of the play by saying that it is not necessary to wait for the final day of a life in order to pass judgment on it: she herself, even before she goes down to Hades, already knows that her destiny is nothing but unhappiness.[19] Life is unpredictable ... A well known, generalizing topos of exits is turned upside down as an entrance statement. We are only at the fourth line of the drama, and the phrase 'before going down to Hades' is a remarkable utterance for a character whom the audience will actually see go down to Hades in the course of that very same day. Sophocles' perspective of irony may seem no different from the examples we have taken from Ovid, but a significant distinction exists. Ovid's heroines – and the case of Theocritus' Cyclops is again particularly relevant – are conditioned by an intertextuality which is not simply mythological, but specifically literary. In tragedy the irony arises from that knowledge of myth which the dramatic text reactivates in the spectator through a continuous triangular movement at the characters' expense. (It would be silly to deny that literary consciousness, allusivity and intertextuality are present in Attic tragedy: but there is still, I believe, a difference in degree.) The youthful Cyclops and Ovid's heroines, on the contrary, are caught up in a conflict of literary codes and genres; the reader hesitates about their place in the literary tradition; they are characters who attempt to rewrite their own story in terms of a new and different code. It is not by chance that this conflict and indecision is generally derived from the contrast between such traditional genres as epic and tragedy, and such a new and private genre as love poetry.

Different genres diffract our perceptions and multiply differences. From our vantage point, we see love poetry framed by more powerful codes. We are superior to the heroines, we know the unavoidable ends – but while we look at their illusions from the vantage point of irony, we are framed too: our ironical vantage point is built on the acceptance of a master fiction which controls us as we control intertextual ironies.

No one can read Ariadne's epistle without thinking of Catullus 64, but not everyone is prepared to accept the consequences of this link. This new Ariadne is more restless and dynamic than any other heroine: she runs around, climbs up rocks, shouts, gesticulates – just as if she had been let out of a prison, the prison of the static character of the Catullan ekphrasis. The new Ariadne roams around like a possessed Bacchante (10.47-8) and of course she is about to meet some even more frenzied Maenads (cf. Catullus 64.254ff.) – but for Catullus she was immobilized in the *statue* of a Bacchante (64.61 *saxea ut effigies Bacchantis*), a paradox of frozen energy. Ovid's Ariadne has got a bed and a bedcover to complain to (10.51ff.): this is a topos of erotic poetry (*torum repeto ... strataque quae membris intepuere tuis ... lacrimisque toro manante profusis ... 'lectule ...'*),[20] and certainly not very realistic in the setting of a deserted shore.

Nothing remains of Theseus except a bed and bedclothes: a bed which will not 'show' the two lovers together any more (*non ... exhibiturus erat*, 10.52). It is useful to recall (as Florence Verducci has done[21]) that Ariadne made her entrance in the Roman literary world as the decorative element on a bed, exhibiting herself to visitors on a bedcover: oddly enough this was, in fact, a marriage bed, like the one she is addressing in Ovid. The Ovidian letter gestures towards its origins in the ekphrastic tradition.

The temporal context of the letter within the myth is more or less the same as that of the animated ekphrasis on which it is modelled: but the Ovidian reader is invited to a more complex response. The myth has a divided future: Theseus and Dionysus; the deserted woman and the sleeping beauty.[22] The letter is poised between the conventional model of the lamenting Forsaken (10.80 *quaecumque potest ulla relicta pati*) and the promise of a surprising epiphany. Many of Ariadne's remarks leave room for unorthodox and involuntary associations of ideas, and point to two separated areas of foreshadowing: the rescue by Dionysus, and the fall of the house of Theseus.[23]

Meanwhile, as we know, Theseus is sailing away. Ariadne wakes up in the dead of night and strains for a glimpse of his ship in the moonlight (conveniently provided by Ovid: 10.17 *luna fuit*). This is a dark setting which Catullus, impeded by his purple backdrop, could not allow himself to depict. At last (10.30) it looks as if Ariadne has seen the sails, but the following line should qualify this statement:

> vidi praecipiti carbasa tenta Noto.
> Aut vidi aut fuerant quae me vidisse putarem

fuerant quae me: tamquam quae me: etiam cum me: aut vidi aut etiam cum te vidisse putarem *Bentley*: aut vidi aut tantum quia me vidisse putavi *Madvig*: aut vidi aut tamquam quae me vidisse putavi *Palmer*: ut vidi haut umquam quae me meruisse putarem *Housman*

Line 31 could be reconstructed in various ways.[24] Housman, for example, corrected it to *ut vidi haut umquam quae me meruisse putarem*, 'when I saw the sails, a sight I would never have thought I deserved'; for him the basic meaning is obviously that Ariadne definitely sees the sails but in her indignation does not believe her own eyes. This is exactly how Catullus describes Ariadne at the beginning, 64.55 *necdum sese etiam quae visit visere credit*. But as we have already implied, the situation is different: Ovid insists on the darkness of the night, on the physical difficulties in seeing, and on Ariadne's hope of making any kind of contact whatever. His Ariadne is not (or at least not yet) indignant: she is fighting for her life. Soon afterwards we see her making desperate signals to attract the attention of the lover who has left her behind:

candidaque imposui longae velamina virgae
scilicet oblitos admonitura mei
(10.41-2)

and this signal is well chosen, because a white cloth ought to catch the eye against the darkness. If we take line 31 in the most promising form offered by the manuscripts

aut vidi aut fuerant quae me vidisse putarem

we can now translate it confidently as 'either I saw the sails, or they were just as I thought I saw them, I was able to see them'. This meaning is supported by two illustrious poetic models, two sentences in which someone 'sees or thinks he sees' something elusive in a gloomy setting. In Apollonius (4.1477) the hero Lynceus, with his portentous lynx-eye, tries to see Heracles from an enormous distance: just as someone who wants to see the moon at the beginning of the month 'sees or thinks he has seen it'. We also remember Aeneas trying to glimpse the shade of Dido, *per umbras / obscuram* (*Aen.* 6.4522f.): once again there is the analogy of one who sees or thinks he has seen (*aut videt aut vidisse putat*) the new moon, indistinct against a screen of clouds. In both examples there is darkness on darkness, vision at a breaking point, difficulty in trusting the senses.

Thus Ariadne says she has seen sails bellying in the wind: *vidi praecipiti carbasa tenta Noto* (10.30), but then she corrects herself: either she has seen them, or she was able to think she had seen them (after all, we might add, she wanted to see them at all costs). But why all this uncertainty? The white sails of a ship ought not to be so difficult to see on a moonlit night. If Theseus received her letter he would understand, and might then make up for his lapse of memory. The fact is that, as Catullus tells us (64.227-45), he is sailing homewards with *black* sails, which are by no means easy to see against the sea by night: this is why Ariadne is so uncertain. If Theseus were to see the white sails (10.41 *candida ... velamina*) that Ariadne is waving to attract his attention, he might realize[25] that he is making a fatal mistake: the *candida ... vela* (Cat. 64.235) should be substituted for the *infecta ... lintea* (Cat. 64.227), the *fallacia vela* (Ov. *Ib.* 493) that will be the cause of his father's death. Forgotten on the shore, the girl is in mourning (10.134 *maesta*; 137 *lugentis* more; 145 *lugubria pectora*): but Theseus' ship brings an inappropriate sign of mourning (Cat. 64.234 *funestam ... vestem*) which will bring death to his beholder, as a compensation for Theseus' desertion. Consider also the last prayer of the heroine (10.149, in the last distich of the epistle):

Flecte ratem, Theseu, versoque relabere vento.

Verso ... vento is a bit surprising: at this stage of the story, Ariadne speaks about Theseus as a voluntary betrayer, and preoccupation with weather conditions seems out of place. Perhaps Burman was right in suggesting *verso ... velo*. What Theseus should do is to change his course (*Her.* 13.132 *dum licet ... vertite vela!*), but the Latin also suggests 'change your sail' before it's too late.

Ars patet arte sua: characters writing about their story written by others: I know that so far I have not done much to defend the poetic merits of the *Heroides*. Many readers think that allusiveness and dependence on mythology are faults in a text which is only worth reading for its psychological interest. But maybe these two aspects are not incompatible. The heroines' struggle for control over their own destinies in the face of adverse or even impossible conditions is dramatic for the very reason that these destinies have already been recorded and written down: these women are in fact writing against the grain of the classical authorities. The idea of allowing 'feminine' voices to make themselves heard through the gaps in the opus of the past is full of possibilities, which are by no means limited to intertextuality and poetics. Once again I want to stress that we too, as readers, are caught in the process of irony, because our ironical reading needs an external vantage point, and this 'external' vantage point turns out to be based on the acceptance of master fictions. These naive, sentimental little fictions are framed as illusions by more powerful texts: but irony cuts both ways, and the superiority of the reader exposes the nexus between tradition and fiction.

Reflexive allusions

But we shall now go a little further into the world of artifice and erudition. We have already mentioned the idea of a text which in a certain way identifies its model, and so becomes self-conscious, self-referring.[26] On my reading of selected passages, Ovid's Phaedra, Medea and Deianira remind the reader of their origins as constructs of the tragic scene, and Ariadne even draws particular attention to bedcovers, after having been introduced to Roman culture as an image on a marriage bed. The Roman poet re-enacts origins, pointing to continuity and difference.

We know that here too the example comes from Alexandrian poetry, and it would be difficult to neglect Callimachean precedents. We are a few lines into the first hymn when a simple sentence, *Krêtes aei pseustai* (1.8) opens a vertiginous perspective. At the beginning of his 'Hymn to Zeus', Callimachus is not sure whether Zeus was born in Crete or in Arcadia, and asks the god to make the point clear. Our quotation seems to suggest (though this is not certain, and it would be an unprecedented move in the hymnic tradition) that the god actually replies, even though in only three words: 'Cretans always lie.' Readers perceive a strong quotation effect: this is a famous saying, not exactly a proverb, but a quotation from an almost legendary poet and holy man of the remote past, Epimenides. This distant authority is already inscribed in a tradition: the text of Epimenides seems to be modelled on a famous line of Hesiod's *Musenweihe*. Anyone who recognizes the source of the quotation sees a recession of mirrors opening up in front of him.[27] Epimenides was a poet who recounted the birth and infancy of Zeus: thus we have here a god who reconstructs his own origins by quoting a human informant, better, a literary text – just as his poet Callimachus could have done himself. But Epimenides was also a Cretan, and this sentence offers a ready-made example for handbooks of logic: a statement that renders the truth of its own content unprovable. Thirdly, the weight of the tradition behind Callimachus affirms that Zeus really was born in Crete. This is, however, a dangerous mainstream: Cretans are also famous for pointing out a grave of Zeus, and regard the god as a warrant for their tradition of pederasty.[28] So the poet has good reasons for turning away from the Cretan tradition: but if we admit that the god is a Cretan, like Epimenides, then we must apply Epimenides' self-implying statement to him too, with the result that we are back to square one. The authority that Callimachus' text derives from the past has the effect of endangering his own credibility, and exposes the connection between fiction, tradition and antiquarian research.

The Callimachean example is an extreme one, but points to a more general quality of literary allusion: in the process of alluding to predecessors, poetic texts discover a potential for self-reference. Allusions always focus on individual models but, to some extent, every allusive text makes also some broader reflexive statement: 'I am poetry', or 'fiction', or 'I belong in a tradition'. Augustan poets are particularly interested in this potential because they write in a tradition which has rich articulations and separate canons. I will be speaking again about Ovid's *Heroides*, but I would not liken this mode of allusivity to an Ovidian peculiarity, typical of the 'excessively literary poet' as opposed to his 'restrained', 'classical' predecessors. I will select a short Virgilian example to show that we are dealing with a continuous tradition. When readers meet Dido they become aware of a shocking novelty: this character owes many features to the model of tragedy. Various stages of Virgilian narrative gradually reveal her as having elements in common with, for instance, Phaedra, Medea, Alcestis, Pentheus, Ajax, Andromache, Helen and Evadne. I list these influences merely to assert that there is no dominant, individual 'source': every single allusion points to a common factor and Dido enters the epic poem as a complex voice of tragedy. This is a reference to genre, not to single exemplary models, and we have to accommodate this reference within our reading of the *Aeneid* as an epic.

A great deal of industry has been put into reconstructing a proper tragedy of Dido, with act divisions, scenic actions and the like, but this is not my preoccupation here. I am more interested in attempts to show that the Virgilian text is a self-conscious part in this debate on the appropriation of the tragic code.[29] Aeneas arrives at an unknown harbour, described by the narrator (the epic voice) as a *scaena* (*Aen.* 1.164). Later, he visits Carthage, and notices among the buildings going up a very unusual sight in heroic times: foundations for theatres, theatrical scenery in construction (1.427ff. *lata theatris / fundamenta ... scaenis decora alta futuris*). It almost seems as if the Carthaginians are setting the stage for Punic tragedies to be performed. Aeneas has learned of Dido's earlier history – a dark story worthy of the Atridae – from his mother Venus, who is disguised as a huntress: Venus is wearing buskins (1.337 *cothurno*), the typical marker of tragedy in Roman culture. Later on, when Dido is sitting in her magnificent dining-hall, we see her profiled against *aulaea* (1.697f.), rich hangings: a luxurious setting, but the most common use of the word in Latin denotes curtains in a theatre. Thus, even if in a fragmentary, subliminal form, we are not completely unprepared when the epic voice, with a bold stroke, presents Dido as a tragic character brought on to the scene by an actor: *aut Agamemnonius scaenis agitatus Orestes* (4.471). We are in the fourth book but the germs of the story – and the scenic apparatus – were already set in Book 1. Along similar lines, perhaps, Ovid opens the Theban sequence in the *Metamorphoses*, an extended cycle of stories linked by a common tragic matrix, with an odd image: the Sown Men of Thebes rise out of the ground like a theatre curtain going up.[30] For a moment the reader is like the spectator of a tragedy: these epic poets are glossing their operations outside the epic code. Interestingly, Dido is *dreaming* when she is compared to an actor *performing* Orestes.

Reading is dangerous

Again we can take some cues from the *Heroides*. As a text it is erudite, rich in models of different kinds and, as we have seen, in literary self-consciousness. It is also a text in which the procedures of writing and story-telling are used not only as the form but also as material for the content. From this angle I would like to examine the last 'double' *Epistulae*, the correspondence between Acontius and Cydippe. Like all the other texts in the *Heroides*, these final pages tell a story which is well known: there is an illustrious model in Callimachus' Aitia. Acontius throws an apple on which there is written (more or less) 'I swear by Artemis to marry Acontius' and Cydippe fails into the trap: she picks up the apple and reads its cunning message. Betrothed to another, Cydippe falls ill, and the cause of her illness is, an oracle reveals, the work of the offended goddess. In order to escape from this situation of involuntary oath-breaking, Cydippe agrees to marry Acontius, because the god Apollo has announced through his Delphic oracle that this is the only possible solution to the problem. Ovid places Acontius' letter in a significant pause in the story: Cydippe is ill, the end is coming. This position has a striking consequence: the letter is explicitly presented as a replica of the more important message, the apple that Acontius as in the model (Callimachus) has made use of as an

insidious means of communication. Acontius refers to that message as a
scripta ... caute littera (20.40), which is also a satisfying definition of the
epistle itself (cf. *AA* 1.455; 457). Writing and repetition will be the main
concerns of my reading (which will be, of course, very selective).[31]

Acontius starts from a negative move (20.3 *nihil hic iterum iurabis
amanti*), but his letter glides into repetitions: *verba licet repetas ...* (20.11).
En iterum scribo (20.35) is a remarkable confession, since every letter in
Ovid's *Heroides* is normally a 'first' act of writing. His invitation to Cydippe, *perlege!* (20.5) is an insidious echo: *perlege!* (21.111) was the nurse's
invitation to read the tricky words on the apple. Cydippe is now aware that
reading is dangerous (note the pun in 21.146 *vir mihi non isto more
legendus (!) eras*), and understands that an epistle can be a repetition of
the fallacious apple: *succedat epistula pomo* (21.147). Of course, Ovid too
is repeating: he is repeating Callimachus. This procedure is revealed at the
crucial point where Acontius writes: 'say again the words of the oath',
recitetur formula pacti (20.153); *lecta tibi quondam nunc quoque verba
refer* (20.216). If Cydippe obeys

> mittitur ante pedes malum cum carmine tali –
> ei mihi! iuravi nunc quoque paene tibi!
> (21.109-10)

she will bind herself by a second promise: in reading Acontius' (and Ovid's)
epistle, she will be made to repeat the other, absent, words that she has
already read on the apple – and which have been read, I presume, in the
text of Callimachus' *Aitia*.[32] This is a tantalizing moment: the Latin text
stops before reciting the formula of the Greek model. The apple with its
text comes into the Ovidian text as an emblem of the model that the Latin
imitator intends to recall, but not to reproduce: *iurare in verba alicuius* is
always a sign of excessive subjection. Interestingly, Cydippe sees the
message as a *carmen*: this is appropriate for an oath, which is also a kind
of binding spell, but also of course for the Callimachean model.

It is interesting to note that at the end of Acontius' letter the apple is
even reduplicated physically. Acontius wants to display an effigy of it, an
image of the apple that will demonstrate the efficacy of its message by
means of an inscription: a new inscription, after those carved by the
Callimachean Acontius on trees and on the apple itself. The inscription is
a distich:

> causaque versiculis scripta duobus erit:
> 'Effigie pomi testatur Acontius huius,
> quae fuerint in eo scripta, fuisse rata'.
> (20.240-2)

There is a strong mirror effect. Acontius ends his story by displaying a
causa ... versiculis scripta duobus – a precise allusion if one remembers

that the model for this story is to be found in a poem entitled 'Causes' and composed in elegiac couplets. His ex voto re-evokes both the object itself and its origin in a text.

Callimachus' pair of lovers have now become the authors of letters, and both of them, in their own ways, show themselves worthy to continue the work of their original author. Acontius is, as he was in Callimachus, a simple young man rendered expert and astute by love. 'Love himself was the teacher of Acontius ...' (fr. 67.1 Pf.). In his first-person repetition of this statement, Acontius underlines that Amor has been a teacher in *verbal* art: *dictatis ab eo feci sponsalia verbis* (20.31). Another powerful stimulus was the *puella: sollertem tu me, crede, puella, facis* (20.28); the Ovidian lover is a manipulator of words inspired by a woman and dictated by love. The poetics of Roman elegy, as we shall see later, provides an area of comparison: *Amor ... me docuit* (Prop. 1.1.4-5); *Venus ... perdocuit* (Tib. 1.8.5-6). Acontius describes his success as a victory of witty discourse: *te mihi compositis, si quid tamen egimus, arte / adstrinxit verbis ingeniosus Amor* (20.29-30). This is in fact a witty statement: on a first reading, *arte* goes with *adstrinxit*, because the message is a binding spell, a kind of *katadesmos*. Bondage is a recurring theme in the letter, but the metrical position of *arte* allows a second reading: *artĕ compositis verbis* would be a good Ciceronian definition of manipulative rhetoric (*De or.* 3.196 *verbis arte positis moventur omnes*). Acontius is learning the art of writing.[33]

Cydippe, on the other side, ill and obliged to write in secret, is a suitable embodiment for some well-known qualities of Callimachean art. Her frail body, *gracilem* (21.17) as a result of illness, responds to the precepts of a 'thin', *leptaleê* Muse.[34] The effort involved in writing (21.27ff. *verba imperfecta repetita fatigat labor*; 247 *calamo lassavimus*) and the refusal of length (20.243 *longior infirmum ne lasset epistula corpus*; 21.248 *officium longius*) are typical requisites of any author who aspires to be part of the Callimachean tradition. The message of the apple is seen, in a symmetrical perspective, as something 'learned', which requires 'learning' in order to be understood: *verba ferens doctis insidiosa notis* (Acontius, 20.212); *docta fui* (Cydippe, 21.184). Slenderness, toil, brevity, doctrine are a familiar pattern of Roman Alexandrianism.

The story had begun with a chance meeting in a famous resort of religious tourism. Cydippe recalls her journey: attracted by its fame, she hastened to visit Delos (21.79). We might ask ourselves if this fame has anything to do with Callimachus' 'Hymn to Delos'. Finding it difficult to land, she addresses the island: *'Quid me fugis, insula? ... Laberis in magno numquid ut ante mari?'* (21.85-6). The question captures the central point of the story told in the hymn. Cydippe herself remarks that her letter is not supposed to be a Blue Guide: *neque enim meminive libetve / quidquid ibi vidi, dicere* (21.103-4), but the only two sights that she mentions correspond to two famous images from two Callimachean hymns: the altar made of horns in the 'Hymn to Apollo' (21.102 with *Apoll.* 62-3) and the palm-tree in the 'Hymn to Delos' (21.102 with *Del.* 209-10). These cross-references lead us to the repetition of a famous scene from the *Aitia*. As we have seen, Cydippe remembers that she has enacted this scene, but avoids repeating the exact words of the *carmen* (21.109-12). If she pronounces the formula, she will fall into the trap a second time. If Ovid reproduces his model, he will be an imitator in the trap of repetition, one who swears according to the formula of his model. For Ovid the *carmen* (21.109) consists of a combination of two texts, that of Acontius and that of Callimachus, inscribed on the same apple. In responding to her nurse's *perlege* (21.111), Cydippe comes very near to a literal repetition of the words of a 'great poet':

> insidias legi, magne poeta, tuas.
> (21.112)

The irony directed against the 'great poet' Acontius is redoubled by the awe that the imitator shows in respect to his own great but insidious predecessor.

Cydippe's letter rushes towards a solution which covers exactly the Callimachean story: the answer given by Apollo's Delphic oracle forces the girl's parents to accept Acontius as a son-in-law. The Ovidian version is a problematic passage, very badly transmitted; however, some points can still be made:

> is quoque nescio quam – nunc ut vaga fama susurrat –
> neglectam queritur testis habere fidem.
> Hoc deus et vates, hoc et mea carmina dicunt:
> At desunt voto carmina nulla tuo!
> Unde tibi favor hic? Nisi si nova forte reperta est,
> quae capiat magnos littera lecta deos.
> (21.235-40)

Apollo's intervention shows that Acontius is the victor – the victor, it is interesting to note, not only as a lover, but also as the author of approved texts: the language of 238-40 (*carmina ... favor ... nova ... reperta est ... littera lecta*) suggests a true literary 'success story'. Line 238 is difficult and possibly corrupt, but at least a general meaning seems to be clear: a wandering rumour whispers or insinuates (*susurrat*) that the god demands the keeping of the oath. Interesting, the *detailed* speech of Apollo *reported* in the Callimachean original (fr. 75.20-38ff.), and *directly* received by Cydippe's father who was consulting the Delphic oracle, has become a *fama*: there are other examples, in Roman poetry, where *fama* becomes a mediator and an analogy for the literary tradition. 'Rumour' functions as a substitute for 'literary influence': we have already commented on the 'fame' of Delos in 21.79. There could be even a more precise link: Callimachus introduces the god's message as an *ennuchion epos*: in fact, the speech will be difficult, learned and winding, so *ennuchion* could be taken to mean 'obscure', and *vaga fama susurrat* would be an apt way of capping this Callimachean point.[35] Anyway, the wandering, whispering rumour exonerates Ovid from close repetition of a Callimachean text: the oracle 'fades', like the oath. So, Cydippe capitulates to a god, to a *vates*, and to *carmina*: every kind of *carmen* is on Acontius' side (237-8). The use of *carmina*[36] suggests a metaliterary effect: Acontius wins through inscription and oath, through oracles, through his (and Cydippe's) letter and finally through the Callimachean *carmina* which warrant the end of the story. The identity of the *vates* (237) has proved difficult to assess: Van Lennep suggests that he is still Apollo, *deus et vates*, 'god and his own prophet'; Palmer brings on to the scene 'seers whom Cydippe's friends may be supposed to have consulted on her behalf'. There are no other traces of these prophets in Ovid's text; and Callimachus, for his part, clearly states that it was Apollo himself who gave the complete explanation. Callimachus takes advantage of an opportunity to put words into the mouth of his favourite god, the truest 'advocate of Callimachean poetics'.[37] The answer is rich in erudition and indirectness, a good sample of the poetics of the *Aitia*. The Roman reader sees a recession of *carmina*, and a mysterious *vates* who conceals a tribute to the authority of Callimachus. In this way the poet is paired with his patron, with implications that the author of the *Aitia* would certainly have appreciated. The epistolary collection ends by conjuring up the Greek *princeps elegiae* and his victorious *carmina*. Reader and rewriter of Callimachus, Ovid has exploited to the full a story in which the acts of reading and writing play a fundamental part, and has made of it a conclusion to a poetic book of heroic epistles, a book in which the act of writing itself is (by implication) exalted to the rank of heroic action.[38]

'The Origins of Latin Love Elegy'

This reading of *Her.* 20-1 has focused on the idea that the epistles are not only imitations of Callimachus, but texts which are self-conscious about their intertextual origins. These epistles 'stage' their derivation from a Callimachean original. This may seem a subtle distinction, and my analysis may have overworked it; but I was trying to underline features which will be useful as I start, finally, to examine literary reflexivity from a different angle.

Two kinds of premises can be made. First, Acontius is not a typical character in Ovid's *Heroides*. He is not a famous mythical name, as eighteen or nineteen other 'authors' in the collection are. He owes his existence to a single Callimachean tale, presented as 'history' by Callimachus himself. In this history he features as a successful *writer*: his decisive move is not acting, but writing. According to that premise, he is the only character in the *Heroides* to *achieve* something through writing.

Secondly, *Her.* 20-1 differ from many other *Heroides* (double and single) in that they have, and acknowledge, a model which is *elegy* (not, for instance, narrative or dramatic poetry, to be metamorphosed into Ovidian elegy).[39]

This last point becomes more important if we recall a sketch of Ovid's poetic career. Ovid's double *Heroides* represent his latest work in love elegy: Ovid has made every possible effort to demarcate his 'sad' elegies from Pontus and his earlier amatory work. *Her.* 20-1 seem (on the manuscript evidence) to have a final position, both in the writing of letters, and in the composition of love elegiacs. They are also, incidentally, the latest compositions we have from Augustan love poetry. And Acontius is, of course, from more than one point of view an elegiac hero. He comes from the most successful love story in what is, in general, an elegiac masterpiece, the *Aitia*. More than that, he has a long career as a role model for Roman love poetry. The Callimachean narration is largely imitated before Ovid starts to rework it but, more than that, it is appropriated, and receives a new programmatic force. As we will see in the Appendix to this chapter, Catullus 65, a crucial text in the development of Roman elegy, seems to play on Acontius' seductive apple. But in general, the elegiac poets focus on a different part of the Callimachean original. Desperately in love, Acontius becomes the solitary lover who goes to the woods, addresses trees, and carves 'beautiful Cydippe' in the bark. This is where he becomes a prototype: the solitary lover reappears, as an explicit Callimachean influence, in important texts like Propertius 1.18 and the first love poem by Virgil, *Ecl.* 2, and the Gallan/Virgilian texture of Eclogue 10.[40] In this last poem, which represents Gallus as the model for Roman love elegy, we see the poet carving 'love' on the trees

> ... tenerisque *meos* incidere *amores*
> arboribus: crescent illae, crescetis amores.
>
> (10.53-4)

Of course, Gallus is famous for writing *Amores*, so this is an intense metaliterary moment. Acontius carving the trees becomes a model not only for the Roman lover, but for the Roman lover and poet. His writing on the trees is seen as a germ of elegiac poetics: in Prop. 1.18 the poet's voice is cast in the role of Acontius.

The importance of this appropriation cannot be overstated. Augustan poetry *needs* Callimachus for complex reasons, which include the politics of poetics, and sometimes have little to do with the poetics of the originals. A powerful, creative misreading of the *Aitia* is badly needed, if Callimachus has to provide the precedent and warrant for Roman love elegy. So, the episode of Acontius and Cydippe (see Ov. *Rem.* 381-2) is very influential for a complex poetic strategy: through this allusion the elegist 'proves' that his Callimachean allegiance has a basis; through the theme of writing 'beautiful Cydippe', the Callimachean character becomes a project for the 'subjective' Roman poet.

I believe that this recession of appropriations and misreadings is important for Ovid's imitation of Callimachus. The theme of writing is, again, relevant, but now with a different emphasis. From the original, Ovid selects not the over-exploited solitary lover (and writer), but the successful writer of love apples. The focus shifts from writing 'Cydippe' to seducing Cydippe through writing. Writing as seduction would be, of course, an apt way of describing the poetics of Roman elegy: this is poetry which represents itself as *practice, werbende Dichtung*. As we have seen, this new Acontius is archly conscious that his writing is dictated by Love and the beloved: *sollertem tu me, crede, puella facis* (20.28); *scribere iussit Amor* (20.232). This is elegiac poetics in a nutshell (*iussit Amor*, for instance, is a tag from Tibullus, 1.6.30).[41] These statements sound like typical openings of a poem, of a collection of poems based on courtship and love at first sight. Acontius is now aware that he is a model for Propertius and his fellow poets. Ovid's readers are witness to the (re-)birth of modern love elegy in Rome: an artful practice nurtured (alternatively, or simultaneously) by the feeling of love and by a reading of Callimachus. Here we have it both ways: Love dictates, and Callimachus too. In a few moments, the Callimachean hero will discover the *servitium amoris* (20.90 *ipsa tibi dices: 'Quam patienter amat!'*) and the love triangle (20.149 *improbe, tolle manus!*).

Ovid has rediscovered the Acontius story as a convincing 'plot' for Roman elegy as a whole: a genre which claims seduction through writing finds its archegete in Acontius, who has made a woman accessible through a cunning manipulation of words. Now we can understand better why epistle 20 closes on the idea of Acontius literally writing poetry, and a distich. He explains his production as a votive epigram (20.237ff. *quod si contigerit ... votivo sanguine ... ponetur ... testatur ... fuisse rata*: a thorough rehearsal of the topoi and markers of dedicatory epigrams, indeed). This is very fitting, because, when an Augustan poet reflects on the origin of the elegiac format, votive epigrams are likely to be introduced as predecessors of elegy: *voti sententia compos*, according to Horace (*AP* 76).

This is why I would read the Acontius epistle not only as a reflexive imitation of Callimachus, but also as a re-enactment, a recapitulation of ideas familiar to modern scholarship ('The Origins of Latin Love Elegy'). I believe that Augustan poets are sometimes tempted to use allusion this way: to recreate a kind of myth of origins (a bit as rituals usually construct their remote beginnings). One could try to show that there is a genealogical dimension in allusive art, and link this idea with the tendentiousness which is so typical of Augustan poetics: these poets devote great energy to inventing predecessors, reshaping genealogies. Acknowledging a debt to such a remote predecessors and 'inventors' of forms as Sappho and Homer,

Hipponax and Hesiod, could not be an innocent act, an 'honest' scholarly footnote. But this, of course, is the project for another study.

Appendix: elegiac apples

My case for reading in *Her.* 20-1 a kind of 'recapitulation' of Roman elegiac tradition would gain some support from a certain reading of Catullus 65: if one accepts that Catullus (19-24) is alluding to the Callimachean story of Acontius, then the *volubile malum* would not be a newcomer in Roman elegy at all.

This is of course a controversial point, and my rehearsal will be very selective. Wendell Clausen has shown, in a powerful reading of Catullus 65,[42] the opportunity of accepting a specific Callimachean allusion in that particular context. The poem is offered as a preface to a translation from Callimachus (65.16 *carmina Battiadae*), and is likely to have a programmatic function: its companion piece, 66, certainly has a programmatic force in importing Callimachus' *Aitia* to Rome. The style of poem 65, far from being humble and deliberately uncouth,[43] is a deliberate attempt to re-evoke the difficult elegiac manner of Callimachus, with its long rambling sentences, parentheses, unexpected turns and changes of mood. Moreover, someone (some say Catullus) has placed this poem as an introduction to Catullus' elegiac oeuvre; poem 116, at the other end of the collection, has been shown to be no less programmatic,[44] and carries another reference to the effort of reworking Callimachus (116.2: *carmina Battiadae* again). If we accept that the position is significant, then some other details acquire a certain programmatic emphasis. Catullus starts from a crisis in his poetical career: grief and mourning are diverting him from the Muses. The (paradoxical) result is poetry, poetry of mourning. There is a strong tradition in Roman culture (not, apparently, in Alexandria)[45] connecting the birth of elegy with lament, *querela, e e legein* and the like. There seems to be an implicit, but deep connection between his personal loss and the choice of elegiac form. A line such as

semper maesta tua carmina morte canam[46]
(65.12)

is highly suggestive in this perspective. The following simile, the nightingale, fits very well with the poet's voice, and particularly with a voice of lament. With *semper ... canam*, I would suggest, Catullus has actually become a nightingale, while being still a learned poet: there is Greek evidence for an etymological connection between *aêdôn* and *aei + aeidô*, possibly with a Callimachean model.[47] *Aêdonides, aêdones* are attested as a symbolic reference to poetry and (possibly) as a title for poetic collections of elegies. The nightingale simile will be adapted by Virgil (*G* 4.511-15)[48] when the *illustrandum* is Orpheus' poetical activity after the loss of

Eurydice: Orpheus has become a singer of laments and carries some features of a proto-elegist. All these tenuous clues point to a shared area, where elegy appears as a mediator between poetry and grief. This area of metaliterary reference (if that is the word: Catullus is showing that his poetical choice has roots in personal experience: elegy nurtured by grief) has to be further combined with the unexpected turn to *carmina Battiadae*: again, there is a common theme, elegy (nurtured by assimilation of Callimachus).

It seems to me that the final section of 65 could be read in this frame of reference. The situation has no strict parallel in Ovid: but Cydippe blushes (21.114 *sensi me totis erubuisse genis*) as the anonymous girl does in 65.24 (*huic manat tristi conscius ore rubor*).[49] And the apple, of course, rolls down. The poem answers a request for *carmina Battiadae*, so it would be a nice touch to offer something from the *Aitia*, though in a devious way, before 66 actually begins.[50] The apple, after all, had been described by Callimachus; more than that, it had been inscribed by Callimachus. As far as we know, the apple carried a *text*, a Callimachean text which is central to the Acontius elegy in the *Aitia*. A written message could be an apt way of connecting Catullus' text with the master of elegy:[51] nothing can be proved, but certainly the apple in Ovid can be seen as an important signifier of elegiac writing. Accepting the apple written by Callimachus, Roman elegists frame a reference to the model they are claiming to appropriate.

6

Tropes of Intertextuality in
Roman Epic

vaga certat imago
Valerius Flaccus

The terrain I have to cover is inviting but so vast as to cause me worry, and I must consider how to spend the space available without seeming too diffuse and impressionistic.[1] A critical tradition from which we have all learned has accustomed us to systematic analyses of very narrow contexts that alternate with theoretical detours of wider scope. It is difficult then, at least for me, to avoid taking this long hallowed path. Still, I will refrain from presenting my personal 'Top Ten' allusions in Latin poetry.

I have thought of a possible alternative route. We are used to treating intertextuality through time-consuming examples that elicit textual pleasure and then require laborious generalizations. But if we focus on the self-consciousness of intertextuality we can at least erect a supporting framework for our observations. We will no longer be detecting relations between individual texts, but rather the ways these relations are represented and the tropes that translate them, figures that precipitate and render them visible. It is possible then to compile a short repertoire of the ways Roman culture mirrors and mediates its intertextual consciousness.

I have chosen the field of epic poetry for at least three reasons. First, it is a well-identified and internally coherent literary genre. Second, it makes strong references to its tradition while still abstaining from explicit citation. Epic poems do not enjoy that freedom of citation so obvious in other literary genres;[1a] even their proems tend to cite their models indirectly. Whoever reads the first words of Silius Italicus' *Punica*, *ordior arma*, has little doubt that its basic meaning is, 'I am beginning: here is a poem in the Virgilian epic tradition.' Yet it is important that there is no direct reference to Virgil. So too, Valerius Flaccus does not name Apollonius Rhodius in his proem, even if his insistence on Apollo is suggestive and revealing on many levels.[2] Only the *Achilleid*, the last epic poem of the classical period (a text unfortunately not dealt with here), explicitly mentions one of its models in its proem (1.3-4: *cantu / Maeonio*).[3] Finally, even though Roman epic poems are poetry books composed within a literate

civilization and for a reading audience,[4] they tend not to mention, and even
to suppress – once again on account of some self-restraint or censorship –
their materiality. These poets sing, speak, remember, and call upon the
Muses, and perhaps no one would have even bought an epic book that
contained expressions like 'I write', or even worse, 'I read'. More to the
point, no epic character is ever caught reading books. No Roman epic
author can resort to effects like those in Shakespeare, in *Titus Andronicus*
for instance, where a character reads a passage from Ovid's *Metamorphoses* (from the story of Tereus and Philomela, naturally),[5] or the effect
produced when the dark hero of *Apocalypse Now* keeps on his bedstead a
copy of *Heart of Darkness*.[6]

Ironically enough, the only exceptions to this avoidance of explicit
admissions to non-orality are found only in connection with the most
ancient and 'primitive' of Roman epic poets. It is the pre-modern poet
Naevius who 'writes' (Enn. *Ann.* 206-7 Sk.) and has books circulating
among his heroes (Naev. *Bell. Poen.* 4 B.).

But I have lingered on this written prehistory of 'oral' epic only to
highlight how self-reflexive and derivative is Roman epic. Every time
interpreters use these adjectives as if they were negative value judgments,
they miss the chance to realize that Roman poets have anticipated them
and pre-empted their criticisms. They slyly hint, 'we are poets of the study',
'we are late-comers', 'this is literature', while the modern critic, still a
Romantic at heart, misses their confessions and mistakes for failed imitations of spontaneity what are instead sophisticated and ironic admissions
of guilt. Naturally, this way of conceptualizing literature has but little to
do with the question of poetry's relation to 'real life'. Naevius himself had
seen much more warfare than some actual pre-Homeric *aoidoi* and some
bards of Roncisval or Hastings. This did not stop him from being a
self-conscious literary figure in addition to being a veteran of the first
Punic War.

Beginning at least with Virgil, books in epic become scarcer and decla-
rations of poetics ever more oblique. For this reason, it becomes interesting
to trace the evolution of certain canonic themes and formal conventions of
epic poetry, what in the title of this chapter I have chosen to call 'tropes of
intertextuality'.

Fate and fame

We can start by marking some modes of discourse which possess metaliterary properties and which act as good vehicles for transferring intertextuality into narrative plots since they pertain to the ideas of transmission
and interpretation. Fate, fame, memory and prophecy are among the most
effective of such modalities. In a poet like Virgil, operations such as
recalling past deeds, interpreting destiny, prophesying the future, and
spreading fame are all to some degree linked to an intertextual awareness.

Despite a diversity of contexts, these always serve to open the narrative plot to preformed discourses (that is, pre-existent and heterogeneous discourses). The action of the *Aeneid* is suspended between an already written past and an already written future, and thus Fate mirrors the tradition that Fame reworks and diffuses. The future is accessible in the procession of shades in the Underworld, where the density of memories leads one to think, as Glenn Most has remarked, that the world beyond is also a sort of library.[7]

Fate and Fame, both 'communicative' words related to *fari*, perform important and complementary functions in Virgilian epic. One could say briefly that Fate delineates the horizon of action, and Fame expresses its result by translating deeds into words. In a story so deeply bound to tradition, the level of Fate tends to coincide with the constraints imposed by the epic tradition and the legendary plot. In some cases it is even hard to distinguish Fate's role in the action from the role of literary genre and the work's implicit programmatics. Love between Aeneas and Dido runs counter to the will of Fate, but also contradicts the generic canons of epic since it represents, on more levels than one, an intrusion of materials outside and not provided for in the epic code (e.g., erotic-elegiac, erotic-tragic). The dialectical overcoming of the deviant Carthaginian episode ends up being therefore a victory for epic no less than for Fate.

Thus the *Aeneid* tends to produce a story in which tradition, reworked by the narrator, becomes Fate, and in turn uses Fate as the compass and necessary curb on the meandering path of tradition and literary influences. In the *Metamorphoses* Ovid, one of the most acute readers of Virgil, offers a precise comment on this tendentious identification of narration and Destiny. Towards the end of the *Metamorphoses* – just in time, since the poem has had little to say about Fate – Jupiter informs Venus that there is an archive of Fate built of bronze, iron and steel (*Met.* 15.808ff.: *aere ... solido ... ferro ... adamante perenni*), and there the certain destiny of the Julian family has been spelled out for all time. Jupiter has read, memorized, and can now recite it (15.815: *referam*). The god's prophetic powers have now become more bookish than they were in the *Aeneid*. Now he has access not only to an indefinite and solemn will of Fate, but to an indestructible and quotable text filed away for all eternity. What follows clearly shows that Jupiter can speak thus because he has read the *Aeneid*, and he is going to replay for Venus' benefit – who must be a little absent-minded, cf. 815: *ne sis etiamnum ignara futuri* – the prophecy concerning the fate of the Julian line that he had already expounded for her in *Aeneid* 1. The weighty and lasting stability of Fate's record in Ovid alludes to the success of the *Aeneid*, which has at once gained the status of an epic masterpiece and has also consecrated the imperial destiny of the Julian line.[8] The success of this epic-dynastic union is so great that Ovid's Jupiter addresses Venus' anxieties with the implicit reproach, 'Haven't you read the *Aeneid* yet?' (We should not see this solely as irony. Ovid is interpreting the ambitions of a poem so different from his own in order to show that there are other available routes for Roman epic.)

As I have said, Fame plays a complementary role in Virgil's epic project. We will see later on the metaliterary significance the fame of Aeneas assumes in the description of the temple at Carthage. For now, a general observation and an example may suffice. We have seen that Fate is quite willing to be associated with an idea of tradition conceived of as a closed and immutable text – specifically, the tradition Virgil adopts with all its weight, and the *Aeneid*'s ambitions of becoming the final word for its community. Fame is not simply a reflex of this project, even if it is the case that, beginning with Homer, epic action and epic song converge on the common goal of producing *kleos*, 'fame'.[9]

In reality, I would say rather that Fame reacts to the fixity of Fate with a more fluid and shifting imagery. Not by chance, the *Aeneid* celebrates Fame's triumph precisely when it comes time to divulge a 'fact' that is the most scandalous of the poet's innovations to the epic-historic tradition. I mean of course the story of clandestine love between the founder of the Roman line and the founderess of Carthage.[10] Virgil enjoys emphasizing that his poem is not only the fruit of a tradition already written – and 'fatally' embraced – but also productive of new fame. Divergence, difference, and varying transmission are typical of Fame, in opposition to the sacred fixity of Fate. What matters is to see that Fate and Fame (among many other things, of course) are two divergent ways to imagine the relationship between a poet and his intertexts and between a poet and his work.

Dreams

Fate which guides actions and Fame which makes them known do not exhaust epic's methods of joining diverse worlds and of transmitting traditional knowledge. It is interesting to examine more specific modes in which preformed discourses are transformed into narrated action and influence its progression. Before going into prophecy (for which see below) we can pause for a moment to discuss dreams and otherworldly revelations. Dreams have a Homeric tradition of their own, but it is well known that Virgil puts them to new and diverse uses. Our focus here will be the same as that which I pointed out at the beginning, that is, the search for 'tropes of intertextuality' within the fundamentally traditional narrative language of Roman epic.

Aeneas' story is set in motion by a dream vision. Hector's shadow visits the sleeping hero and shows him a way to safety and a mission he is to accomplish. Readings of this passage have shown that Hector's apparition nearly takes on the force of a new proem for the *Aeneid*. This return of a deceased Homeric hero serves to invest Aeneas with the status of hero for a new epic.[11] It is not without significance that the poem's action is set in motion by the summoning of a former Homeric hero's shade at exactly the point when Aeneas begins to exist as an individual character.[12]

The other revelation crucial for the poem will not be a return of a ghost in dream to Aeneas, but a vision of a soul in the otherworld. The borderline between the two modes of manifestation is rather slender, and Aeneas ends up leaving Avernus through the gate of False Dreams (6.895-8). Anchises expounds for Aeneas the universal laws of the cosmos and his descendants' role in history. If Hector called him to action and safety, his father Anchises will give him an overall vision and motivation for action.

I am intrigued by a feature that both these two otherworldly revelations have in common. They both betray the influence of the proemial dream that opens Ennius' *Annales*, that great 'primal scene' where the appearance of Homer's ghost inspired and authorized Roman epic. Like Hector, Homer appeared in a dream. It also seems that both apparitions wept. Further, Homer was characterized by the exclamation *ei mihi qualis erat*.[13] In turn, as Anchises will, Homer wept, praised the *pietas* of his successor, and illustrated universal laws of nature and of the destiny of souls.[14]

Thus these two crucial episodes of revelation and contact with the world beyond are influenced by both Homer – true in general for the *Aeneid* – and, more specifically, Ennius' Homer. Ennius had summoned up his Homer from Hades; in the same manner Virgil depicts his dead informants. Aeneas draws inspiration from figures who look back to the programmatic proem of the *Annales*, the very text that had justified imitations of Homer in Latin epic. Since the *Aeneid* tends to deny space to overly explicit programmatic passages,[15] this translated return of the Ennian dream has a greater value and implies a literary genealogy. To revive Hector (this time truly *mutatus ab illo*) is to revive Homer the father, and at the same time to revive Ennius the father (from whom father Anchises will draw no few linguistic traits as well, as E. Norden has documented in his commentary on Book 6).

Prophecy

Just as an allusion that recalls and returns to a literary past can complicate a dream, so too can prophecy open an intertextual window. We have already observed the density of relation between epic poetics, the idea of fate, and the tie that binds together plot development and repetitions of things 'already written'. Being in itself a separable and to a certain degree preformed utterance, prophecy too serves well to create an interface not only between different time periods inside and outside the narrative, but also between different texts. A discussion of characters like Apollonius' Phineus, the numerous prophets in Lucan, Valerius, and Statius, and Virgil's Sibyl, might lead us too far away from the matter in hand. I have chosen, instead, a brief example that I hope will also be representative.

Apollo, the god who sets the *Iliad*'s plot in motion, also provides impetus to the *Aeneid*. Having arrived at Delos, Aeneas hears directly from the god's voice a goal for his travels – which will turn out to be Italy – and a promise of a great future dynasty:

> hic domus Aeneae cunctis dominabitur oris
> et nati natorum et qui nascentur ab illis.
>
> (*Aen.* 3.97-8)

It is intriguing that this prophecy, so decisive for the Roman poem's plot, is basically the replay of a famous passage in the *Iliad*:

> νῦν δὲ δὴ Αἰνείαο βίη Τρώεσσιν ἀνάξει
> καὶ παίδων παῖδες, τοί κεν μετόπισθε γένονται
>
> Αἰνείαο βίη Τρώεσσιν – A. γένος πάντεσσιν   Strab. 13.1.53 (C 608)
>
> (Hom. Y 307-8)

In a truly Alexandrian move Virgil has Apollo recite two Homeric lines and introduces a learned variant: 'he will rule over all', instead of 'over the Trojans'.[16] *Cunctis ... oris* picks up and amplifies *pantessin*, a reading which someone, in order to construct a retrospective prophecy and a 'Roman' interpretation of a Homeric text, wished to interpolate in place of the original *Troessin*. This was surely not an initiative lacking a geo-political edge. The imitation/rewriting enables Aeneas to leave the Troad instead of pinning him there on the authority of Homer, which in itself might render void the legends of Rome's Trojan origins.[17] But what interests me here is the literary more than the political consequences of this procedure. An Apollo who quotes the *Iliad* in some sense turns the entire *Aeneid* into a continuation of the *Iliad*'s prophecy, where Poseidon had clearly stated, 'Fate wills that Aeneas get out of here alive' (20.302). It could not be said more clearly that Virgil wants to continue Homer. But as was noted a moment ago, this also implies rewriting Homer. The imitator produces a 'new Homer' suited to his needs, not a reproduction based solely on traditional readings of the Homeric text.

The prophecy thus concerns not only Aeneas' future but also the *Aeneid*'s poetic programme. But there is a problem; a poetic text that greatly influenced Virgil in his formative years had criticized the imitation of Homer. I am referring to Callimachus' *Hymn to Apollo*. In this poem at once religious and metaliterary, Envy attacks the poet who cannot sing 'like the sea' (i.e. like the great Homer),[18] and the god responds with the famous critique aimed at the 'Assyrian river'. From Catullus onward, Callimachus' Apollo is regularly cited as the authority who holds back the revival of Homerizing epic. From this perspective, it is curious that the episode of Aeneas' visit to Delos is based on two Callimachean hymns, those to Delos and to Apollo.[19] The prodigy accompanying Apollo's epiphany as Aeneas relates it is inspired by the epiphany announced by Callimachus at the beginning of his most programmatic hymn. In sum, an Apollo not lacking Callimachean traits authorizes both Aeneas' mission *and* Virgil's Homerizing programme. The prophecy is also a way to hold together his Homeric and Callimachean impulses, two forces irreconcilable perhaps, but still active within this daring epic's experimentation. (At the end of Book 3, Aeneas takes one of Odysseus' companions on board and has him tell, first, the episode of the Cyclops, and then also a kind of erudite catalogue of Sicilian cities [3.690-1] that seems modelled on Callimachus' aetiological elegies.[20] This is perhaps another – slightly audacious – way of joining what seemed incompatible qualities, epic sublimity and Callimachean erudition.)

The relation between prophecy and tradition in Virgil may deserve further explication, but I have space for only one additional brief comment that at least allows us to continue our focus on the end of Book 3. After the soothing catalogue of Sicilian cities and their origins, Aeneas' narration takes a dramatic turn and reports the sudden death of Anchises while the fleet is in Sicily. Aeneas' sorrow is understandable: 'nobody had foretold to me this bitter grief, neither ominous Caeleno, nor Helenus the prophet ...' (3.712-13). But Aeneas' emotions are also perfectly in tune with the reader's reaction: indeed, no one had foretold (i.e., *prae-dicta*) Anchises' death in Sicily – not Naevius, who had Anchises reach Latium, nor Ennius, who does the same (for once in agreement with his predecessor), nor even does Cato offer this account. Virgil alone, the first as far as we know, separates so soon the founding hero from his father. We get the feeling of a sudden turn that combines Aeneas' shock with the surprise of learned readers. In this shadowy space of prophetic discourse Virgil grounds his authority as a reformer of the tradition.

Images

Epic poets have another important strategy for intertextual framing. Past texts can resurface in new texts not only as preformed discourses (fame, oracles, dream revelations) but also as illustrated texts, so to speak, images that mediate allusions to literary models. I am speaking of what, in our modern jargon, is usually called ecphrasis.

Virgil already offers the greatest possible development of this strategy. The temple at Carthage depicts Aeneas' past and summarizes at the same time the Homeric and Cyclic heritage the *Aeneid* needs in order to get its new story underway. It surprises Aeneas that his fame in battle has already gained universal notoriety:

> bellaque iam fama totum vulgata per orbem.
>
> (1.457)

But the language of Callimachean poetics makes possible a metaliterary reading for this lines as well: 'wars made trite by fame (*omnia iam vulgata*) through the spinning of the epic cycle', *orbis* being the Latin term for *kyklos* in literary criticism of the time.[21] The temple at Carthage summarizes the influence of Greek epic and the Trojan cycle while at the same time framing and distancing it. After having reread the story on the temple, Aeneas will be ready to become the narrator of a new version of Troy's capture and the *nostoi*. The ecphrasis thus works here – as will become a general tendency in Latin epic – as a gathering up of intertextual energy and a space for reflection upon the relationship with one's models. (We are not that far from the film hero who reads a novel by Conrad. What makes these strategies more tolerable probably is the difference in artistic *media*: cinema and literature, literature and monuments.)

Complementary to the temple at Carthage, the shield of Aeneas establishes a relationship with another epic tradition, that of annalistic and celebratory epic. The scene's chronological organization, largely modelled on Ennius, allows us to read into the future a potential epic about Rome, one that Virgil did not wish to write and that he offers as merely a figurative miniature. Here too it is evident that the ecphrasis serves to embrace tradition and to negotiate its influence. The poem's third substantial ecphrasis, the door of Apollo's temple at Cumae, allows Virgil to zoom in on his relationship with a third epic tradition, that of Alexandrian narrative verse. Before Aeneas is brusquely torn away from this distracting reading, these images have the time to suggest allusions to Catullus 64 and Callimachus' *Hymn to Delos*.

The epic experiments of the Flavian period exhibit the tenacious vitality of the same metaliterary and self-reflexive tradition. Statius' *Thebaid* presents his readers with neither a temple nor a shield, but with a somewhat uncanny artistic object (2.267-88). Harmonia's necklace displays a *serial* history of madness and crimes,[22] like the *series* of horrors that Statius promised in his proem. The way it is knit together is itself a series of sorceries. The ecphrasis finds in the object an evil energy perfectly fitting Statius' new poetics and his relationship with the sanctity of tradition. The necklace is a painstakingly assembled collage of fragments and remains from the mythological past, among which one finds ashes from Jupiter Tonans' lightning bolt and a lock of Tisiphone's hair, the Fury who is the most powerful locus of supernatural power in the poem. The gold-wrought miniature and the *sudor* required to perfect it smell of erudition, *poikilia* and Alexandrian *labor limae*, but collaborating also in its forging are the Telchines, 'known for their creations' (2.274) – those evil demons who with their epic programme had laughed off Callimachus' curses.[23] Moreover, the work is still constructed by the Cyclopes who, as Statius ironically comments,[24] had been trained to produce greater works (*docti maiora*). The power that had forged the epic shields of Achilles and

Aeneas has had to be warped to fit a new web, a miniature of disorder and madness suited to the cosmos of a deviant and claustrophobic epic.

One might expect less dynamic solutions in the world of Valerius' *Argonautica*, since the model of Apollonius offers a sure compass for reading his whole poem. But even Valerius does not miss the opportunity to complicate through ecphrasis his relation to tradition. Having finally reached Colchis and before undertaking any action, the heroes find them-selves reading a massive artistic edifice (5.407-55), a storied temple that bankrupts any other model of epic ecphrasis in that it recapitulates from the beginning the entire history of the Colchians, the myth of the Golden Fleece, and goes so far as to foretell the future fate of Jason and Medea – a quiet *coup de théâtre* worthy of this underestimated poet.[25] If they had had time to analyse the images – and luckily they do not – the Argonauts might have seen the whole story culminate with a flying chariot hovering over a Greek city stricken with grief. For just a moment the ecphrasis threatens to swallow up the story's protagonists – and Roman readers with them – in the reading of an already written myth, rendering any develop-ment of plot futile by anticipating it in full.[26] By foreshadowing Medea's tragedy in Corinth, Valerius shows that he has pondered upon the in-tertextual strategy used by his epic model. The third and fourth books of Apollonius are focused on the expectation of an oncoming tragedy, and just as Apollonius was writing for readers of Euripides, so now Valerius writes for readers of Euripides, Apollonius, Ovid and even Seneca.[27] The disturb-ing clarity of the vision of this solar temple lures readers into an intertextual maelstrom, and Valerius has the audacity to define this ecphrasis, incomprehensible to its addressees, as an *error* (5.455: *quin idem Minyas operum defixerat error* ...). Medea's flight, a sort of apotheosis of crime, is featured as the conclusion in order to offer a subversive response to the ideal ending sketched out in the proem. There, in his official platform, the poet had declared that he intended to conclude with the pious ship Argos' assumption into heaven (1.4).

The model of Apollonius can also be integrated into the perspective of alternate traditions. Apollonius had refused to narrate the building of the ship aided by Athena, a theme already exhausted by 'singers of long ago' (A.R. 1.18-19).[28] With feigned naivety Valerius assumes the role of the outmatched narrator, and supplements his model with an ecphrasis of the Argo (1.121-49). We thus discover that the ship was decorated with images unknown before. The theme, stories of heroes living before the time of the Argonauts' expedition, has the standard function, codified by Virgil with the temple of Carthage, of summarizing the past and offering a model for the future. But the images chosen here – the marriage of Peleus and Thetis, the Cyclops courting Galatea, the battle between the Lapiths and Centaurs – cannot but refer Valerius' Roman audience back to a specific tradition of Latin mythological poetry, Catullus 64 and Ovid's *Metamor-phoses*. The ecphrasis not only supplements the story with its backward glance, but also enriches the work's intertextual programme. On top of Apollonius, Valerius is also heir to neoteric epyllion (which had probably already influenced Varro's Argonautic epic) and to Ovid's great mythological *summa*.

An overlooked example from Silius Italicus (6.653-716) adds an unexpected twist to this tradition.[29] For the first and only time in the history of epic ecphrasis, the artifact is described and then, in nearly the same breath, wiped out forever:

> in cineres monumenta date, atque involvite flammis!
> *(Pun.* 6.716)

Hannibal discovers at Liternum a portico decorated with frescoes commemorating Roman victories in the first Punic War. For the only time in the tradition of ecphrasis we gaze at an object of art through the eyes of one who hates it and will soon destroy it. (Silius must have reflected upon the fact that monuments in epic are not destined to last. Epic is a poetic genre that erases the memory of and replaces the monuments it described. The Achaean wall at Troy must vanish: the epos is the only remaining trace of the war. The numerous monuments built by the words of Virgil are ephemeral for readers of the *Aeneid*, with the sole exception of the Ara Maxima, an isolated relic of the heroic age.) In Silius, Hannibal hatefully scans the images of Roman victory and before levelling them vows a celebratory ecphrasis to commemorate Carthaginian victories in the second Punic War. Finally, we are given to understand, Carthage will have her own ecphrasis, one that pays no honour to the victors. We are reminded with a bit of embarrassment that Virgil had given life to an originary Phoenician-Punic monument only to inscribe upon it – an outrage to the conquered – the charter myth for Roman culture, Troy. The ecphrasis Hannibal plans sounds like a possible subversion of Silius' *Punica*. It is no accident that the last word, the climax of the project, *Tonantem* (6.713, 'Capitoline Jupiter hurled down from the Tarpeian rock'), is the same word that closes the entire epic poem (17.655ff.).

But why does Silius allow Hannibal to destroy the memory of the first Punic War? The *Punica*'s proem had already explained that there had been three wars against Carthage, but that the second one deserves greater attention because it was then, and only then, that Rome came close to annihilation (1.8-14). In becoming the singer of the second Punic War, Silius secures the legacy of Ennius, and this poet not by chance is featured in the *Punica* as a military hero (a completely fictional depiction, as Silius himself must have known), a warrior who carves out a niche for his own fame in the subject matter of his own poetic song (12.393ff.).

While planning an epic poem entitled *Punica*, Silius was probably not unaware of another poem entitled *Bellum Poenicum* devoted to the first Roman-Carthaginian War. Driven by competition with Naevius, Ennius had merely summarized that war, concentrating all his energy instead on the war against Hannibal. Silius now offers a summary and synoptic chart of that remote annalistic scheme, a *longus rerum et spectabilis ordo* (6.657). The formula that opens the ecphrasis (657: *monimenta ... signata ... quis inerat ...*) had been coined by Naevius for one of his epic ecphrases (fr. 12 Buchner: *inerant signa expressa, quomodo Titani ...*).[30] Now Silius employs ecphrasis to recapitulate themes on which Naevius had no doubt focused attention: the consul Appius' contested declaration of war, the heroism of Regulus, Lutatius at the Aegates, and Erycinian Venus' participation in the Roman victories in Sicily.[31] Verification is impossible since we do not have Naevius, and it might even be the case that Silius had not read him.[32] But the destruction of the monument clearly signifies a homage – a self-consuming homage at that – to a forgotten predecessor, one whom the new poem's programme marginalizes in favor of Ennius. It is ironic to think that Silius represents Ennius in the role of heroic warrior in the Punic wars (12.393ff.),[33] a role in actuality played by Naevius – as Silius presumably would have known – and which is now transferred to his rival and competitive successor.[34] Once again the ecphrasis serves to draw in influences but also marginalize them, so as to keep them under the control of the new work's intertextual programme. The reproduction of stories through figurative art, and the transcription of artifacts into verbal ecphrasis, both act as markers of the intertextual appropriation that fuels with its complexity every new epic enterprise.

Echoes[35]

In a culture so lacking in technical reproduction as compared to our own, one cannot underestimate the role of the echo as an icon of repetition and poetic memory. Poets, for whom it was vital to learn to speak in voices not their own, inevitably encountered this natural artifice. I will not go into yet another reading of Ovid's myth of Echo, which still might hold in store some intertextual pleasure, but I will close instead with an example from Valerius, one that I now admit might be included on my top ten list of favourite intertextual chords.[36] Consider his version of Heracles' search for Hylas, a myth already treated by no fewer poets than Theocritus, Apollonius, Nicander, Varro Atacinus, Virgil, Propertius, etc. This is, in short, the nth time that Hercules has been desperately seeking his lost love and calls out the name of the absent boy:

> rursus Hylan et rursus Hylan per longa reclamat
> avia: responsant silvae et vaga certat imago.
>
> (*Arg.* 3.596-7)

What could be simpler than a name and its echo? Obviously, an echo cannot create a new voice.[37] This voice repeats a repetition that we have already heard:

> his adiungit, Hylan nautae quo fonte relictum
> clamassent, ut litus 'Hyla, Hyla' omne sonaret.
> $\qquad$ (*Ecl*. 6.44-5)[38]

Virgil's presence is supported by the rare use of *responso* (*Aen*. 12.757), by the significant doubling of *rursus*,[39] and above all by the echo of another acoustic phenomenon from the *Eclogues*:

> non canimus surdis: respondent omnia silvae
> $\qquad$ (*Ecl*. 10.8)

But if the woods from *Eclogues* 10 are made to resound with a cry and its echo from *Eclogues* 6, the result will be for once a dialogue between texts – appropriate to the title of this book.[40] Valerius has his *silvae* repeat the name *Hylas*, a word containing the Greek equivalent to *silva* – *hulê* – producing a perfect convergence of signifier and signified.[41] After so many poets in successive competition, the myth has once again found a summarizing formula capable of both synthesizing the root and the aetiology that animate it, and of manifesting the awareness of an echo-like and derivative condition serenely accepted. Indeed, to close my own argument with Valerius' clever final comment: *vaga certat imago*.

Some Points on a Map of
Shipwrecks

One of the most curious souvenirs for sale in the tourist shops of Seattle, when I was there for a conference on intertextuality (April 1995), was called *A Map of Shipwrecks*.[1] It was a map of the jagged coastline of the Northwest dotted with points plotting the sites where ships, both old and more recent, have gone down. Having begun with the idea of keeping a 'ship's log' for the conference, I then settled on the less ambitious idea of sketching out some points for a map of critical shipwrecks to be drafted. I have perhaps been influenced by the brilliant metaphor of a young philologist, Jeffrey Wills, in his new book on (among other things) repetition and allusion in Latin poetry: 'One reason why theoreticians and practitioners of allusive criticism often pass like ships in the night is that the cross-cultural scope of one and the language-specific technical acts of the other quickly diverge, leaving little room for generalizations about technique.'[2] With this book, Wills has helped to improve the naval traffic on the sea of intertextuality and stylistics, whose waters, moreover, are often perilous to navigate.

I believe the papers gathered in this collection justify a less pessimistic outlook,[3] and my present survey, though targeting difficulties and even impasses of research, still holds some grounds for hope as well. After all, there is more than one way to use a map of shipwrecks. Those who see it as a record of defeats and errors miss the chance to use it as a guide for safer sailing, or lose the pleasure of dreaming that the map holds traces of underwater treasures.

My travel notes for the conference have synthesized eight theses that I would like to present as moments of provisionary consent among scholars from different places and backgrounds and en route to results often only imperfectly compatible. They are my answer to a question implicit, I believe, to the whole set of problems posed for the conference: what is changing in research on intertextuality, what critical attitudes are gaining ground at the expense of others in a field of study that has not been 'invented' by anyone in particular and that is as old as criticism itself, or better yet, as old as poetry and self-consciousness. Here then are eight points that seem worth highlighting as possible preliminary sites for cooperative effort, while at the same time marking out divergences from the classical philology of the recent past.

(1) Intertextuality is an *event*, not an *object*. It is not a thing, a fixed given to be analysed, but a relation in motion, even a dynamic destabilization.

This idea, which seems to be surfacing in several contributions, sounds like common sense to commentators and interpreters who know all too well how to take various kinds of critical 'snapshots' of an intertextual 'event' occurring in transit between two texts.[4] Many corollaries of this image still need to be disentangled, but one is dear to my heart at present. Given a text that refers to another text, no critical authority exists that can establish a priori (a) how much of the text alluded to is present in the alluding text, and how much instead must be 'left behind'; (b) whether the prevailing sense must be one of similarity or of difference; (c) whether one should view intertextuality as a process or as a result, as an operation ever in progress or as a final product.

(2) Readers move from texts to models, and in so doing – if they are interested in literary density – they become aware that the text was produced in the opposite direction, from the model to the text – not from new to old, but from old to new. Therefore every allusion, when detected, entails a glance towards the production of the text and the figure of the author.

To deny intentionality does not mean being able to exclude this glance toward the production of the text. But it must be insisted that (a) our lack of authentic documents (such as biographical materials, autographs, letters and rough drafts) weakens the role of the author in classical philology. (b) The author's intention is only one component in a play of forces that also includes the textual reception 'foreseen' by the author; both are only strategies, not ends, of reading. (c) The relation that joins a text to a model involves the interpretation not of one text but of two. Both these interpretations are ever on trial, in process, and continually influencing one another. The new text rereads its model, while the model in turn influences the reading of the new text – indeed when recognized, it often has the power to do so. We are all aware that a widespread procedure consists in taking the meaning of the allusion as open, problematic, negotiable, while the meaning of the model is thought to be reasonably certain and univocal. Surely we all need some stable ground to work with, but this sort of gentleman's agreement might conceal some dangers. Do we mean perhaps that models belong to a positivist epistemology, while for imitations we can freely apply rules of post-modernism? Or is it that for the interpreter the polysemy of the imitating text can be limited by the univocal certainty of knowing how the imitator received the model? This is a bizarre compromise that turns the author – complex by definition when composing – into a simpleton reader.

(3) *Intermezzo: a case study in plagiarism.* Classicists, condemned to work with ancient fragments of a dead culture, often fantasize about gaining direct access to information. I will try to console classicists with a real-life anecdote – it will not be, I swear, a reworking of something out of Seneca the Elder. I have a friend, older, of literary talent, but who nonetheless has had very few of his poems published. His youthful poetic vein later took the path of teaching and criticism. This part-time poet, let us call him L, had some poems published many decades ago in a literary journal thanks to the help of an already established author whom I will call Eugenio Montale. After some years, L discovered with a shiver of recognition a couplet he thought was his own in a new collection by the great Montale. In the years to come L, a refined but not famous author, had to deal with the unsettling feeling of being the owner of one of Montale's memories. This feeling, both resigned and ironic, came to a sudden end a few days ago. On rereading Montale's text more carefully, and perhaps with some detachment, L realized that the similarity must be due to chance. He stopped regarding it as an appropriation.

As you see, not even direct access to authors can grant one privileged entry into the laboratory of intertextuality. L had all the right keys – he knew the model by heart, it was his own, he knew the possible channel, that is, he knew that Montale had in fact read his poem – but still his judgment changed over time. The similarity now seems to him no longer intentional but casual. The possibility that a third person, namely a critic, might have noticed it has always been next to nothing, given the small circulation of L's poems and the enormous mass of texts published in Italy right after the war. From this example I draw two conclusions. First, the study of intertextuality is often accused of exaggeration. This may be true in relation to the texts that we have, but every new discovery of papyri shows that the circulation of allusions and influences visible to us is only part of a larger reality. Secondly, there is no reason to despair of the objectivity of our sampling methods. Our research is part of any normal humanistic activity: it is imprecise, conjectural, rhetorical and subjective. But there is no discipline in the humanities lately which has remained immune from this sort of self-criticism.

(4) It seems that no work on the art of allusion can get underway without a word of justification for the most scandalous of classical allusive texts –

> invitus, regina, tuo de litore cessi
> (*Aen.* 6.460)

– even if one has to admit that the recent tendency is to forgive Virgil for having given us so much to work with in only fourteen syllables. Almost all recent contributors insist on the problem of pathos, and the spectrum of solutions inevitably remains very broad.[5] Among these, it is argued that (a) Virgil frees the potentially noble register of the original from the pathos of its context; (b) the pathos in the original undermines the pathos of Aeneas, or of Virgil himself; (c) the original is much more serious and painful than one usually thinks, since Catullus has added something not there in Callimachus (e.g. his brother's death, cf. poem 65), and Virgil has reread it in this somber key. I do not feel uncomfortable when faced with this fluctuation of opinions. As we have seen, allusions are combinations of two texts both needing interpretation, with each interpreting the other, not the combination of one text already 'closed' and another still 'open'.

It is not necessary to repeat all the difficulties I mentioned above. After all, they have all appeared, to no one's surprise, in the critical discourse on this allusion. How much of the two contexts are meant to interact? (Oriental queen, catasterism, forced separation, the merciless steel ...) What prevails, similarity or difference? – see the preceding paragraph – operation or result? – Callimachus and Catullus elegize epic, Virgil epicizes Callimachus and Catullus.

The case of *invitus* ... is memorable because there are, strictly speaking, not two but three texts in question. It is surprising how few interpreters include in their readings Callimachus' enigmatic elegy, a sentimental and surreal poem that might well have been easy for Virgil and Catullus to grasp, but it is certainly not for us. This brings me to my present contribution to the question, which focuses on a formal detail. One of the few facts from which to begin seems to be that Virgil differs from Catullus almost solely in using a masculine form, *invitus* instead of *invita o*. The delicacy of this retouching draws attention to its expressive value. The verse has lost a pathetic interjection ('oh'), a heavy assonance (*o ... tuo*), and an elision, *-a o*. Hence Virgil improves Catullus and constructs him, technically speaking, as a pre-classic predecessor; simplified and re-polished, the verse of course sounds more serious and sincere.

This argument is valid insofar as Catullus 66 is an elegy in Latin, but it might fall short if one thinks Catullus 66 is (also) a translation of a Callimachean elegy. Might Virgil too be interested in this aspect? Maybe so, since Callimachus indeed played some role in his poetic apprenticeship. But how could Virgil render Callimachus through Catullus, seeing that a homo-linguistic model is superimposed upon a hetero-glottic one and that, at any rate, the two models speak as one in the voice of a lock-of-hair-become-a-star?[6] We do not have the Greek model for *invita, o regina*, but we know that both poets featured a lock of hair swearing 'by your head, o queen', and that this oath influenced the Virgilian context. (Aeneas swears not by the head of Queen Dido but 'by the stars' – an intriguing choice in light of the astral element in Catullus/Callimachus.) Of course, we are not allowed to reconstruct a Greek model from its reflection in *invita, o regina* ... When such enterprises were still popular, around sixty years ago, Barber and Lenchantin hazarded a hexameter beginning with *akon* ('unwillingly'). It might even be the case that a close echo of this formula is preserved in Greek by Apollonius Rhodius, when Medea's swears her oath:

> ... ἴστω ἱερὸν φάος Ἠελίοιο,
> ἴστω νυκτιπόλου Περσηίδος ὄργια κούρης,
> μὴ μὲν ἐγὼν ἐθέλουσα σὺν ἀνδράσιν ἀλλοδαποῖσι
> κεῖθεν ἀφωρμήθην·

> (*Arg.* 4.1019-22)[7]

But the comparison between Catullus 66 and the fragments of Callimachus allows us to draw at least one inference. Wherever comparison is possible, Catullus has a 'lock' (It., *ciocca*) speak, while Callimachus has a 'curl' (It., *ricciolo*). In short, Catullus has rendered as feminine an object that the Greek poet intended as masculine – a *coma* in place of a *plokamos* or a *bostruchos*.[8]

The modern use of titles such as 'La Chioma', 'Die Locke', etc., has obscured this difference to some extent. Taking some chances on the lacunae, and on an author of proverbial unpredictability, I would not rule out the chance that Callimachus had something like *invitus* rather than *invita*, suitable to a deserter like Aeneas more than to a runaway braid like the Catullan lock.[9] Thus Virgil might have had Aeneas borrow Callimachus', not only Catullus', word. To continue this speculation, one should not think the allusive process hinges entirely on innovation. The paradigm of originality conceived as divergence from and variation of a model – the driving force in Latin philology in the first half of the twentieth century – is not the only way to conceive of the intertextual process. Perhaps every single word in the pathetic formula of *Aeneid* 6.460 had been used before at some time or other. But allusion works even when it is a choice of possibilities all of which have already been employed in the tradition, not only when it adds a new twist. This is so much the case that not even Virgil has exhausted forever the potential in this quotation.

The life of our formula, in fact, does not end with Virgil. There are poets, like Ovid, who provide an implicit commentary on the relation created between Callimachus, Catullus and Virgil.[10] Indeed, there has been at least one poet not frightened away by the joint authority of Callimachus, Catullus and Virgil. Here are the lines in Statius where Achilles, returning to being a hero, takes his leave of Deidamia:

> nec ego hos cultus aut foeda subissem
> tegmina, ni primo te visa in *litore*: *cessi*
> te propter, tibi pensa manu, tibi mollia gesto
> tympana.

> (Stat. *Ach*. 1.652-5)

Invitus, regina, tuo de *litore cessi*.

After Catullus and Virgil, the phrase *litore cessi* is so memorable that
Statius can afford to wedge a strong pause, a shift in syntax, between the
two words. But can one also say that after Callimachus, Catullus, and
Virgil the act of imitation still has strong relevance? In particular, one may
doubt that the presence of Callimachus/Catullus still has value, given the
strong magnetic attraction that Virgil exerts on Statius' epic. Not by
chance, the context of the *Achilleid* is speaking about a hero leaving his
beloved – Achilles leaves Deidamia just as Aeneas leaves Dido. But if one
looks deeper, Achilles does not say, like Aeneas, that he is leaving his queen
unwillingly. Being less tactful than Aeneas, though, he uses the phrase in
question to make clear that he would not have approached her shores if he
had not seen her. Staying with her is not an option, as Aeneas tells Dido.
Achilles too must leave, after having postponed his heroic destiny on
account of his attraction for Deidamia.

Somewhat like Aeneas, Achilles had undergone a transgressive experience on those shores. Worse than Aeneas, he lived in Skyros like a woman,
and dressed as a woman he conquered his Deidamia. If Aeneas had become
subject to a woman (so Mercury says at least), Achilles has gone so far as
to become female. In his indecorous *prepon*, the peculiar key of the scene
in Statius, one can feel the presence of Callimachus and Catullus. Against
all probability, they have not been overshadowed by the intervening
Virgilian influence. One only need consider what Achilles is saying before
he falls into the famous quotation *litore cessi*: 'How could I have endured
those feminine hair-styles ...'. *Hos cultus* indeed, what other model is more
appropriate than a text whose main protagonist, for the only time in the
history of literature, is a feminine haircut? Achilles is quoting not only the
Aeneid but also the *Lock*. More precisely, he is setting in contrast the
Aeneid and the *Lock*. The allusion strikes with devilish precision the
sensitive nerve joining the Lock's femininity and Aeneas' rather doubtful
heroism, a hero who for a moment spoke in the tender voice of a royal curl.
The allusion offers interpreters of Virgil, and among them Statius, an
interminable debate on the meaning of a text that continually cries out for
justification, 'against my will (*invitus/invita*) I left you' – causing a crisis
of categories in literary genre and sexual gender. It truly seems that
separation and confusion are constitutive features of this obstinate little
phrase.[11] The problem of sexual identity posed by the new context is
recapitulated in the allusion's genealogy. Words with a long history of
uncertain gender move from an ambiguous Callimachean masculine to a
Catullan feminine to a troubled Virgilian masculine.[12]

(5) (Connected with the preceding.) The idea that pinpointing models can
above all be a way of restricting and binding a text's meaning is an illusion.
Experience teaches that tracing intertextual relationships enriches and
complicates reading, setting up dialectical tensions, more than it closes
and simplifies interpretation. Poetic self-consciousness shows us the way.

The duel between Aeneas and Turnus at the end of the *Aeneid* is not only the revival of a duel between Homeric paradigms – Achilles vs. Hector – but is a contest between interpretations of these paradigms. Which of these two is Achilles and which is Hector, and at what times? Who has more right, Achilles the avenger or Hector the defender of his city? There is also a battle for influence, a dispute in which the Virgilian text directs the reading of Homer, while the possible readings of Homer reflect back upon Virgil. It comes as no surprise that the slaying of Turnus elicits conflicting reactions among readers. To say that Virgil wants to signify something *because* he alludes to Homer at a certain moment in the plot (the strategy typical of Knauer in his fundamental *Die Aeneis und Homer*) means that one believes intertextuality is nothing but a message to be deciphered – while instead it is more like a code than a message. One should contemplate the fact that reading Virgil entails reading Homer too. If one must read Homer in a simple manner, as is somewhat necessary when our main text is Virgil, it is best not to forget that intertextuality involves the interpretation of at least two texts, not of one alone.

(6) Dealing with intertextuality does not imply taking sides in a debate, more or less implicit, between formalist and historicist readings of ancient texts. The polemic between formalist and historicist readers has long been exhausted, and the last Japanese snipers isolated in the jungle should have been informed of this by now.[13] There is no real contradiction between reading a text 'in history' and reading a text within its intertextual dynamics. Even the distinction between 'form' and 'content', between 'ideological' and 'artistic' goals, is a highly toxic convention for those who truly wish to write literary history. It is not at all true that the more a text is intertextually charged, the less it is linked to a political and social context. It might be true that studying Sallust's use of Thucydides is a different activity than studying allusion in Alexandrian poets; but these two areas still share problems of method, and it would be wrong to label the first as 'history of ideas' and the second as 'art for art's sake'. When I read Callimachus' line, 'kings come from Zeus' (*Hymn* 1.79), I am grateful to critics who lead me to appreciate the refined Alexandrianism of the Hesiodic quotation, 'kings come from Zeus' (*Theog*. 96). Yet I am even more grateful to those who lead me to see that this quotation poses the problem of cultural and political change, and exposes conflicts between diverse conceptions of the relation joining poetry, persuasion, and authority. In the same context Hesiod had also said, 'singers come from the Muses and Apollo; kings, on the other hand ...'. Callimachus does not repeat this statement, and the context of his hymn to Zeus makes one think that the whole question of authority – whether monarchical, religious, or poetic – is a living problem for Callimachus and his readers. The problem of method – what is the value of citing, what is the role of omissions side by

side with explicit quotation – is interwoven with the 'history' of poets and kings – be it Hesiod's kings or the Ptolemies. A conference on intertextuality can be many things, but it is surely not the place for celebrating a mistaken formalism's triumph over a mock historicism. Similarly I find it a mistake to create an opposition between the formalism of intertextual studies and the political engagement of 'gender studies'. Why should a literary criticism attentive to questions of sexual difference be an alternative to intertextual studies? Patricia Rosenmeyer's thoughtful contribution to this conference shows how interwoven feminine voices and poetic memory are in Sappho, suggesting a model of intertextuality *cum differentia* that we would do well to consider.[14] As I have tried to show above with the frivolous example of the Lock, even in a completely masculine poetic genealogy the gender (as much as the genre) of the allusive voices can make some difference.

After all, even in the recent development of new historicisms and cultural studies one sees the tendency to recuperate the legacy and methods of a 'formalist' intertextuality.[15] I would like to take up briefly from this perspective a poetic text perhaps ripe for reconsideration. The mysterious poetess 'Melinno of Lesbos' opens her so-called 'Hymn to Rome' with praise of 'Rhome, daughter of Ares', and concludes her fourth and final sapphic strophe with something even more unexpected:

> ἦ γὰρ ἐκ πάντων σὺ μόνα κρατίστους
> ἄνδρας αἰχματὰς μεγάλους λοχεύεις
> εὔσταχυν Δάματρος ὅπως ἀνεῖσα
> καρπὸν ἀπ' ἀνδρῶν.
>
> (*Suppl. Hell.* 541.17-20)

Melinno's rating as an artist is not very high (cf. below, no. 7, for this aspect of the problem); dating her is tricky as well: is she before Augustus, since she praises Rome but not an Emperor (Wilamowitz)? Or is she after Trajan, for reasons of style and metrics?[16] Finally, the text has at least one great difficulty – should *ap' andrôn* be amended to *ap' agrôn* (Bergk) or *aroura* (Bücheler)? Among modern treatments Bowra's is perhaps the best,[17] and inevitably a little apologetic. He asks us to consider that Melinno is not lacking literary models. She does have some poetic skill, and the strange image of Rome as a grain field continually producing new and frightful warriors cannot be understood without recalling the myth of Jason in Ares' field as found in Apollonius Rhodius. The warrior sons of the earth spring up thick and straight like heads of grain, ready and eager for battle:

> οἱ δ' ἤδη κατὰ πᾶσαν ἀνασταχύεσκον ἄρουραν
> γηγενέες· φρῖξεν δὲ περὶ στιβαροῖς σακέεσσι
> δούρασί τ' ἀμφιγύοις κορύθεσσί τε λαμπομένῃσιν

Ἄρηος τέμενος φθισιμβρότου· ἵκετο δ' αἴγλη
νειόθεν Οὐλυμπόνδε δι' ἠέρος ἀστράπτουσα.

(*Arg.* 3.1354-8)

My problem is not so much the rehabilitation of Melinno (even if in point 7 below we shall see that this evaluation is serious business) as much as the possibility that nowadays this text might be rediscovered by those who study the relationships between Greece and Rome from a historical and cultural perspective. For now I would venture to say that this hypothetical but not implausible rediscovery should also accept with patience the discourse of style and intertextuality. We do not know for whom and in what context Melinno composed her poetry. But it is in Greek and rich in references to Greek culture. The occasion might have been (but we cannot be certain) a celebration and homage to the leading nation of the empire. Just another voice in the choir, perhaps; but nonetheless it remains a 'Greek' voice. It is possible that the allusion would lead its Greek audience into problematic reflections, an audience with a collective memory readier than the Romans' to recall Jason, and Cadmus himself for that matter. After all, Jason and Cadmus, both archetypal Greek heroes, had been paralysed and horrified by the spectacle of a ploughed field bringing forth armed soldiers rather than grain.[18] These menacing fruits of the earth had then engaged in fratricidal warfare. The fertile harvest of Demeter balances the initial image of a city sacred to Ares, whose name is the Greek word for 'Force'. Melinno has combined in a single image the ideas of peaceful fertility and inexhaustible violence. It may be the case that her hymn is not merely an act of cult devotion to Rome, but also a contribution to the Greek image of the ruling power. The allusion to Apollonius suggests a visualization shared by the audience members because it is mythical and iconographic. But at the same time it shows the contradictions, more or less conscious, imposed by this visualization: Rome-Demeter, fertile mother of armed ranks. Without this long 'detour' into literary allusion, this possible 'positioning' of the audience with respect to the text might never have emerged, or might have been detected only in an impressionistic or generic manner.

In conclusion, the more literature talks about itself, the more it talks about the world. The exasperated and cryptical Callimacheanism of Augustan poets is also a political gesture, just as Livy's allusions to Sallust count as an ideological programme. Literature deals with literature which deals with real life. Poetic sources are not simply reflective bodies of water, as demonstrated by a poet we have just accused, then acquitted, of having an omnivorous memory:

> I have kneeled down in delirious love
> over the Castalian Spring
> but not one drop of water reflected
> an image of me.

Even if real life must undergo its metamorphosis, as the same poem goes
on to warn us:

> I have never seen
> the waters of piranhas. Whoever plunges there
> reaches shore a heap of fleshless bones.[19]

(7) The study of intertextuality presupposes a certain level of trust in the
ability of the authors we wish to analyse. This lending of credit presupposes in its turn something we do not like to name but which still exists in
our field – value judgments. The language of evaluation has always been
implicit in studies of poetic reuse. It is important to remember this since
every judgment is subject to continual re-evaluation. Virgil 'improves'
Matius, he 'transforms' Catullus, and Statius 'emulates' Virgil. The use of
'transform' shows that Catullus is in the same league as Virgil, while
Matius' day of glory does not seem to have arrived (perhaps, lacking
further fragments, it will never arrive). But for Statius the times are ripe,
and 'transforms' now sounds better than 'emulates'. This re-evaluation has
a simple effect. The critic's lens moves from the model's influence to the
transforming activity of the imitator. After some decades of this interpretive practice, an author such as Statius migrates from the heading of
'Virgilian reception' to the heading of 'creative imitation'.

In Italy there are several scholars who have greatly contributed to texts
which for a long time have been unjustly discounted: Imperial Age epic
both Greek and Roman, Greek parodic verse, Roman theatre, epigram,
and other 'minor' Hellenistic and Roman genres. Better studies of these
authors have had the effect of widening the canon. Every new reading
unearths new riches of meaning created by the intertextual competence of
authors who, not long ago, were considered uninteresting or even incapable of such productivity. It goes without saying that progress in this field
has always been achieved by critics who have to some degree 'made
themselves enjoy' the texts they study. But our current rhetoric of criticism
precludes the formation of value judgments, of a hierarchy or canon, as a
goal for reading. Literary histories tend more and more to avoid elaborat-
ing on the respective merits of the authors and periods they treat, just as
commentators refrain from admiring virtues and scolding defects of texts.
The language of criticism has become objective.

Surprisingly enough, evalution, which had been discarded as an *end*,
re-emerges as a *premise* in philology, most often an implicit one, a trade
secret of philologists. This circumstance reminds us that the problem still
exists. The situation we live in is continually shifting. When I began to
study Greek and Latin texts, a certain – let us call it a 'rich' – way of
studying textual models was normally applied to authors like Theocritus,
Virgil and Catullus, a little less to Aratus, Apollonius, Lucan and Ovid, and
much less to authors like Meleager, Seneca, Valerius, Statius and the

Greek novelists. Then it happened, progressively, almost imperceptibly, that the canon had widened, and the frontier is still moving. In homage to this trend Stephen Hinds and others have focused on examples drawn from 'decadent' and 'silver' Latin poetry. It is a trend that continues to encounter tacit resistances, every time one compiles sombre lists of 'parallels' and 'imitations' without a word of comment – just as ninety years ago one did for Virgil – or every time one presupposes that excessive reliance on tradition renders the effects of allusion null and void. On the contrary, it is evident (to me at least) that among the next protagonists in this widened canon are not only Statius and Silius, but also Nonnus and Claudian as well as certain medieval authors who need to be liberated from 'poor' and impoverishing reading habits. Whether we like it or not, in order to appreciate the memory of the poets we must put a little trust in their skills.

(8) But all of the above may be concealing a pitfall, the notion that what is *complex* is also *beautiful*. I think that this concept is somewhat implicit in modern studies of intertextuality. The development of these studies is upheld by the idea that reuse constitutes creativity and that complexity is a positive value. Without this foundation we would not have moved very far from the *furta Vergilii*, or the tables of sources ('Virgil's debt to Theophrastus') popular at the beginning of the century. This idea however is not an eternal and necessary presupposition. Many readers of poetry in various ages of western history might have rejected, misunderstood, or considered it of little interest. Do simple poetic texts still exist? The question seems to underlie a very intriguing debate that has developed around Horace *Odes* 1.38:

> Persicos odi, puer, apparatus;
> displicent nexae philyra coronae;
> mitte sectari, rosa quo locorum
> sera moretur;
>
> simplici myrto nihil adlabores
> sedulus curo: neque te ministrum
> dedecet myrtus neque me sub arta
> vite bibentem.

In a 1993 talk entitled 'Tying down Proteus', R.G.M. Nisbet reacted to a criticism levelled by Don Fowler concerning the commentary of Nisbet himself (and M. Hubbard) on Book 1 of Horace's *Odes*.[20] According to Fowler, the commentary is inadequate because it does not take into account the programmatic value that 1.38 assumes as the concluding poem in *Odes* Book 1.[21]

Given that Nisbet and Fowler represent, for generosity and acumen, the best of both generations, I want most of all to avoid playing the arbiter for this dispute, and I hope I can do justice to both scholars with a couple of minor clarifications. First of all, Fowler has never used 1.38 to lobby for some perpetual freedom of over-interpretation. His argument is based on normal philological and historical criteria. The probability that 1.38 plays a programmatic role derives from the culture of poetry books in which Horace participates, as is shown for example at 2.20 and 3.30. Fowler deals with 'closure' as a literary historian. It is tendentious then to present this case – as Nisbet seems to be doing in his cry of alarm addressed to British high school teachers – among a series of examples of critical relativism, of the cult of indeterminacy, and of arbitrary over-reading.[22] Nevertheless, one of the preoccupations expressed by Nisbet has a convincing ring. Is there not a chance that *any* poem Horace might have put at the end of Book 1 could receive the same treatment? And if this is the case, what can critics say about 1.38 that is truly specific to it? Is it true that the meaning of a text is determined by its position? As I have already made clear, I do not think this critique is specifically addressed to Fowler or to recent trends in criticism. The critical position that Nisbet finds dangerous, because it paves the way for metaliterary and non-specific readings, had already been put forward with the utmost clarity by Giorgio Pasquali. A final word like *bibentem* (with its crown of vine-leaves) becomes meaningful when positioned at the end of a poetry book written under the influence of Alcaeus and looking back to his symposium lyrics as its model.[23]

Once this avenue has been opened it is hard to stop more modern critics from continuing down its path. One can note, for example, the connection between the poem's linear development, the aversion to redundancy (*Persicos ... odi apparatus*), and the ideals of Callimachean stock. One recalls that the woven wreath is the icon of the poetry book in what for the Romans was among the most influential models for the *Gedichtbuch*, the 'Wreath of Meleager'.[24] (It is intriguing that among the various plants in Meleager's Wreath the myrtle represents Callimachus.)

Yet the position of 1.38 in a poetry book is food for thought. Not only because the book ends here – unless one thinks along with L. Mueller that 1.39-40 have been lost in the manuscript transmission! – but also because it immediately follows 1.37. The short poem 1.38 ending with *bibentem* follows a grand ambitious ode that starts off with *nunc est bibendum*. If we are not quick to shift gears, and perhaps we should not be, *Persicos odi apparatus* will turn our minds back to the theme of an oriental queen's great fall that dominated 1.37.[25]

We are not obliged to think that myrtle and (later on) late roses tell us only about poetic choices. Poetry is never purely self-reflexive and self-referential. The ancient tradition usually connects myrtle to Venus and love. Does 1.38 maybe have an erotic flavour as well?[26] More simply, ancient culture tends most of all to see myrtle as an evergreen. For his private party the poet wants only this plant, and refuses greenhouse roses which are always at the point of withering. It is hard to ban a reading of

1.38 in the very terms that Horace made binding for the secular European tradition of lyric with its focus on existential time.

But the problem that unsettles a great commentator like Nisbet remains. Are we right to so complicate the reading of a poem the explicit theme of which is 'simplicity at banquets'? *'In my simple way* I took this to be a recommendation of simplicity of life.'[27] So protests the commentator on Horace with a clever play on words, in which identification between interpreter and his author could not be taken any further. The ambiguity of the word 'simple' unite Nisbet and Horace against the complicated efforts of less-gifted readers who superimpose their own extravagance on the simplicity of the original. But this rhetoric of simplicity has a double edge. Both Nisbet and Horace probably reached their enviable simplicity after many complex attempts, with many discarded hypotheses, many wide-branching theories pruned down to the stump. It might be more accurate to say that 1.38 is a poem on the *achievement* of simplicity. Perhaps Eumolpus already understood this when he said *Horati curiosa felicitas*. Ironically, Horace's message to the *puer* is precisely this: 'don't uselessly complicate things',

> simplici myrto nihil adlabores
> sedulus curo

but he says this in one of the least linear constructions in all of Horace's lyrics, and with a surplus of labour imposed on the simple reader. The words allow for at least three syntactical combinations. To be sure, Nisbet and Hubbard's commentary is rigorous in rejecting many metaliterary overgrowths: *nihil adlabores*. To arrive at this point they limit references to tradition and focus on something like a poetic 'subgenre' from which 1.38 draws inspiration, a tradition of Hellenistic epigrams in which the poet addresses his servant giving instructions on how to prepare a banquet. The direction in which they point should, I think, be taken seriously. Among the poetic texts we know of, and arguably known to Horace as well, these are the only ones really comparable to 1.38. All the rest – Callimachus, Meleager, poetics, love, the book of odes, the passing of time – come afterwards, granted that these should enter the picture at all. It is a commonly accepted practice among us academics to identify a literary tradition and to use it to delimit and specify an individual text's references.

But even here the reading seems to me reversible. In accepting the terms of discussion selected by Nisbet's commentary it is even harder to protect 1.38 from the complications engendered by its reading. When we compare Horace with his Greek predecessors, we are struck by how complicated the task of preparing a banquet could be. How many flowers, wines and ointments were compiled on these elegiac grocery lists! The comparison brings to the fore all that the Latin poet has done away with, not only what he says he does not want – *odi, displicent* – but also all that he has passed over in silence. 1.38 is not only a programme striving for simplicity, but also the simplification of an exuberant and densely detailed intertext. Yet I am not sure that this is really a 'simple' reading of 1.38. Intertextuality brings back into the reading those refined entanglements whose absence the poem proudly celebrates. Readers must take it upon themselves to repeat a little of the author's work, and once again the result cannot be separated from the process. I find myself again in the midst of a complex and complicated reading, and it is here that I must stop, because I have become – along with my aesthetic horizon – part of the same problem I hoped I might regard from the outside and thus resolve.

8

Allusion and Society:
Ovid the Censor

As a poet and a critic, Josif Brodskij has been an inspiration for contemporary lovers of Ovid. One of his last published interviews (in the Italian magazine *L'Espresso*) restated his enthusiasm for Ovid and he quoted, as one of his favourite lines in Roman poetry, the following Ovidian hexameter: *sic ego nec sine te nec tecum vivere possum*. A moment of embarrassment followed this statement. A learned Italian journalist objected that the line actually belongs to Catullus or better – he corrected himself – to Martial, and lamented the usual lack of double-checking references that afflicts Italian journalism. On this last point one must agree, and I am sorry to say that it took some time for me, a professional Classicist, to realize that Brodskij was in fact right: he was quoting *Amores* 3.11.39. The counter-attribution to Catullus and Martial was not simply a slip: the Ovidian line belongs to one of the most Catullan passages in Ovidian elegy,[1] and Martial appropriates *Amores* 3.11.39 verbatim in epigram 12.46.2, *nec tecum possum vivere, nec sine te.*[2]

This little contemporary incident attests to a reality that should be familiar to every student of 'arte allusiva': imitation of a famous poetic predecessor opens up a two-way traffic, where imitations 'read' their models but also models 'read' imitations, and appropriation is both an active and a passive process. A model can be powerful enough – within a specific interpretive community – to appropriate the imitation which strives to appropriate the model. In other words, since the familiarity with a certain Catullan manner is so widespread, and Ovid is actually writing *à la manière de* Catullus in a large part of 3.11, it is only logical that someone should read the line as Catullan. By accepting this legacy, Ovid has in fact jeopardized his own control over the poetic tradition.

The main point of this chapter, however, is that precisely when he was pretending to be somebody else, Ovid was in fact being much bolder than it is normally realized. Since reading Brodskij's praise of the line, I have come across its unlikely source. In 131 BCE the censor Q. Caecilius Metellus Macedonicus, cos. 143, gave a speech *de prole augenda* or *de ducendis uxoribus*: this exhortation to marriage features the only other Latin occurrence (so far as I know) of the phrase *nec cum nec sine (aliquo) vivi posse*.

> in censura dixit ad populum de ducendis uxoribus, cum eum ad matrimonia capessenda hortaretur ... 'sed quoniam ita natura tradidit, ut nec cum illis satis commode, nec sine illis ullo modo vivi possit, saluti perpetuae potius quam brevi voluptati consulendum est.'
>
> (Gellius 1.6.1 = *ORF*[3] fr. III)

There are two reasons why I think the similarity is not coincidental:

(1) The whole speech had its celebrity revamped in Augustan Rome through an impressive event of political intertextuality: the Princeps reperformed the whole text of Macedonicus in the Senate,[3] and forcefully implied that it was still applicable to modern Roman society:

> Q. Metellus censor censuit ut cogerentur omnes ducere uxores liberum creandorum causa. exstat oratio eius, quam Augustus Caesar, cum de maritandis ordinibus ageret, velut in haec tempora scriptam in senatu recitavit.
>
> (Liv. *per.* 59; cf. Suet. *Aug.* 89.2)

(2) The line immediately before 39 declares (again in a pointedly Catullan mood) that the poet succumbs to Corinna's sex appeal but indicts her immorality:

> aversor morum crimina, corpus amo

and *morum crimina* is a clear self-reflexive index for the 'censorial' background of the next line – an allusion to a Republican censor recently appropriated by Augustus' new and impressive censorial stance.

I will shortly elaborate both observations with reference to the problem of chronology and to 'censorial' themes in the *Amores*. But first of all I would like to mention briefly two implications that transcend the frame of the present. (1) It is normal to contrast Ovid's libertinage with Augustan repression, but this mental habit obscures a more general issue, which is certainly more important than others to a modern *regard eloigné*. The two texts can be seen as conflicting but, from our modern vantage point, they are also collusive: the censor and the elegiac poet share a gendered language which represents woman as a 'necessary evil'. (2) The sophistication of the Ovidian poem could easily construct Macedonicus as a *durus senex* of a reactionary past, but this reading – this Ovidian reading of the model – has the effect of obscuring a more accurate reading of the censorial speech. Metellus is in fact being witty and showing a remarkable rhetorical competence (as Professor Badian has suggested to me in correspondence): the repetition of *vivere* collapses two different references, i.e. 'matrimonial life is impossible', that is, unbearable to the individual Roman male citizen (and similar tags must indeed have been tested on

Augustus' own marriage to Livia ...) but also 'marriage is necessary to the life of the Roman community'. He could even have been aware that a similar tag – 'neither with nor without them' – had currency in Greek culture (cf. Ar. *Lys.* 1038-9,[4] and 'Susarion' PCG 3-5).[5]

Ironically, the Metellan fragment has often been quoted as relevant to another elegiac context, a nest of allusions to marriage laws and old-fashioned *senes* in Propertius' second book.[6] R. Reitzenstein made a brilliant but misguided attempt to enlist Augustus and Metellus to explain Propertian polemics,[7] and S. Commager revived the idea for passages like 2.30.13-16, *ista senes licet accusent convivia duri ... illorum antiquis onerantur legibus aures* and even 2.7.14, *nullus de nostro sanguine miles erit.*[8]

The link has been proved impossible by Ernst Badian,[9] who conclusively explained that in 28-25 BCE Propertius cannot possibly be reacting to Augustan initiatives in the field of marriage and *mores*. Even more obviously, Propertius is not answering the Augustan appropriation of Macedonicus, an event that firmly belongs to the official discussion of marriage laws in the years 18/17. But this chronological difficulty is invalid for Ovidian love elegy. I see no problems in accepting two mainstream ideas: (1) Ovid wrote most of *Amores* 1-3 no earlier than 20 BCE and was revising and publishing the definitive collection not earlier than 10 BCE;[10] (2) the crucial years for the debate on *de maritandis ordinibus* and *de adulteriis* are 18-17,[11] and the issue remained critical for many years afterwards.[12]

A more precise dating is beyond my competence, and certainly beyond the scope of this chapter. Suffice it to say that an Ovidian response to the Augustan revival of censorial speech in the years 18 and after is compatible both with literary analysis and with historical evidence. I will come back to issues such as elegiac morality, adultery, censorial control, and the like in a moment. But first let me observe that the usual approach, if one wishes to forestall this kind of reading, is to stress that the *Amores* is a juvenile and apolitical product, as opposed to that later poetical flirtation with disaster which is the *Ars amatoria*. Does one need to assume that the politically sensitive poems were written after the season of the *leges Iuliae* and their aftermath, within the sensitization of public opinion that is so evident in the late Horace? The poems could be 'innocent' because written before.

My first problem with this approach is that this is exactly the approach we find in the late Ovid.

> Quae decuit, primis sine crimine lusimus annis.
> *(Fast.* 4.9)

With parallel ingenuity, *Tristia* 2 convicts Tibullus of the crime of being a forerunner of the *Ars amatoria*. Ovid is not the most reliable witness on which *carmina* are *crimina* and which ones are not. The question of why the *Ars*, and not the *Amores*, provided a body of evidence against Ovid is not relevant here.[13] My second problem with the 'juvenilia' approach is that this puts too much weight on the vexed crux of the first edition of Ovid's *Amores*. The text we are discussing here (the only one available to us and perhaps the only one ever available to a general audience)[14] is a three-book edition prefaced by a witty epigram stating 'We are three books; we used to be five; a reduced *poena* – for the reader'. Apart from the suggestive use of punitive terminology, it seems to me that this epigram, far from being a disclaimer, actually stresses the responsibility of the 'poet as editor' for his text. If the collection derives from a selection of previously written pieces, how would the reader know that, say, 3.11 predates the marriage legislation, or that 2.19 is unaware of the adultery law?[15] Even a reader deeply involved in a philological search for traces of the first edition would have had to admit that Ovid's decision to publish the collection after the Augustan moral reform was an acceptance of that moral climate as a cultural context in which the work was destined to be appreciated.

The allusion to the censorial speech on marriage[16] is inseparable from a pattern of *nequitia* that is especially noteworthy in Books 2 and 3 of the *Amores*. The poet cruises and finds a girl under the portico of Apollo Palatinus (2.2.3-4), a few yards from the prince's door. 2.2 and 2.3 feature a miserable eunuch watching the girl, the first instance of a pattern of growing tension and repression. 2.4 combines language of censorial control (v. 1, *non ego mendosos ausim defendere mores*) and Catullan self-analysis, thus looking forward to 3.11. 2.7.1 introduces the poet as a *reus*, playing on the two meanings 'defendant' and 'guilty'. 2.13 and 14 explore an elegiac approach to abortion. The final poem in the book alludes to a husband who could be subpoenaed as a pimp,[17] and the final word is *veta!* Book 3 has two impressive poems based on the Catullan language of passion as (anti-)marriage, 11 and 14.[18] A selection of 'censorial' lexica from the two poems includes, for example, 3.11.38, *morum crimina*; 42, *ad mores ... malos*; 45, *parce per o lecti socialia iura* (based on Tib. 1.5.7 *parce tamen, per te furtivi foedera lecti*); 50, *coactus amem*; 14.3-4, *nec te nostra iubet fieri censura pudicam / sed tamen ut temptes dissimulare rogat*; 52 *et quam, si nolim, cogar amare, velim* (cf. Liv. *per.* 59: *Q. Metellus censor censuit, ut cogerentur omnes sumere uxorem liberorum creandorum causa*). The two poems construct Corinna as a Lesbia-like mistress, magnetic and abject, experiment on her an exaggerated version of the marriage imagery so typical of Catullus and Propertius, and at the same time evoke censorial control. This last effect is particularly teasing in 3.11, since the mistress is exposed as a target for moral reform, but at the same time the argument that the poet cannot live 'with or without you' is culled from a protreptic to marriage passed over from Metellus to Augustus. This is not simply a revisitation of Catullus: by incorporating a discourse of moral control, the elegiac poet is hammering together erotic *nequitia* and a Roman discourse that had always been a source of authority, the analysis of *mores*.[19] Before we reach the resumption of the topic in 3.14.1, *non ego, ne pecces ...*, we know that Ovid is serious about *matrimonia capessenda*; 3.13, the only poem in the collection (apart from the magnificent 2.6) which has no immediate bearing on eros and elegy, informs us that he has a wife and joins her in attending festivals of Iuno.[20]

Thus far I have only been suggestive, and the ideal reader of this chapter (as an anonymous reader has pointed out) is not allowed to decide whether Ovid is, (1) challenging the new morality, or (2) claiming – as Catullus had – to impose traditional standards of morality on his own unsanctioned relationship, or (3) condemning the persona he has played throughout the *Amores* collection, or finally (4) invoking censorial stand-ards to dismantle his failed relationship with Corinna. If pressed, I would certainly answer that the first option cannot really work if we do not take options 2-4 seriously enough. But allow me to be less allusive and try, instead, to narrate a plot that would underpin the workings of intertextu-ality in 3.11.

On a formal level, we might say that Ovid is recapitulating the origins of Roman elegy by means of an unparalleled density of Catullan echoes. In an even more formalistic reading, this recapitulation is performed by condensation: different aspects of a Catullan discourse about love, which were positioned at discrete textual loci in the Catullan collection where they could be perceived as connected yet contradictory, are now forced to cohabit. These include: (1) *amor* as a love/hate polarization and oscillation; (2) the collision between the poet-lover and traditional morality; (3) an indictment of the *puella* as a source of immorality (a tension sharpened by conjectures on Lesbia's status, since Ovid's own construction of Corinna shows elegy's power both to generate and to forestall such speculations); and (4) the collusion between the poet-lover and traditional morality in the troping of love-as-fidelity, love as family, love instead of family. In a considerably less formalistic reading, this appropriation, exploration and energization of Catullan tensions is now happening – as the Macedonicus allusion reminds us – within a social context where a discourse about marriage and morals has a different intensity. Elegy must now renegotiate its voice in a paradoxical society where the *traditional* mores of the Catullan elegist are facing the *new* discourse of Republican censorship.

Appendix: The 'two editions' of Ovid's *Amores* and the implications of the introductory epigram

The idea that Ovid's elegiac collection was published in two editions is very persistent in modern scholarship: even those who are deeply sceptical about two editions for Apollonius or Virgil's *Georgics* tend to accept this for Ovid as an exceptionally clear-cut case.[21] The reason for this is not the presence of attested variants, or surviving prototypes, belonging to the first edition: not a single word survives from *Amores* 1-5, while we do have testimonies (whatever their value) about Apollonius' *proekdosis*. The reason is simple that the poet himself declares, in the prefatory epigram to the new work, that *Amores* 3 is the successor to a homonymous work in five volumes.

People who spend a great deal of time with Ovid are often the most cautious in pressing the issue of a 'first edition'. J. McKeown (1989), for instance, on the first page of his commentary, states that the epigram 'provides, in fact, the only explicit testimony that the collection as we have it is a second edition'.

I wish to put slightly more emphasis on his restrained assessment, since I am interested in showing that the issue of dating individual poems in relation to the question of two editions can become a stumbling block for interpretation, and that further, the whole question of reconstructing a first edition has had a misleading importance in contemporary scholarship.

My starting point, of course, is the famous *Qui modo Nasonis fueramus quinque libelli* .... The normal reaction to this epigram has been that Ovid presupposes a reader already familiar with the *editio plenior* and invites him to be more favourable to a shortened edition of the same work. But I would accept G.B. Conte's suggestion ([1985] 62-5) that Ovid's wording presupposes familiarity with *Ille ego qui quondam*, the tetrastich prefixed to some texts of the *Aeneid*. (Both Conte and I believe that the lines are not Virgilian, but are indeed quite early, and were composed to create a transition between the previous rolls of Virgil's oeuvre and the new poem, *Arma virumque* ...) If this suggestion holds water,[22] the Ovidian epigram is amusing in a slightly different way than it is normally believed. Ovid is in this case alluding to a text which marks the *Aeneid* as a new, and indeed unexpected, product by the self-same author of two previous celebrated masterpieces, the *Eclogues* and the *Georgics*: all hexameter poetry, but ranging from pastoral to agriculture to military epic.[23] With the same kind of pride the *Amores* epigram introduces a previously unknown artist to the Roman public. The name, Naso, is of course necessary – no *ille ego qui* ... here, and the difference between *modo* and *quondam* could also be pointed from this perspective (cf. the use of 'once / now' in Artemidorus *AP* 9.205, quoted by McKeown [1989] 4: in this kind of epigram one expects *quondam*, not *modo*). The epigram in fact says 'We were five books of elegy, now we are three: a reduced *poena* – for the reader'. Apart from the suggestive use of a punitive terminology (see above for the language of incrimination in the *Amores*), what is interesting here is that Ovid is cashing in on his previous achievements in much the same way that 'Virgil' does in the *Ille ego* ... Instead of having published *quondam* the *Eclogues* and *Georgics*, his claim to popularity is having published – *modo* – *Amorum libri quinque*, a vanished masterpiece whose only original merit is having been subjected to a drastic diet. Could *Amorum libri quinque* have existed only to create a witty introduction to *Amorum libri tres*? This would be the same kind of literary existence which belongs to the epic of *Amores* 1.1 and to the Gigantomachy of 2.1. The analogy is probably too crude. But note what McKeown says ([1989] 76, n. 8): 'one may reasonably doubt whether Ovid felt any pressing motivation to collect his elegies for publication ... despite the *Amores'* evident popularity, the first edition has disappeared without a trace. This may indicate that the original books had a very limited circulation.' In other words, the modern concept of edition is more convincing when applied to the extant text.

By alluding to *Ille ego* in his preface, Ovid scores three more points: (1) he emphasizes his commitment to the elegiac genre, a reference which will run through all his later proems, including the *Metamorphoses* proem; (2) he drops all the conventions of retrospective modesty and absolute beginning (*audaxque iuventa*, and the like) just as, in the closing elegy of Book 1 (1.15) he will surpass all previous self-congratulations and immortality claims made by already established poets such as Propertius (in his book 3) and Horace (in his book 3); and (3) he presents a CV which already includes, then rejects as too boring, a collection of elegies one book longer than Gallus' homonymous collection, the founding text of Roman elegy. Finally, by shrinking his collection from five to three, the *auctor* (a curious designation for one who subtracts instead of increasing: McKeown [1989] 5) proves his Callimachean credentials. So the importance of the so-called 'first edition' is more in the speculations and implications it raises[24] than in its actual circulation or – even – existence.

Notes

1. Continuities

1. Dörrie (1971) 66.

2. Palmer (1898) 13; Housman's contributions, which came out in *Classical Review* starting in 1897, are listed and summarized at pp. liv-lix. For Purser's contribution see ibid. pp. v-vi.

3. See Housman (1899) 172.

4. See Lehrs (1865) 49ff., reprinted with a short introduction in Lehrs (1869) ccxxiiff. (this was made available to me courtesy of E.A. Schmidt). Lehrs' emendation at 3.44 appears in the asterisked note on p. ccxxix.

5. For the same idea see also Dido in *Her.* 7.113ff.: *durat in extremum vitaeque novissima nostrae / prosequitur fati, qui fuit ante, tenor*. In an opposite sense, note *Pont.* 3.3.84 *et veniet votis mollior hora tuis*, used by Bentley to correct *inceptis* into *votis* (modifying accordingly the preceding *venit* into *veniet* – a detail not indicated in Dörrie's apparatus). In my view none of these parallels is particularly decisive. Surprisingly enough, no critic cites the text which is certainly the 'aural' model for our line: *Prop.* 2.28.15-16 *sed tibi vexatae per multa pericula vitae / extremo veniet mollior hora die*, in a very similar context. This is the only attestation of the nexus *mollior hora* before Ovid, and the structure of the verse is a valuable argument in favour of *malis*.

6. It follows that the 'night' that Briseis calls to mind at the start of the letter (v. 19ff.) is the 'night of the spies' of the *Doloneia* – she is perfectly right not to venture out! Note also that the letter's temporal frame coincides with the short pause before the *Iliad*'s plot reaches its dramatic resolution. Briseis writes after having been informed of the failed embassy (*Il.* 9), and she fears that Achilles may set sail the next morning (v. 57: *cum crastina fulserit Eos*). Homer's reader knows, on the contrary, that the morning will bring an unexpected resolution: it is the day of battle when Patroclus dies and Achilles' wrath comes to an end. On the importance of temporal 'intercutting' for understanding the ironic poetics of the *Heroides*, Kennedy (1984) 413ff. provides valuable observations, dealing specifically with the intersection between the epistle of Penelope and the *Odyssey*.

7. A vast bibliography in Geisler (1969) 300ff. Additional material in the apparatus of Lenz's edition ad loc., who lists, in a not very successful polemic with Kenney, the scholars in favor of *Rhesus*. It is worth noting that Bornecque in his Budé edition prints *alius ... Rhesus* without mentioning that the manuscript reading is *aliquis*.

8. See Kenney (1958) 172 n. 5, and (1959) 258 – rightly followed by Lazzarini (1986) 145. See Kenney and Geisler for the distribution – in itself inconclusive – of variant readings in the manuscripts.

9. The most logical and ingenious defence of *Rhesus* is proposed by Paola Venini in her review of Lenz's edition (Venini [1965] 480). She observes, building upon Lenz, that one should not downplay the importance and notoriety of Rhesus (according to Kenney, he was famous only for having been killed in his sleep; see also Geisler [1969] 301). In this regard, she draws attention to lines 380ff. of Euripides' *Rhesus*. Indeed, in the tragedy Rhesus swaggers on stage hurling threats against the Trojans; in a boastful tirade he even threatens to capture Odysseus and have him impaled (vv. 510ff).

At any rate, even in this tradition (strictly connected to a particular dramatic speech) it is clear that Rhesus is someone who *has been summoned* to war by the Trojans. Moreover, he has arrived very late and Hector complains to him about this. *Socios ad arma vocat* cannot mean 'he calls his Trojan allies to battle': this allusion would be meaningless if it referred to someone coming to fight only in the ninth year of the war. For the use of this expression for someone who *promotes* a war, see instead Ovid, *Her.* 16.350: *nulla tamen Minos Cretas ad arma vocat.* In our case one might think of either Agamemnon or Menelaus.

Finally, and this seems to me the strongest reason, the whole context calls for Circe to mention something that would make Ulysses *worry*. Rhesus, who has been dispensed with in the *Doloneia* with incredible ease, does not seem the best candidate for evoking memories of danger and toil. For all of the above, though I will now go on to explore the implications of the reading *rursus*, I will no longer insist on the inadequacy of *Rhesus*.

10. See Geisler (1969) 296ff., who provides numerous references also for this aspect. However, the theme was already well documented in Castiglioni (1908) 55, 59 and note.

11. Goold (1965) 99.

12. See below, n. 22.

13. It goes without saying that anachronisms are visible only when projected against the background of a precise poetics, in this case a poetics of extremely careful chronological framing. The anachronisms so common in Shakespeare's plays do not exist as such, since the poetics to which both the author and his audience are committed does not make them perceptible (as when Aristotle is quoted in *Troilus and Cressida*). Every poetics has its own margins of tolerance, based on an implicit contract between author and reader. Naturally anachronism becomes less pointed if it is based on a tacit analogy. A case of this kind in Ovid has recently been pointed out by Hardie (1985) 17 n. 40. The *Metamorphoses* stages an oratorical duel between Ajax and Ulysses over the arms of Achilles. Ulysses argues that a shield so ornate does not suit an owner like Ajax (*Il.* 18.483ff.):

> scilicet idcirco pro gnato caerula mater
> ambitiosa suo fuit, ut caelestia dona,
> artis opus tantae, rudis et sine pectore miles
> indueret? neque enim clipei caelamina novit
> Oceanum et terras cumque alto sidera caelo
> Pleiadasque Hyadasque inmunemque aequoris Arcton
> diversasque urbes nitidumque Orionis ensem:
> postulat, ut capiat, quae non intellegit, arma.
>
> *(Met.* 13.288-95)

Ajax is viewed ironically as some sort of *nouveau riche*, a rustic who wants to acquire objects of art which he does not at all understand. Odysseus may be insinuating indirectly that the subject matter of the shield is much better suited to himself, the hero destined to see the cities of many men and who knows, as the captain of a ship, the world and the constellations (see *Od.* 5.272ff., where the lines on the stars from *Il*. 18 are repeated word for word). But naturally the idea of a hero who receives the gift of a shield with *incomprehensible* ornament does not come from Homer. Rather the hero who does *not* understand (who cannot understand) the images of the divine shield is Aeneas:

> Talia per clipeum Volcani, dona parentis,
> miratur rerumque ignarus imagine gaudet
> attollens umero famamque et fata nepotum.
> (*Aen*. 8.729-31)

It is to this analogy that Ovid's line (13.295) looks back with a touch of irreverence. The anachronism is here only indirect, and coincides with the irony of misreading. An exact parallel reference could be found already in Ajax's counter-argument (*Met*. 13.103ff., noted by Labate [1980] 28ff. His article, strangely enough, was overlooked by Bömer in his well-informed commentary, who cites instead passages of little relevance). Ajax underlines the fact that the glittering weapons of Achilles are not suitable to one whose forte is nocturnal ambushes. The essential link comes not from the *Doloneia*, to which the words of Ajax certainly intend to allude, but from the Virgilian episode of Nisus and Euryalus, in which the glittering of weapons plays a disastrous role. In conclusion, both Ajax and Ulysses quote explicitly an episode from the *Iliad* and implicitly one from the *Aeneid*, which in turn was clearly meant to imitate the corresponding Homeric episode. The Achaean audience attending the debate knows and takes for granted the *Doloneia* and Achilles' shield, just as Ovid's complicit audience knows and takes for granted Euryalus and Nisus, and Aeneas' shield. 'Implicit' anachronisms of course occur in other authors (see e.g. Sophocles, *Aj*. 1285ff., and commentaries). But in Ovid the phenomenon seems to me more strictly bound to a specific overall vision of literature and myth.

14. *Ars* 129ff. is expounded by Rosati (1983) 161 n. 124. Apollonius Rhodius (2.707-10) highlights the same contradiction, adopting a point of view that betrays greater theological preoccupations. Apollo, when he killed Python, *still* had his youthful curls – but the poet corrects himself immediately and apologizes. No, he writes, Apollo still has, and always has, his handsome uncut locks, *permanently the same*.

15. On the wide diffusion of the motif, see Phillips (1953) 53ff.

16. See *Aen*. 3.272ff.: *effugimus scopulos Ithacae, Laertia regna,* / *et terram altricem saevi exsecramur Ulixi*. This passage, in my view, should be compared to *Od*. 13.352-4:

> Ὣς εἰποῦσα θεὰ σκέδασ᾽ ἠέρα, εἴσατο δὲ χθών
> γήθησεν τ᾽ ἄρ᾽ ἔπειτα πολύτλας δῖος Ὀδυσσεύς
> χαίρων ᾗ γαίῃ, κύσε δὲ ζείδωρον ἄρουραν

This is the moment in which Odysseus, after such long suffering, recognizes his island. *Effugere* and *exsecrare* are gestures that invert the joy with which Odysseus kisses the *zeidoros* 'earth'. The epithet 'giver of *zeal* ' was interpreted as *'life*-giving' already in the time of Aeschylus and Empedocles, and may thus have prompted Virgil's *altrix*, given the exceptionally intense pathos of the Homeric context. For a similar interpretation of the pathos in *zeidoros* and *physizoos*, cf. Hainsworth's (1982) note on *Od*. 5.463. See also *Il*. 3.243, the passage that enabled Ruskin to theorize his famous 'pathetic fallacy'.

17. Virgil's interest in chronography is clear in many places. For the particular problem of dating the fall of Troy, see Grafton-Swerdlow (1986) 212ff.

18. Or was it Odysseus' *ship* (see *Od.* 12.407ff.)? Commentators (see above all Haupt-Korn-Ewahld ad loc.; Bömer ad loc.) only mention this latter passage as a model. Certainly, *ratis* usually means 'ship' in Ovid (and it is chosen here for its phonetic aptness: *NeRITIaeque RATIs viderunt fRAgmina*: 14.563). Nevertheless, if Ovid intended a translation not of Homeric *neus*, 'ship', but of Homeric *schediê*, 'raft', what other term was available? Also, *fragmina* does not get us very far: in both passages Homer emphasizes the violent shattering of the ship and the fate of the remains. However, there are still some details arguing in favour of the episode in *Odyssey* 5: (a) the idea of the protective intervention of the nymphs could have been suggested to Ovid by the same episode in which Leucothea 'who was once mortal' (5.334), 'took pity' (336) on Odysseus' misfortunes and helped him in the storm; (b) the next episode Ovid recounts, the petrification of the Phaeacians' ship, takes place in the waters off Scheria, the same waters in which the raft is wrecked; (c) the episode in *Odyssey* 12 is chronologically *prior* to the Virgilian metamorphosis of ships into nymphs (one should recall also that Odysseus remains with Calypso for seven years), while the episode of petrification falls after this (it clearly takes place a few days before the end of the *Odyssey*, ten years *post Troiam captam*: cf. instead Bömer on 14.563-5). The chronology is coherent when one accepts the episode of the raft as the model. Bömer (loc. cit.) seems convinced that Ovid is not interested in this kind of synchronicity. But in *Met.* 14.70-4, Ovid deals specifically with Odysseus passing by Scylla – the episode of *Od.* 12 to which *Neritiae fragmina ratis* could refer – and states that *after* Odysseus passed by there (14.71: *sociis spoliavit Ulixen*), Aeneas arrived in the same area (*mox eadem Teucras fuerat mersura carinas / ni prius ...*). This progression is completely plausible if one considers the temporal intercutting of the two poems.

19. That Circe is at home in Latium is proved, on the one hand, by mythical and geneological connections she has with characters like Latinus (her son by Odysseus, according to a very old tradition!) and Picus. And on the other hand, from a geographical point of view, the Circeum is considered the first locale in ancient Latium one encounters when coming from the south (see Scyl. *Per.* 8; Pliny *NH* 3.56). The placement of Circe in Latium is also important for Virgil, and it is one of the elements motivating the position of the episode in the narrative structure of the *Aeneid*, which occurs right on the border between the end of Aeneas' wandering and the presentation of ancient Latium. For the wealth of traditions connecting Circe to Italy, see e.g. Boas (1939) 39ff.

20. It is worth noting that Geisler refuses to trace this connection, when his own analysis of *non hic* seems to make it inevitable: 'in der Stellung des *hic* R. 281 liegt ein doppelter Sinn: "Hier wird kein neuer Krieg um Troia entbrennen" und "Nicht *hier* (sondern in Latium) [!] wird Troia neu entstehen" – die Göttin Circe scheint in die Ratschlüsse der Götter eingeweiht zu sein' ([1969] 300).

21. And already in *Am.* 2.12.21, *femina Troianos iterum fera bella movere / impulit in regno, iuste Latine, tuo, iterum* was the focal point of allusion, see *Aen.* 6.93, *causa mali tanti coniunx iterum hospita Teucris / externique iterum thalami.*

22. It is natural that Circe promises 'this land as a whole' as the kingdom for Odysseus, and Virgil's readers know perfectly that this entire land will soon be a battlefield upon which the future of the kingdom will be decided. In saying this, I would not go so far as to discard Bentley's conjecture *tuta*, which after all, from our point of view, is even more open to ironic implications. Nevertheless, as Geisler notes ([1969] 303), the nexus *tuta sub regno tuo* stresses, perhaps even too much, the safety of the country instead of the confidence of Odysseus, upon which the context hinges. In favour of *tuta* one can read the arguments (in my view not very conclusive) of Goold (1965) 99, and of Henderson (1979) 77. (See also Luck [1961] 225, [1962] 148, who surprisingly advances *tuta* as his own proposal.)

An argument that seems worth noticing is the possibility of an allusion to Virgil, *Aen.* 3.384ff. (the prophecy of Helenus, a passage commonly cited as depending upon the predictions of Homer's Circe): *ante et Trinacria lentandus remus in unda / et salis Ausonii lustrandum navibus aequor / infernique lacus Aeaeaeque insula Circae / quam TUTA possis urbem componere TERRA*. In that case, Ovid might be insinuating that the land destined to be *tuta* for Aeneas could not be such for his archenemy Odysseus.

In light of this, v. 283 *hic amor et pax est* could have a similar Virgilian model: *Aen.* 4.347 *hic* [in Italy!] *amor, haec patria est*. In this case we would encounter again the double analogy Circe:Dido :: Odysseus:Aeneas, enriched by a contrary movement (flight from Italy: travel towards Italy); see n. 12 above. But the echo between the two lines is too weak to make a convincing case.

23. On the various forms of this motif 'words to the winds', see the informative contributions of Hross (1958) 135ff. The most traditional use of this topos is in the context of one who is *leaving*, the empty promises and oaths that a lover leaves unfulfilled behind him: Catullus 64.58ff. *immemor at iuvenis fugiens pellit vada remis, / inrita ventosae linquens promissa procellae ...*; 64.142, *quae cuncta aerii discerpunt inrita venti*. The inverted motif, now applied to the woman *abandoned*, is perhaps yet another touch of irony for readers who know Virgil: in this case *inrita* means not only 'ineffective' but also 'groundless, false'.

24. Conte (1985) 39.

25. Verducci (1985) 270.

26. The original nucleus of the present lofty element could go back to Zenodotus' version of *Il.* 4-5, but the real importance of that model, also in relation to the Greek tragedians and Catullus, continues to be debated in great detail (Zetzel [1978] 332; Renehan [1979] 100; Thomas [1979] 475; Dee [1981] 39ff.). Even closer, in my view, is the way Euripides' Andromeda speaks, a classic and impressive example of the *relicta* (see Eur. *Andr.* fr. 121, 122 N.²). We are clearly dealing with a *Pathosformel* that eventually lost the traces of its origins. See also Hross (1958) 87-9.

27. Reeve (1973) 332.

28. For the attempted corrections, cf. Dörrie's apparatus ad loc. (and more recently, Cadoni [1982] 191ff.). Housman fixes the problem of *quis scit an* followed by indicative by proposing, interestingly enough, an inversion of *forsitan* in the preceding line. But he also remarks that a grave difficulty at the end of the pentameter remains unsolved. There, the elision *insula habet* is unacceptable in light of normal Ovidian practice (e.g. Platnauer [1951] 90 and n. 1). The correction *insula alat*, which still enjoys some favour, is not therefore a real advance. But what is not brought into the discussion is the reference to tigers, on which more below, accepted in all the reconstructions so far advanced.

29. On the origins of the motif, cf. the exciting debate between Maass (1889) 528ff. and Perrotta (1931) 371ff. Another good parallel text is Hor. *Carm.* 3.27.61-6.

30. On this point I agree with Tarrant (1985) 75 n. 3. Tarrant finds lines 88 and 93-5 absurd (points *b d*, and *e* in our list), and thus proposes to expunge only the lines in question and to insert 96-8 between 81-7 and 89-92 (p. 72ff.).

31. See Bonner (1949) 150. On the relation between the *Heroides* and rhetorical ethopoiea, see more recently Russell (1983) 11ff.

32. Unconvincing therefore is the proposal of Stégen (1960) 360, implicitly refuted by Reeve (1973) 332 n. 1. The authenticity of v. 95 in this context is defended more convincingly by Marg (1960) 505, who proposes a lacuna after 95 and hypothesizes, among other things, an allusion to Bacchus, but in a slightly different sense than the one suggested below. Different, and hardly pertinent, is the case of *Met.* 8.51, where Scylla declares that she wants bird's wings to fly to her lover.

33. Unrealistic but not at all unproductive: it is precisely the obvious epistolary fictiveness that forces Ovid's Ariadne to recast her own experiences. This motivates the slight sense of detachment and self-reflexiveness that separates Ariadne in the *Heroides* from the Ariadne of Catullus. See also Schmidt (1967) 495.

34. On the importance of this tradition, which melds together the two phases of the myth in an atmosphere of pseudo-religious sensuality, see McNally (1985) 152ff.

35. Verducci (1985) 272 finds slightly ridiculous Ariadne's fear of seals ('the notoriously peaceful seals'), but her remark does not do justice to Ariadne. Seals are frightening and appalling also to the hero Menelaus and his crew, inured to all the dangers of the sea (see *Od.* 4.404ff.). On the irony of the entire passage, cf. Hross (1958) 88.

36. See e.g. Kiessling-Heinze (1968), commentary on Hor. *Carm.* 3.3.13, and more profusely, Bömer on *Fasti* 3.668. For Ariadne on the chariot drawn by tigers, it is enough however to recall *Her.* 2.80. Steier (*RE* 6.1 col. 952), in a minor oversight, refers this passage to Cybele, as does Richter, *Kleine Pauly* col. 826; for both s.v. *Tiger*.

37. This shorthand recasting of the Catullan model is an operation symmetrical with the insatiable expansion proposed by our passage in the *Heroides*. The parallel illustrates how Ovid conceives the countless possibilities of retelling any given story.

38. In Nonnos' version (47.447). On the similarity of the atmospheres of Nonnos and Ovid, there are good comments in Castiglioni (1908) 40ff.

39. For the present phase of the myth in Ovid, cf. Hollis (1977) 124; and see Prop. 3.17.7-8, with comments ad loc. of Fedeli (1985), who carefully distinguishes the different versions of the myth and the katasterism: *te quoque* [sc. Bacchus] *enim non esse rudem testatur in astris / lyncibus ad caelum vecta Ariadna tuis.* See also *Fast.* 3.510: *'Pariter caeli summa petamus' ait.*

40. See Citroni (1986) 111.

41. For the following argument, see the important reading of Hinds (1985) 13ff., some of whose observations I employ here.

42. In the context of the proemium the connotation of 'refined, polished', to which now the term *rude* is set in opposition, was based on *deducite*. See Kenney (1976) 51ff.; Gilbert (1976) 111ff.

2. Narrativity and convention in the *Heroides*

1. The traditional order of the epistles has a good chance of being Ovidian, but I would prefer not relying too heavily on this. In regard to their 'not requiring an answer', this is not the only reason to distinguish sharply the *Heroides* that stand alone from those that are coupled, the latter being almost certainly later, on account of style, metre, internal parallels, etc. Here I will not refer, therefore, to epistles 16-21, which pose rather different questions of poetics (see Barchiesi 1999b).

The idea that the epistles cannot have a response seems to be clearly implied by Penelope's letter. The initiative taken by Ovid's friend Sabinus, who composed some responses from the heroes (e.g. from Odysseus himself; see *Am.* 2.18.27ff.) might have been a lighthearted and intentional violation, something a prankster would do (but still in the Ovidian spirit, given Ovid's passion for unmasking literary conventions in all their arbitrariness). At *Am.* 2.18.32 (*quodque legat Phyllis, si modo vivit, adest*) one almost perceives a playful distinction on Ovid's part, based on the strict temporal set-up typical of epistles 1-15. The situation in which Phyllis is writing does not allow any time for response. (In this case, the words *quam cito* at v. 27 are all the more ironic.)

2. Good observations on this point in Kennedy (1984) 413ff., one of the first works to illuminate the problems of poetics posed by the *Heroides*. Meaningful also are Fränkel (1945) 36-9, and Della Corte (1973) 39ff.

3. See vv. 63-5, 99 (*nuper*). This is clearly the *terminus post quem* for Penelope's letter. In Homer, Telemachus delays telling his mother about his travels to Pylos and Sparta, and when he finally resolves to do so (at 17.107), the soothsayer Theoclymenus adds that in truth Odysseus is not only alive, but already home and preparing to punish the suitors (17.152-61). Penelope considers the news a dubious prophecy. Immediately afterwards, in a dramatic montage of events, Homer narrates how Odysseus, disguised as a beggar, approaches the house of his birth and is recognized by his aging dog.

Also, the motif of Penelope entrusting letters to all strangers passing through is in a certain sense the development, almost the inversion, of a Homeric suggestion. At 14.372ff., Eumaeus tells Odysseus that Penelope often takes in travellers and asks them news of her husband, and among them there are often impostors – Odysseus, strangely enough, is the last of these impostors.

4. In the eighteenth-century epistolary novel, a work in 'many voices', the superior vantage point of the reader is provided not by intertextual knowledge, but simply by the circumstance that no character has access to the whole picture. Only the reader, who is directly complicit with the author, can patch together the points of view of the individual narrators into a coherent design. On the poetics of this important narrative form see Rousset (1976) 81ff. On illusion as the unifying realm for Ovid's works, see the fundamental essay on the *Metamorphoses* by Rosati (1983).

5. See the feminist rebirth of the *Heroides*, now as the marginal voice, in Brückner (1985), and Schubert (1985) 76ff.

6. I have the feeling that any attempt to infer too much from *Ars* 3.346, *ignotum hoc aliis ille novavit opus*, ought to be drastically curbed on both sides of the question. The claim for absolute novelty clashes with the catalogue of debts that any philologist can easily compile following the usual method of *Kreuzung der Gattungen*. On the other hand, the discussion concerning the degree to which the *Heroides* constitute a new genre, a new *Dichtart*, runs the risk of spinning its wheels. In my view at least, it is clear that the *Heroides* begin a new 'game' with rules created ad hoc. None of the objections made against the truthfulness of Ovid's declaration seem convincing. It is true that the habits of the Roman poets would lead one to expect the solemn chant of *Primus ego* .... But any claims to originality (and of original 'importing' from Greece) need to be read in their precise context. In the *Ars* Ovid is not parading his masterpieces for future generations, but is busy listing the cultural commodities that might enrich the dowry of a well-to-do young lady (after all, the following advice, in vv. 349ff., recommends learning how to dance). In such a context, there is no room for an *exegi monumentum*, but it would be wrong to dismiss the importance of *ignotum ... novavit*. When he talks about the *Amores*, Ovid does not make similarly far-reaching claims and does not make himself the founder of a school (that would have been rather difficult, after having mentioned, six lines before, Gallus, Propertius, and Tibullus).

7. See in general Conte's introduction to Lazzarini (1986) 11, useful for my argument for its analysis of Ovid's early relationship with Roman elegy (relativistic, unmasking of conventions, self-reflective), and more generally, for its recognition of the nature and function of the literary genre. Stroh (1971) 190 n. 59 rightly includes the *Heroides* (as *zweckhaftes Brief*) in the genre of elegy. If one considers the concrete elegiac sources that nourished the *Heroides*, the importance of Propertius book 4 (Arethusa, Tarpea), though well known, still deserves to be emphasized.

8. Lechi (1979) 83ff., brought a new approach to the question of the exemplum in elegy (on Penelope, see esp. p. 87, and on Briseis, pp. 88ff.).

9. This nexus is commented upon by Fedeli (1980) 130.

10. See Scivoletto (1976) 71 (and more generally, 57ff.); other useful remarks in Labate (1984) 41 n. 44. See also the jealous atmosphere in Laevius, fr. 18 Mor.

11. On the figure of Briseis in love poetry, see in general Pasquali (1964) 491, Nisbet-Hubbard (1978) 70. It might also be useful to consider the widespread iconographic motif of Briseis' *abduction*, portrayed in the manner of a sentimental romance; on this, see the useful contributions of Frangini-Martinelli (1981) 4-13.

12. See the lucid synthesis in Fedeli (1986a) 294, and in general the important essay by Lyne (1979) 117.

13. The brilliant formulation of Kraus (1950-1) 60.

14. Briseis as a *geras* (= *munus*), widespread in the Homeric account of Achilles' wrath, is here taken up by the first-person narrator in a gesture recurrent in the allusive grammar of the *Heroides*.

15. On *queri, querimonia* and similar terms, as sometimes connotative and often technical terms for elegy, see e.g. Hinds (1987a) 103ff. with bibliography; also Baca (1971) 195ff. (though rather disappointing).

16. See, first of all, Fedeli (1980) 282, who in commenting upon Prop. 1.11.23, examines very carefully the direct functioning of the Homeric model in the language of Roman elegy.

17. A certain resemblance between Ovid's Briseis and Tecmessa has been well noted by Wilkinson (1956) 229 n. 3.

18. See Paduano (1982) 195 n. 32; Rossi (1977) 15; Easterling (1984) 4. See also the fine close reading of Kirkwood (1965) 51ff.

19. An instructive example of these delimitations of sphere and pertinence is the way Briseis' epistle employs the embassy to Achilles in *Iliad* 9. Briseis confidently hopes to convince Achilles where the Achaean ambassadors have failed (for her posture cf. Tarpeia in Prop. 4.4.59-60). In the beginning she lists, with great exactness, all the promises made by Agamemnon in order to pacify Achilles (vv. 27-38). But Briseis emphasizes that she alone has the weapons (elegiac, to be sure: arms to wrap around his neck and eyes to look into his, vv. 131-2) that will win Achilles over. So far the two worlds are only parallel. But one argument made by the Homeric ambassadors crosses over the line into Briseis' sphere: i.e. the apologue of Meleager which, as we know, Phoenix employs in vain to appease Achilles. Homeric scholars have often noted, beginning from antiquity, that it is a rather strange example. To be precise, we have here the story of a hero who refuses any and all offers to entice him back into battle, just as Achilles himself will do. The example is thus marked by failure from the start. But Phoenix himself says that in the end the only person able to persuade Meleager was his highly beloved wife Cleopatra. The apologue thus fits Briseis better, who can construct a clear parallel between herself and Cleopatra and can appeal to the power of love (vv. 91ff.).

We know well enough that the epic world will in the end prevail: Achilles will return to battle not on account of Briseis' beautiful eyes, but for exclusively epic reasons (heroic vengeance, restoration of his honour as a warrior).

20. The problems posed by the erotic-elegiac enclave in Book 4, carved out of the epic context of the *Aeneid*, corresponds to a critical zone of conflict in Ovid's poetics. The question is to what limit it is possible to 'force' epic towards other genres without it losing its identity, and this will obviously be crucial when Ovid undertakes the *Metamorphoses* (good notes in Hinds [1987a] 133ff.). In the *Tristia* Ovid has an unforgettable epigram on the 'provocation' embodied by *Aeneid 4*. The context is here tied, as is well known, to a defence of the *Ars amatoria*, but the formulation certainly goes beyond the immediate context:

> et tamen ille tuae felix Aeneidos auctor
>   contulit in Tyrios arma virumque toros,
> nec legitur pars ulla magis de corpore toto,
>   quam non legitimo foedere iunctus amor.
>
> (*Tr.* 3.533-6)

The 'flanking' manoeuvre of the nexus *Tyrios ... toros* (the plural is poignant; see Maas [1902)] 499) has, on the one hand, clear erotic undertones (reinforced less by the potential, well-worn pun on *arma* than by the vague physicality of the next line *pars ... de corpore*), and on the other hand, it introduces a literary paradox. The epic plot (*arma virumque*) is encompassed and framed, so to speak, by Carthaginian eros, but it is also the case, inversely, that this love story, so well known, is properly only a subordinate member of the great 'body' of epic. We also ought not overlook the multivalence of *arma virumque*: it is simultaneously the incipit signal for the *Aeneid*, a metaliterary marker for heroic epos (see Conte [1985] 47ff.), and an allusion, all the more ironic for its unquestionable literalness, to an episode in *Aeneid* 4. Not only has the hero visited Dido's bed, but has also forgotten his arms there (a disastrous forgetfulness), and Virgil draws attention to this with the 'heroic epic' cliché *arma vir-*:

> ... arma viri, thalamo quae fixa reliquit
> impius, exuviasque omnis lectumque iugalem ...
>
> (4.495-6)

21. On the metaphorical sphere of 'flame' and 'wound', see Hardie (1986) 232, with relevant bibliography. On the implications of Dido's last lines (4.661ff.: *hauriat hunc oculis ignem crudelis ab alto / Dardanus*) see the perceptive interpretation of Lyne (1987) 48; see also *Aen.* 5.4ff.: *quae tantum accenderit ignem / causa latet ....*

In Ovid, the shift from *uritur* to the 'programmatic' *uror* (cf. *Am.* 1.1.26) is the clear sign of a border-raid – from an epic poem with elegiac tendencies to an elegiac reworking of epic themes.

22. Conte (1984) 82ff.

23. See e.g. the introductory note to the epistle in Palmer's commentary (Palmer [1967] 339).

24. In the same tone perhaps, the swan – with which Dido unexpectedly identifies at the beginning of the epistle – is represented as *abiectus* (see Kenney

[1982] 424). This term has the connotations 'demoralized, depressed', but also 'humble' (not only of people but also of literary style!).

25. The conversion of the motif is not the sign of an altered ethos (with Ovid's Dido being 'meeker' than the other) but rather an alignment with the pragmatics, the *Werbung*, of the letter. For the comparison with the tone of elegiac propempticon, see e.g. Prop. 1.8.17 (cited by Adamietz [1984] 125). Only slightly different are cases where the lover inveighs against the person who is departing (with accusations of infidelity, appeals to the gods, etc.) but then retracts from fear of bringing down a storm upon the loved one's ship. This typically elegiac mode is reused, for example, in Laodamia's epistle, which hinges on a very sharp change of tone (v. 132: *sed quid ago? revoco? revocaminis omen abesto!*); see also *Ep.* 2. 135-8.

26. For the play on the 'forgotten' sword, see n. 20 above.

27. The beginning of the letter poses grave textual difficulties, but these are of only marginal concern here. The authenticity of the lines that Dörrie numbers 1-2 (omitted by all the principal manuscripts but one) is highly doubtful, also for lexical reasons; what most leaves one wondering is that Dido calls her letter a *carmen*. Even if one accepts influence from the next couplet (the swan's *carmen*), the expression is unparalleled in the *Heroides*, except when the author is Sappho (cf. 15.6). Since the authentic text could hardly begin with *sic ubi* (v. 3 Dörrie), much effort has been spent defending the authenticity of lines 1-2 (cf. in particular Kirfel [1969] 61). From our point of view, it is interesting that the contested couplet contains diction like *moriturae* and *ultima verba*. But even with these lines eliminated, the image of the swan, certainly authentic, serves its purpose as a programmatic frontispiece.

28. For the tragic – or in this context, melodramatic – register of this expression, it is worth noting that *fata vocant* is a Virgilian nexus (*Aen.* 10.471), and that Plato defines the Greek equivalent *kalei hê heimarmenê* as an 'expression suited to a tragic poet' (*Phd.* 115A). The image of a swan that presages its own death also has famous antecedents in Greek tragedy (good observations in Wilamowitz ad Eur. *Heracl.* 110, and Fraenkel ad Aesch. *A.* 1444ff.).

29. The idea that the letter is dominated by a sincere disposition towards suicide is readily dismissed by Adamietz (1984) 121ff. Good observations already by Anderson (1973) 49ff.

30. On Ovid's irony as 'hesitation' with respect to the conventions of various genres, see Conte's introduction to Lazzarini (1986) 23ff., with relevant bibliography cited in nn. 24, 34.

3. Voices and narrative 'instances' in the *Metamorphoses*

1. Namely, in an essay on Ovid's poetics, of which the present work is an approximation. I will deal with two aspects to which I cannot do justice here, that is, the use of narrativity as a theme for narrative, and the relationship between literary genres and the act of narration. (See Barchiesi 1999a and 2002.)

2. Solodow (1988) 38: I cite him without polemic because he has the merit of expressing with the highest clarity the position that is implicitly dominant in Ovidian studies (cf. *contra* Hinds [1987a] 126). On the other hand, I will investigate in the essay promised in n. 1 a problem somewhat connected with the concept of a single narrator, that is, Ovid's tendency to demotivate metadiegetic procedures and reveal their arbitrariness. I follow here Genette's terminology (as in Genette [1976] and [1983]), and therefore by 'metadiegesis' I mean a narrative within a narrative. So also the term 'instance', in the chapter's title and throughout the text, is used in the particular sense attributed to it by Genette's translator Jane E. Lewin: 'The narrating instance, then, refers to something like the narrating situation, the narrative matrix – the entire set of conditions (human, temporal, spatial) out of which a narrative statement is produced' (Genette [1980] 31).

3. In the Greek of Ovid's age *polyeideia* has two distinct meanings: 'metamorphic capability' and 'plurality of literary forms and genres'.

4. These are all problems familiar to readers of Petronius; on the interaction between metadiegesis, narrative frames, and the structure of the novel, see Fedeli-Dimundo (1988) 16-42.

5. The comparisons, obviously more problematic for the fragmentary *Hecale*, receive systematic treatment in Hollis (1983) in his commentary on Book 8. In the *Met*. Theseus' victory over the bull, the mythic situation of the *Hecale*, had already been recalled in the celebration at 7.433ff. (cf. Call. fr. 290 Pf.).

6. The banquet and hospitality as sites of narrative exchange are a common situation in Callimachus, as can be seen in both the fragments of *Hecale* and, even more so, in the *Aitia*. To be sure, the banquet as a metadiegetic device is widespread in all genres and at all levels of narrative.

7. See Kenney (1986) xxviii. One might compare from the *Satyricon* the reaction of Lichas in the inset story of the Lady of Ephesus. There too one narratee of the story is struck more than others because he sees himself reflected in a certain feature of the plot (see Fedeli-Dimundo [1988] 23). The difference is that for Petronius' reader the relation between the story and narratee is mediated and clarified by the preceding narrative of the novel (which presented Lichas, as far as we can gather, as a cuckolded husband); in Ovid this mediating function is supplied not by the context but by the intertext with the Callimachean model.

8. See especially Diller (1934) 25ff.; Büchner (1957) 205ff.; both end up underestimating the comic elements in Ovid's narration, which arise from the high pitch he imposes on his model and are inseparable from this. If it is true, as we are observing, that Ovid 'epicizes' Callimachus, this does not mean that Ovid is somehow 'more serious' than Callimachus.

9. Thus, for example, *attenuate* is the opposite of *sublate ampleque* (Cic. *Brut.* 201) and of *redundantia* (Cic. *Orat.* 108). On the *genus adtenuatum* and *adtenuatio*, see in general *Rhet. Her.* 4.10-11. Cicero defines as 'attenuated' the oratorical style of Licinius Calvus: bloodless, controlled, and accessible to only a few connoisseurs (see *Brut.* 283). As is known, the Roman followers of Callimachus delineate the stylistic ideal of *lepton* by relying upon the rhetorical terminology for the *genus tenue* (cf. Reitzenstein [1931] 25ff., and especially 39ff.).

10. Erysichthon's insatiability appears to be connected to an almost bombastic style that goes beyond the usual level of epic elevation. We catch a hint of this in 8.855, where the hero, who should be simply saying 'o fisherman', displays a periphrasis like '*o qui pendentia parvo / aera cibo celas, moderator harundinis*'. (On the 'pomposity' of Achelous' style see also Hollis on *Met.* 8.549ff.). An amusing parallel in Plautus *Rud.* 310ff.: *salvete, fures maritumi ... famelica hominum natio.*

11. The force of *deducite* in opposition to *perpetuum* has been noted independently by Due (1974) 95, n. 8, Gilbert (1976) 111ff., and Kenney (1976) 51ff. See also Hinds (1987a) 18-20. Of course, one should not forget that *deducite* already has one satisfactory meaning: the narrative is 'brought down' from the origin to its final destination (cf. Dion. Hal. *Ant.* 1.8: *katabibazô ... tên diegesin*).

12. The topos is analysed and well documented by Wimmel (1960) 222ff., 227-33. See also Thomas-Scodel (1984) 339, and Clauss (1988) 309-20. Worth noting also is Ov. *Fast.* 5.662: *leves cursum sustinuistis aquae*; in the *Fasti* the

Tiber has *leves* waters, but in the epic model for this passage (*Aen*. 8.66) the flow of the river is *tumens*.

13. Antimachus is cited with great emphasis on v. 45, and is the most probable candidate for the negative examples in vv. 36-40 (the horse of Adrastus, Archemorus, Amphiaraus, Capaneus), in addition to appearing as a typical antagonist of the Callimachean tendency towards the *lepton*. As a matter of pure curiosity, I mention that Achelous is cited in a text of Antimachus (*POxy*. 2516 = fr. 62.4 Lloyd Jones-Parsons, *Supplementum Hellenisticum*; the editors suspect, but with great uncertainty, that it is part of a proem).

The context of 2.34 is extremely complex, and the choice of examples is probably influenced by this. The struggle between Heracles and Achelous is undoubtedly an epic theme, which Propertius pits against 'slender' love poetry, but one also gets the impression that behind this choice lies an agenda. The Achelous is presented as *fractus ... amore*, which, on the one hand, may allude to the defeat he has just suffered (Heracles vanquishes him and breaks off one of his horns, as Ovid reminds us in *Met*. 9), but on the other hand, it reintroduces into the field of epic the theme of love, which ought to remain, in programmatic terms, in the opposite camp. The effect is subtle: Propertius offers Lynceus choice examples of poetry to be avoided since they do not serve love, but at the same time implies that even there, in the epic genre Lynceus obstinately practices, love makes its weight felt.

14. We know this, thanks to Hinds (1987a), who updates and redefines the position of Heinze (1960).

15. For the encounter, see fr. XXIX, and for the union with the Anio see fr. XXXIX, but also XXXIV, XXXVI, XXXVII in Skutsch (1985) 206-13.

16. On *Amores* 3.6, Suter (1989) 15ff. She pursues the reference to Callimachus in a different direction than the one taken here.

17. I believe this is an important point. Ovid's literary generation had by now been saturated with appeals to the *lepton*, refusals of epic, and the entire paraphernalia of Callimachean poetics. Beginning with his spectacular entrance upon the literary stage with *Amores* 1.1, Ovid brings with him a new breeze and ironically shuffles traditional dichotomies. Using a swollen river as a narrator seems integral to this ironic tendency; the image, by now worn out in its 'defensive' use against epic, now provokes instead a certain aversion, tempting one to regard the situation for once from the opposite point of view. For the somewhat 'dialectical' and problematic approach to Callimachean *imagery*, Horace's *Ars Poetica* offers important insights (fine observations in Brink [1985] 345ff., 208ff.).

18. The history of this motif is traced by Fantuzzi (1980) 163-72. It may be worth recalling that the formula, famous as the incipit for Aratus' *Phaenomena*, was attributed by ancient interpreters of Aratus to an Orphic source (see Fantuzzi, [ib.] 163 n. 1). Callimachus does not use the formula, but begins his first hymn with the name of Zeus.

19. By curious coincidence, *ek Dios archômestha* occurs at the beginning of one of the most infamous and blasphemous pederastic epigrams of antiquity, one by Strato that became the proem to Book XII of the *Anthologia Palatina* (see Fantuzzi [ib.] 165, 168). Note also that Orpheus has just come from singing a *Gigantomachia* (10.149-51), the most elevated of all poetic genres, in which Zeus is the absolute protagonist responsible for super-epic deeds.

20. Phanocles' version of the Orpheus myth contains several *aitia* (see Hopkinson [1988] 178), among which is an explanation of why Lesbos is a 'musical' island, filled with and renowned for song. This explanation is picked up by Ovid in *Met*. 11.50: Orpheus' head and lyre travel towards Lesbos, emitting a feeble lament (see 52-3: *flebile ... flebile ... flebile*). It seems plausible to me that both Phanocles and

Ovid intend to suggest some continuity between the songs of Orpheus and the great love lyrics of Lesbos, which can be seen in some sense as their heir. Alcaeus, for example, might be cited as evidence for this poetic genealogy, in as much as he was a renowned singer of *Paidika* (see Hor. *Carm.* 1.32.10-12).

21. Notwithstanding the scarcity of our knowledge of the *Zmyrna*, a weighty presence of Cinna's epyllion in Orpheus' epyllion seems a probable hypothesis. The only certain point of departure is that fr. 7 Mor. (see Haupt-Korn-Ehwald-von Albrecht [1966] on 10.298ff.) is echoed in the situation of v. 503 and in the tone of moral condemnation in v. 469 (see also v. 474).

22. See Kiessling-Heinze (1968) ad loc.; *Orph.* fr. 245 K.

23. See Segal (1989) 93.

24. The rhetorical matrix, resolved on a higher poetic register by Virgil, is made more evident by the repeated use of *gratulor*, probably a stylistic feature of declamation (see Elder Seneca, *Con.* 9.2.4: *gratulor sorti tuae, provincia, quod ...*; 10.4.9: *gratulor tibi, Roma, quod in conditores tuos homo non incidit*).

25. For a similar contrast between localization and characterization, see Fedeli (1986b) 10ff., who discusses how the modesty of the lady of Ephesus in Petr. 111.1 is at odds with the connotations of the toponym Ephesus, a seaport associated with loose standards of morality. Some degree of ironic relativizing should be seen also in *Met.* 10.331ff., where Myrrha envies the fortune of faraway peoples among whom incest is allowed. It is not said what regions these people inhabit, but readers used to the polarities of ancient ethnography would be tempted to answer 'in the Far East' – the only problem is that, with respect to Orpheus, the heroine is already an oriental character.

26. For the proverbial lack of sexual restraint among Thracians, see also *Her.* 5.5; Men. fr. 794 Sandbach. The *Met.* also offers the parallel case of Boreas, featured as an unrestrained rapist of young girls (6.685ff.), and of Pyreneus, a Thracian king who has the disconcerting goal of raping the Muses (5.269ff.).

27. It should not be passed over in silence that also in another of Orpheus' performances, his song that persuades the residents of Hades, the role of the audience is much emphasized (10.40ff.), much more so than in the corresponding Virgilian model (see Segal [1989] 24).

28. See 10.143ff. *inque ferarum / concilio medius turba volucrumque sedebat*; 11.1: *animosque ferarum*; 11.20ff.: *attonitas ... innumeras volucres anguesque agmenque ferarum*; 11.42ff.: *auditum saxis intellectumque ferarum / sensibus*.

29. Note also 7.386ff.: *cum matre / ... concubiturus erat saevarum more ferarum*.

30. [Translators' note: In the US the expression 'strive for five' is a slogan referring to the recommended daily number of servings of vegetables.] Aggressive, but in the end healthy, is the position of Solodow (1988) 164ff. My only reservation is that I do not consider valid any generalizing argument based on the unpopularity, or rather the popularity, of Pythagoreanism in Rome.

31. Dion. Hal. 2.59ff. (cf. Cic. *Tusc.* 4.1; *Rep.* 2.28; Liv. 1.18.2-3). For the history of the coupling of Numa and Pythagoras and on its decline in the Augustan age, see Gabba (1966) 158ff. Skutsch (1985) 263ff. dismisses the idea (for which Ovid scholars are mostly accountable) that Numa's Pythagoreanism may have had a model in the *Annales* of Ennius. Note also that the other two places in Ovid where Pythagoras is Numa's teacher are rather uncertain. In *Fast.* 3.153ff., it is explicitly stated that Egeria, Numa's wife, is a source alternative to Pythagoras. In *Pont.* 3.3.44, the account is introduced with *ferunt*, which gives it a sense of distancing, especially when nothing of this kind is found with the other teacher-student couplings cited in that context (though they too are endowed with little historical weight: Eumolpus / Orpheus, Olympus / Marsyas, Chiron / Achilles).

32. For *silentes* in the sense of 'the dead', see Hor. *Epod.* 5.51; Ov. *Met.* 13.25; Sen. *Med.* 740; for the use of *silentum* at end-line, see Prop. 3.12.33; Verg. *Aen.* 6.432ff.: *silentum / consilium* (the *silentum* at Mat. 8 Mor. comes from the adjective *silentus*; this is not clarified by Norden ad *Aen.* 6.432).

33. This contrast is due to the fact that the apostrophe to mortals is an outworn and required feature of the repertoire of didactic diatribe. Lucretius had powerfully remotivated the cliché with dramatic effect, when he introduced Nature addressing a man (as Everyman) with the word *mortalis* (3.933). After the poet's long analysis dedicated to death and its dread, the term is stripped of its inertia and becomes the emotional keynote of the entire argument. The use of the apostrophe in the mouth of Pythagoras has an opposite effect: the didactic marker is demotivated by its unsuitability to the context, or else (a more troubling hypothesis), it works to dismantle the logical premises of the context. (Those who believe the seriousness of Pythagoras' consolatory message in Ovid would do well to reflect upon the sarcastic message of the extraterrestials in Kurt Vonnegut's *Slaughterhouse Five*: 'we will all live forever – no matter how dead we may sometimes seem to be').

34. The term should be taken in the widest possible sense, to include the entire growing mass of *pseudo-Pythagorica*, as well as autonomous figures, such as Empedocles and Epicharmus and their Roman successors, who contributed in varying degrees. The progress of knowledge in this field makes attempts – such as that of Georges Lafaye – to connect Ovid with specific sources ever more improbable.

35. Ovid is one among those narrators who could be called 'suppressive', because they frequently allow us to perceive that their narratives rest upon a selection of information, and that they do not cover 'everything' that might be said at any given moment of the story. The term 'suppressive' is used in a slightly different sense by Sternberg (1978).

36. At least for a didactic text of around 400 lines. The process by which the markers of a particular literary style are 'densified' with respect to normal practice corresponds to what we usually call parody. However, as is known, it is not easy to draw a definite line between parody and intertextuality when the quoted text is itself so 'over-coded'.

37. For the tradition of this peculiarly didactic formula, see Schiesaro (1984) 150. See also *Hal.* 69; in the entire corpus of Ovid there are only three other instances of *nonne*.

38. See Conte (1990).

39. The line uniting Aristaeus to the context of the *Georgics* is drawn by Conte (1984) 52: '[Virgil's Aristaeus] is not only the ideal model *of* a person who receives and applies those teachings but also a complete model *for* a person who will receive and apply [the teachings of the *Georgics*] ... the fable of Aristaeus is nothing other than the translation, into the dynamic form of a story, of the literary didacticism that underlies the whole poem and foreshadows its reception.' Like Numa, Aristaeus is a civilizer and an antecedent for religious and sacrificial practice. For an attempt to resolve the contradiction by attributing bloodless sacrifice to Numa, see Plut. *Num.* 8.15.

40. The allegorical function of the two names seems almost inevitable, and it is surprising that this exegesis gained no favour before Skutsch (1959) 114.

41. The *Iliad* parallels are listed by Ovid commentators ad loc. For the memory of Mars (*Met.* 14.812ff.; cf. *Fast.* 2.483ff.), and of Ariadne (*Fast.* 3.469ff.), see Conte (1985) 35-40.

42. On Panthus, see e.g. *Aen.* 2.318 cum Serv. auct. ad loc.; schol. *Il.* [AB] 12.211; [T] 15.521; Pind. *Pae.* 6.74. On Helenus, see *Aen.* 3.359ff.; Williams ad *Aen.* 3.295; *Il.* 6.76. With regards to the oracle at Delphi, Virgil and Ovid take opposite stands; see Paschalis (1986) 47 n. 18.

43. A similar question arises in the *Aeneid*, when Anchises remembers that Cassandra had already said the right thing, but had not been believed (3.184ff.: *nunc repeto ... sed quis ... crederet? aut quem tum vates Cassandra moveret?*). In any case, an optimistic prophecy for Aeneas occurs already in Homer, *Il.* 20.302-8, and Creusa is extremely explicit in *Aen.* 2.781ff.; see also the *Trojan* Sibyl of Tib. 2.5.19ff.

44. A useful account of the question in Bömer's commentary ad loc.

45. Critics usually explain this intrusion of the author as an 'Augustan' commentary. Solodow (1988) 168, thinks, on the contrary, that Ovid's point of view is pessimistic about the destiny of Rome, since *quoque* in line 431 seems to connect strictly the ascent of Rome to the decadence of the other powers. Interestingly, Hollis vacillates between seeing in this passage a deep patriotic impulse (comm. to *Met.* 8 [1970] xix), and later, an incidental comment with respect to the poem's structure (Hollis [1983] 160). One might escape this set of alternatives by dropping the 'authorial' voice and instead taking the narrative situation at face value. Once again, we note that in the *Met.* the 'literal' interpretation, as suggested by the narrative contexts, turns out in the long run to be also the most ironic, relativized, and rich in implications.

46. For the parallels, one should see the subtle reading of Feeney (1986).

47. On Ovid and the eternity of Rome, Galinsky (1975) 44 and 254, is balanced and convincing.

48. In truth, Horace's statements about the eternity of Rome need to be evaluated with great care (see La Penna [1963] 66-8). But Ovid's omission of any temporal reference in his *sphragis*, written with *Carm.* 3.30 in mind, is surprising, and suggests a conscious choice on Ovid's part (see also Galinsky [1975]).

49. E.g. Melville (1986) 1: 'to our modern times'. For an author writing around the end of Augustus' Principate, the closing of a work is problematic; Livy might offer us an instructive point of comparison.

50. E.g. Hinds (1987b) 26, in a different train of thought. For a surreal version of the same theme, cf. instead Prop. 4.6.60: *sum deus; est nostri sanguinis ista fides*. Caesar, looking upon the victory at Actium, finds self-affirmation of his own divinity. Cairns (1984) 167, appropriately reminds us that an offspring can confer retrospective glory on his ancestors. But his proposal of reading *sum deus* as a formula for epiphany has no connection with Propertius' text, in which Caesar is not appearing to anyone. If one accepts *sum deus* (instead of a *facilior* emendation such as *tu deus*) it must be admitted that Propertius is playing with Augustan propaganda, and is pushing to its breaking-point the machinery of retroactive deification.

51. See Zanker (1989) 180.

52. A glimpse into iconographic propaganda (see Zanker [1989] 39, 180, 206, 235ff.) shows that the presence of the *sidus Iulium* is strictly linked to a dynastic point of view. On an ideal diagram the high points would coincide with the Civil Wars (particularly up to Naulochus) and, after a dormant period, with the politics of adoption. The star reappears in order to shine on the young princes, Gaius and Lucius Caesar.

53. An exception is Galinsky (1975) 258ff., who is clear-minded and precise in comparing Ovid with Horace and Virgil, but in my view does not go far enough in accepting the 'realistic' implication of Ovid's position. Galinsky considers the rhetorical feel of the praise of Augustus to be justified and inevitable, for the reason that formulas grow old and are hard to update. But leaders grow old as well, and the problem of succession for Augustus casts a shadow over the entire finale of the *Met.* (a poem where persistent tensions between order and chaos, repression and disorder run from one end to the other, and the whole is pervaded by a sharp and objective perception of power relations and of hierarchies).

54. In *Met.* 12.542ff., Nestor begins his speech with the famous topos of *renovare dolorem*: '*quid me meminisse malorum / cogis*'. He tells of an event in his early youth, and the reader cannot avoid the feeling that the narrator is over two hundred years old, and thus there is no chance, like Aeneas in Carthage, that he will reopen a wound still fresh. So too, in our passage, the reader is forced to notice that the topos '*serus in caelum redeas*' fits the actual age of Augustus *all too well*.

4. Teaching Augustus through allusion

1. Lechi (1993), the best introduction to the *Tristia* that I can mention, focuses on the four 'homogeneous' books; an understandable choice, since the inclusion of *Tristia* 2 in the collection is actually somewhat of an anomaly. On the fruitfulness of comparing *Tristia* 2 and *Epistles* 2.1, there are short but insightful observations in Nugent (1990) 249.

2. Ferri (1993) is an example of how an epistolary text (Horace, *Ep.* 1) can be examined in terms of didactic impulse and construction of addressee.

3. One should regard with interest those studies that explore the connection between power and didactic poetry in Rome, as do some of the contributions in Habinek-Schiesaro (1997). Naturally this mode of inquiry presupposes a rather wide and comprehensive notion of categories such as 'instruction' and 'cognitive model'.

4. Wallace-Hadrill has furnished particularly enlightening contributions in this direction.

5. Brink (1982) 495.

6. Two important assumptions in the letter are Augustus' interest in the revival of archaic Rome, and in all forms of popular entertainment. These are problems with which Horace's poetics must carefully come to (and *be on*) good terms with (see Wilamowitz's note, cited by Fraenkel [1957] 396 n. 1). In the situation of *Tristia* 2, Ovid prefers to highlight the emperor's inclination towards mimes (see 2.514 *scenica vidisti lentus adulteria*).

7. See Burke (1992).

8. Insightful observations in Fowler (1993); see also the set of problems posed by Martindale (1993).

9. A brief account of the *status quaestionis* in Brink (1982) ad loc. (who treats the effect noted by Fraenkel as proof that Cicero is the active model); Conte-Barchiesi (1989) 101-3; see also Traina (1991) 273. The two hexametres are isosyllabic, metrically identical in the coincidence of all the word endings and in the presence of four initial spondees, as well as assonant with respect to sound: *o for**tam **me consule / te principe* (a relevant substitution, as we shall see) *Romam*.

10. The theme of money in 229-48 is another example of how Horace offers his readers problematic alternatives. Choerilus the poetaster is paid cash for his infelicitous lines: *rettulit acceptos, regale nomisma, Philippos* (234). The harshness of the language of commerce (*rettulit acceptos*, see below n. 13), the exotic tone of *nomisma* and *Philippos*, sets up a distant world of venal and megalomaniac

Greeks. The two consecutive Greek terms are signs of both poetic and political bad taste, a style Horace adopts only to denounce the referent. This type of poetry in exchange for minted coins is contrasted with the noble and abstract *munera* (v. 246) that Augustus distributes to Virgil along with the competent praises he gives as a connoisseur of art. This opposition – bad poetry for foreign currency, vs. good poetry for recognition that is more than material – effaces the connection between economic subsistence and the Princeps' protection from which Horace himself benefits. The opening sentence of the discourse *sed tamen est operae pretium cognoscere* (239), gives an emphatic touch of archaic solemnity (see Brink [1982] ad loc.; see also the parody of Ennius in *Sat.* 1.2.37). But isn't it funny that the etymological meaning is so coherent with the theme of this section, 'It pays to know how poets are to be compensated ...'? The epistle to Florus has a less official addressee, and is much less reticent: poverty has drawn Horace to poetry after Philippi, *unde simul primum me dimisere Philippi ... inopemque ... paupertas impulit audax / ut versus facerem* (2.2.49). After the extreme solemnity of *Caesaris Augusti* in the preceding line, the reader has a split second to decide whether *Philippi* here has something to do with *Philippi* of *Ep.* 2.1.234: 'after money had left me helpless ...'. The grandiosity of Alexander, who pays in coins named after his father, is not that far from Augustus', who issues coins with his own portrait. Once again, one must choose between the harmony of the result and the memory of the contradictions (Lefèvre [1988] 344, concludes that Horace, even in the epistle to Florus, is interested in 'nicht die äussere, sondern die innere Situation', and that the accent falls 'auf dem seelischen, nicht auf dem materiellen Nichts').

11. Courtney (1992) 159, even when referring to the well-known testimonies to poor reception of Cicero's line, concludes (contrary to my own reading) that even if Horace knew the line, he did not find it faulty.

12. Baldo (1989) notes the poignant use of *iussa* in the *Ars*.

13. See Brink (1982) ad loc. The commercial metaphor does not seem to be attested elsewhere in poetry.

14. After *grande ... nomen, Nasonem* could contain a pun: now 'Naso' is a big name; critics *non fastidiunt* – 'don't turn up their noses' at it (see the uses of *nasutus, nasus, suspendere naso* in parallel contexts).

15. See e.g. Brink (1982) 488.

16. Probably a play on words; see Barchiesi (1994a) 293 n. 43.

17. Wiedemann (1975) is still fundamental; Nugent (1990) is of interest on the consequences for literary interpretation.

18. The works written in exile are a strange sort of elegiac palinode: the reader always has to hesitate between effacing and re-evoking the elegy of the past. The *Tristia* begin with a line, *Parve (nec invideo) sine me, liber, ibis in urbem*, that resembles in a curious way the beginning of an erotic epigram, Strat. *AP* 12.208: is there perhaps a common model in erotic poetry? *Ex Ponto* 4 closes with a desperate farewell, *non habet in nobis iam nova plaga locum* (16.52); we have a parallel Greek epigram that refers to Cupid's wounds, Archias *AP* 5.98.2. There is some pathos in the fact that the reader can never completely forget that this poet was born for a different kind of poetry.

19. Brink (1982) 37ff., with pertinent bibliography.

20. On Augustus as reader, Nugent (1990) 249, 254, offers good suggestions. Sharrock (1994) is an important work dealing with the *Ars*.

21. I can thus avoid dealing with the historicist objections of Williams (1978) 53-101, in whose view modern readers are chronically incapable of accepting the conventions of panegyric, and thus practise illusory subversive readings. See also Barchiesi (1994a) 24-5.

22. Other implicit examples of the theme in *Tristia* 2 are: (1) the *Ars* is replete with praises of the Princeps (62, *mille locis* – a patent falsehood); (2) *at si me iubeas domitos Iovis igne Gigantas / dicere, conantem debilitabit onus* (333-4); in *Am.* 2.1.12, Ovid begins a Gigantomachy, *et satis oris erat* (*satis oris* = 'enough voice', but also 'brazen faced'); (3) 'who, if not Homer, has told us about the shameful adultery of Ares and Aphrodite?' (337-8); the answer is, for those of us who have read the *Ars*, at least one other, Publius Ovidius Naso; (4) 'others have written on women's makeup' (487), but then what of the *Medicamina faciei* (see Gomez Pallarès [1993])?

Ovid does not try to exploit the circumstance that Augustus himself has dabbled in poetry. But in lines 525ff., as an example of austere mythology, he cites Ajax and Medea, the titles of two tragedies of varying success, composed respectively by Octavian and Ovid.

23. *Venus tuta* recalls the sexual theory of Horace, *Sat.* 1.2.47-8 (and note also *Sat.* 1.4.113, *concessa ... Venere uti*, both cited by Pianezzola, commenting on *Ars* 1.53). But, in Horace, restraint from adultery is the focal point of the discourse, something certainly not true for Ovid's *Ars*. The goddess of sex, moreover, is all but *tuta* in the *Ars amatoria*: in a programmatic passage of Book 2 (on which cf. Sharrock [1994]), Venus is caught red-handed in adultery (2.580-8) and risks heavy sanctions. Five lines after the excursus on Venus and Vulcan, the poet repeats his self-defence of Book 1: *En, iterum testor: nihil hic nisi lege remissum / luditur: in nostris instita nulla iocis* (2.599-600). The reassurance that 'in this light-hearted poetry no robes of matrons are to be found' sounds a bit ambiguous after Venus – a wedded wife *and* adulteress – has been caught in the act and exposed to the eyes of all completely *nuda* (2.580-4).

24. Activity that presupposes free time and which is nurtured by leisure. In 2.235 Ovid has already pointed out that *otium* is a gift from Augustus to his subjects, an old theme of *encomia* (Verg. *Ecl.* 1.6), which in this context however creates a contiguity between the Princeps and the vices which his moral reforms are trying to curb (see Holleman [1988] 391).

25. On 2.358, *mulcendis auribus* and the theme of persuasion, see Nugent (1990) 254.

26. See e.g. Owen (1924) 59, 'the survey in the *Tristia* is of a ... systematic nature ... such as is not often found in Latin writers.'

27. On the reception of Ennius in elegiac poetry, see Jocelyn (1986) 105ff.

28. See Barchiesi (1994a) 18-19, and also Ch. 2 n. 20 above.

29. For (a) see 2.529-30: *bella sonant alii ... pars tua facta canunt*; for (b) see 2.531-2; Prop. 2.34.58; for (c) see 2.533-7; Prop. 2.34.61-4; for (d) see 2.537-8; Prop. 2.34.67-76.

30. It is important that the Virgilian example is the last among the many poets reviewed in the structure of *Tristia* 2.

31. Tib. 1.6.7-8: *sed credere durum est: / sic etiam de me pernegat usque viro.*

32. 1.2.15: *tu quoque ne timide custodes, Delia, falle.*

33. 1.6.9-10: *ipse miser docui, quo posset ludere pacto / custodes. Heu heu nunc premor arte mea.*

34. 1.6.25-6: *saepe, velut gemmas eius signumque probarem, / per causam memini me tetigisse manum.*

35. 1.2.21: *illa [sc. Venus docet] viro coram nutus conferre loquaces*; 1.6.19-20: *neu te decipiat nutu, digitoque liquorem / ne trahat et mensae ducat in orbe notas.*

36. 1.6.13-14: *tunc sucos herbasque dedi, quis livor abiret, / quem facit impresso mutua dente venus.*

37. 1.6.15-16: *at tu, fallacis coniunx incaute puellae, / me quoque servato, peccet ut illa nihil.*

38. 1.6.31-2: *ille ego sum ... instabat tota cui tua nocte canis.*

39. 1.5.74: *solus et ante ipsas excreat usque fores.*

40. Della Corte (1980) 187.

41. In reality, Andromache is frequently cited in the *Ars*, even in sexual contexts that would be more fitting for Thais (2.709; 3.778).

42. The Telchines, enemies of Callimachus, bear the names of characters destroyed by Zeus' thunderbolt. The famous line of Callimachus, 'thundering is not for me, that's for Zeus' (fr. 1.20 Pf.) is sarcasm aimed at them, not merely a literary-critical metaphor. Ovid's Telchines seem, on the contrary, allied with that destructive power that can incinerate the world of elegy.

43. See Ov. *A.* 2.1.2, *nequitiae Naso poeta meae*; Prop. 2.34.55, *aspice me ....*

44. Kennedy (1993) 88-9.

45. Not to mention that in all the books of the *Tristia* the reader has to apply the *same* formula, despite the fact that Ovid's personal fortunes have changed (good observations in Lechi [1993]): just as in the past it was hard to tell apart the Insolent Muse and the real life of P. Ovidius Naso, the Sad Muse now assumes that the poet's life reflects her sadness.

46. Macleod (1980) 178.

47. This is the basic position of Syme (1978); see especially p. 221.

48. For the erotic symbolism linked to apples and fruit gathering, see Littlewood (1967).

49. *Excutiasque oculis otia nostra tuis* (2.224), literally, 'you find the time to examine with your eyes my disengaged poetry', perhaps implies a sort of gaze similar to that of the informer, the 'eye of the King'.

5. Future reflexive: two modes of allusion and the *Heroides*

*Different versions of this paper were read at Harvard, Columbia, Rutgers and Milan (Cattolica) in April 1992: I thank the audiences there, and Federica Bessone, Sergio Casali, Wendell Clausen, Leslie-Ann Crowley, Marco Fantuzzi, Stephen Hinds, Richard Hunter, for help and advice.

1. Goldhill (1991) 249f.

2. Kennedy (1984) 413-22.

3. I discuss the text with more details in Chapter 1 above.

4. Writing as a danger is a central theme in recent discussions of Euripides' *Hippolytus*, e.g. Segal (1986) 93 17f.; Goff (1990).

5. Apart from jokes like 4.166 *eris tauro saevior ipse truci?*; cf. Eur. *Hipp.* 1214 *tauron, agrion teras.*

6. Stinton (1965) 40ff.

7. In this perspective, as Richard Hunter points out, Dido is not even sure about her role as a ghost. Ovid plays a similar trick in *Am.* 3.9.58 (explained by Comacchia [1989] 101): Tibullus is dead and, as everybody knows, he had two mistresses. Delia says to Nemesis: 'I was a happier love than you'; Nemesis replies *me tenuit moriens deficiente manu*, an imitation of Tib. 1.1.60 *et teneam moriens deficiente manu*: she 'steals' a line that Tibullus had dedicated to his former mistress, Delia. Nemesis is (as her name promises) avenged.

8. Again (see n. 4), Ovid focuses on the theme of communication and distortion which is so important for modern readers of the tragedy; on the *Trachiniae*, Segal (1986) and (1981) 94ff.

9. *Semivir* has a further shade of irony: Nessus is of course a half-man (half-beast), and his action is dictated by an excess of masculinity – but this adjective, before Ovid starts to use it in our passage of the *Heroides*, evokes a lack of virility ('effeminate', 'eunuch': Virg. *Aen.* 4.215). See also G. Rosati (1990) 161-5, who has good arguments for keeping *letifero*, but explains the passage without accepting any form of foreshadowing.

10. For a good survey of attested ephymnia see Schmid (1934) 144 n. 8. Wilamowitz, for example, was fond of recovering repetitions skipped by the transmission of the text, so the number of refrains is liable to considerable oscillation, depending on editorial choices. It was, anyway, a striking feature of tragic diction for readers of any age; Ovid could have profited from the hexametrical recycling of tragic ephymnia (Pasquali [1964²] 245; Fantuzzi [1985] 158) attempted by the author of the *Lament for Adonis*.

11. Suggested by Sergio Casali, a pupil of G.B. Conte at the Scuola Normale di Pisa, who articulates this interpretation in his doctoral dissertation on *Her.* 9 (see now Casali 1995).

12. Knox (1986) 210.

13. Well pointed out by Knox, art. cit., 213 and n. 21. The adverb is frequent in comedy, attested for almost all the Republican tragic poets (Naev. 25; Pac. 118; Acc. 508 R.²); in Augustan poetry only Virg. *Aen.* 9.255, in direct speech (as is frequent for words from old tragedy in Virgil: interestingly, the speaker is a very old man) and Ov. *Met.* 3.557, in the story of Pentheus, a passage influenced by Pacuvian tragedy.

14. Given the affinity with Maenadism (*feror huc illuc*), one might suggest Bacchus as a candidate (so, with excessive confidence, Arcellaschi [1990] 292f.); in Euripides, Jason sees a daimon inside her; in Apollonius, of course, Eros is the hidden force. Ovid alludes to the mysterious depths of Medea's *animus*: the ultimate divine presence is impossible to identify, but the analogy with Dionysiac possession suggests a complicity between tragic character and tragic poet.

15. Ovid implies that only tragedy could give her *verba maiora*, i.e. words adequate to her feelings: cf. *Rem.* 375 *grande sonant tragici: tragicos decet ira cothurnos*; *Trist.* 2.554 *quaeque gravis debet verba cothurnus habet*. Cf. Aristoph. *Ran.* 1060-1.

16. See Hunter (1989) 185; 222f.; Hopkinson (1988) 192 ('plotter, contriver').

17. This point has been made, independently, by Stephen Hinds in a paper on intertextuality in *Her.* 12 (see now Hinds 1993), a welcome coincidence in this area of subtle hints and allusions to missing texts. Note also that Amata's frenzy (*maius nefas, maiorem furorem Aen.* 7.386) is parallel to (and a necessary implement of) Virgil's *maius opus*.

18. In Ap. Rh. 3.1107-8, Medea makes an interesting statement: 'I am not identical to Ariadne.' The reader has to unravel different perspectives: 'I will be different: I will not follow Jason as she did with Theseus' (see Hunter ad loc.); '*she* will be like A.' because she will betray father and brother; because she will be betrayed ('after' Apollonius) like Ariadne; '*she* will be different, a tremendous witch and avenger, not a victim like A.'; '*she* will be raised to the skies, like A.' (see Goldhill [1991] 304).

19. There is a vast bibliography on tragic irony in the *Trachiniae*, e.g. Halleran (1988) 129-31 (pointing out the polysemy of *baptô*); a similar strategy can be seen in Ov. *Her.* 10.142 *infecit sanguis*).

20. The address '*lectule*' defines a shared topos of neoteric and early Augustan poetry (Ticidas 1 Morel; Prop. 2.15.2).

21. Verducci (1985) 262ff.

22. Propertius (1.3.1-2) starts with a sleeping Ariadne in an elegy in which he will play, according to perspectives, both Dionysus and Theseus (so A. Wlosok [1967] 352).

23. See e.g. 10.59-60 *vacat insula cultu;* / *non hominum video, non ego facta boum*; this is a topos of unlucky explorations (Hom. *Od.* 10.98 *entha men oute boôn out' andrôn phaineto erga* before meeting the cannibals) but contrast e.g. *OLD* s.v. 'Naxos': 'most fertile of the Cyclades, famous for its wine and worship of Dionysus'. At 10.132 *auctores saxa fretumque tui* is again a topos (starting from *Il.* 16.34-5 'not Peleus and Thetis, but the blue sea and steep rocks are your parents') but it comes near to reality if one pauses to think that Theseus is either the son of Poseidon or of a man who is going to give his name to the Aegean sea. Many topoi used by Ariadne can be seen as the *recto* of a surprising future. On anticipations of the arrival of Dionysus see above, pp. 24-5.

24. Failure to explain why Ariadne is so confused in reporting what she sees (*vidi ... aut vidi aut ...*) has proved a difficult problem. In the light of my interpretation I could accept both the texts offered by N. Heinsius (*aut vidi aut quod erant quae me vidisse putarem*) and Palmer (*aut vidi aut tamquam quae me vidisse putarem*), but they are inferior on stylistic grounds: *tamquam* is particularly weak and looks like an explicative insertion, and *quod erant quae* is clumsy. For less convincing attempts see e.g. Ronconi (1958) 147-8; Giomini (1959) 80.

25. A point made by Verducci (1985) 261. Note that Ovid has *candida ... velamina* where Catullus has Ariadne losing a veil (*amictus*, 64.64 and 68) as a sign of dismay.

26. On imitation and reflexivity I would single out (from different perspectives) Alter (1975); Hollander (1981) ('transumption'; see also Barkan [1991] 41-8); Conte (1986) 57-69 and now Hinds (1998).

27. I am combining some recent responses to this provocative passage: Hopkinson (1984) 140; Goldhill (1986) 27-8; and particularly Bing (1988) 76 n. 42. On the hypothesis that Zeus is a Cretan, his statement sounds like a version of the famous *mentiens* (Cic. *Div.* 2.11 with Pease ad loc.), *ho pseudomenos*. This ill-famed paradox is attested in conjunction with another Alexandrian master: in his funerary epigram (explained by Cameron [1991] 536) Philitas is said to have died of consumption, pondering this enigma (Athen. 401d). Contrast *Hymn. Hom.* 1.6 *pseudomenon*, a traditional manoeuvre to discard alternative versions for the birthplace of a god.

28. The Cretan 'monopoly' on Zeus is connected with a justification of pederasty via the 'invention' of the Ganymede myth (so Plato, *Leg.* 636d) and with the scandalous forging of a tomb of Zeus (Call. *Hymn.* 1.8-9, immediately after our problematic tag). In the *Certamen Homeri et Hesiodi* (94-101) Homer answers the embarrassing question 'sing about something which is not present, nor future, nor past' with a couple of verses about the tomb of Zeus, the ultimate fiction of all time.

29. See e.g. Harrison (1972-3) 10-25; Zetzel (1983) 86 and n. 6; Clay (1988) 195ff.

30. As observed by Hardie (1990) 226 n. 14.

31. Kenney (1970) 388-414, provides the best interpretation and synkrisis with Callimachus. Rosati (1989) 26-9, is helpful on the narrative technique.

32. A dangerous assumption, since the text of the oath transmitted by Aristaenetus and the *Diegesis* (p. 71 Pf.) does not scan and, moreover, it is a notorious *faux pas* to make assumptions about what Callimachus should tell, or omit, in his capricious narrations. My leap of faith is based on the joint evidence of Aristaenetus, Ovid and the *Diegesis*: these three versions, each in his very different stylization, are unanimous in showing that the plot needs the oath as a focal point. Note also that Callimachus is not reworking a well-known mythical story: the elision of a basic moment in the story could not be recovered *ex silentio* by the reader's competence.

33. On the creativity of lovers see also *Her.* 2.21-2 *fidus amor ... finxit et ad causas ingeniosa fui.* Phyllis, 'witty and versed in causes', is, as far as we know (fr. 556 Pf.), a character from the *Aitia*: again, the use of *causae* could be a deft touch of reflexivity. The conceit 'Love makes you clever and eloquent' can be paralleled in a third episode from the *Aitia*, the story of Pieria (in the third book, like Acontius and Cydippe): Aphrodite trains orators superior to Nestor (fr. 82 Pf.). This Callimachean material is of course relevant to the genealogy of the topos *ingenium nobis ipsa puella facit* (on which see the next paragraph).

34. For *gracilis* as a response to *leptos, leptaleos*, see Prop. 2.13.3; Ov. *Pont.* 2.5.26. On female bodies as poetic programmes see Wyke (1989) 118ff.

35. The interpretation of *ennuchion* as a reference to *incubatio* (see Hopkinson [1988] 106) is not so evident, since this is not an obvious practice for the Delphic oracle. Pfeiffer explains '*in adyto*', quoting Aristaen. 1.10 *ho d'Apollôn panta saphôs ton patera didaskei*, and thus discarding any metaphorical explanation. Fr. 765 Pf., however, shows that *ennuchion* in Callimachus could mean 'obscure'. Possibly the adjective connotes not the message – which is crystal clear, for an oracle: 'take Acontius as a son in-law' – but the *style* boldly adopted by Callimachus: Apollo starts from a series of places where Artemis was *not* at the time of the oath, and ends with glosses about Cean history: rituals, the etymology of 'Etesian winds', the migration of quails. The oracle is a compressed version of Callimachus' poetic technique, and *ennuchion epos* could be taken as a humorous self-reference. Ovid explicitly comments on the problem of translating the difficult manner of Callimachus in *Ib.* 55ff. *utque ille historiis involvam carmina caecis ... utque mei versus aliquantum noctis habebunt* etc.

36. In my opinion, the use of *carmina* in 238 ('as inexplicable as in the last verse' Palmer ad loc.) is unobjectionable: every oracle is a *carmen*, and Cydippe sees a *carmen* on the apple in 21.109. Cydippe of course means 'oaths and oracles' and the reader is free to overhear 'every kind of poetry is on your side'. But the use of *mea carmina* at 237 is a real problem: 'Cydippe is not a poet' (Reeve [1973] 336 n. 7). No other character in the *Heroides* refers unambiguously to her letter as 'poetry': 7.1 *moriturae carmen Elissae* is in a distich omitted by the main mss; 15.6 *mea ... carmina* is in a spurious letter – and, moreover, represents no exception: the letter is by none other than Sappho. I would consider emending *mea* to *tua carmina* in 237: 'the god, the vates, and your verses (i.e. the oath, and the epigram which reduplicates it in 20.241-2) all tell the same story: every kind of poetry supports your desire'.

37. See Hopkinson (1988) 102.

38. Both 20 and 21 have a degree of formal closure which is exceptional in the *Heroides* (9.168 is in a very different situation): VALE is the final word. Ovid spares this last word for his last, Callimachean epistles; Callimachus, less obviously, closes his *Aitia* with a *chaire* (fr. 112.8 Pf., in the last distich of the *Epilogue*).

39. Dilthey (1863) 78; Cairns (1969) 131-4; Fedeli (1980) 418f.

40. Kenney (1983) 46-52; Ross (1975) 72f.

41. The genealogy includes Propertius (2.1.4 *ingenium nobis ipsa puella facit*; 2.30.40 *nam sine te nostrum non valet ingenium*) and Ovid himself as poet of the *Amores* (2.17.34; 3.12.16).

42. Clausen (1970) 93. See also Hunter (1993).

43. A very thorough discussion in Citroni (1979) 91-100.

44. Wiseman (1969) 17-18 'The promise is not to keep writing about the brother's death, but to keep writing *carmina maesta* – which means ... to keep writing elegiacs. And, of course, the rest of the collection *is* in elegiacs.' Note also Hinds (1987a) 103-6. On 116 and its implications, Macleod (1983) 181-6.

45. But see below, on nightingales and poetry.

46. As will be evident, I have a vested interest in *canam*, but *tegam* is unacceptable on all counts.

47. Hopkinson (1988) 249 suggests that this etymology is relevant to Callimachus, *Epigr.* 2. For 'nightingales' as poetry see Call. fr. 1.16 Pf. (as integrated by Housman) and *Epigr.* 2.6 (with Gow-Page and Hopkinson ad loc.; Williams [1991] 121 n. 11).

48. The simile shares with Catullus an allusion to Homeric models (see the commentaries). Many have observed a parallelism between Orpheus and the Gallus of *Eclogue* 10. In general, both *elegos* and *questus* can be applied both to nightingales and to elegy; Hinds (1987a) 104, analyses a mythological nightingale-simile from Ovid's *Fasti* and suggests a programmatic nuance. On the Greek tradition see Kannicht (1969) II, 282-5.

49. See also 20.7-8; 99; Aristaen. 1.10 (with a refined poetical simile for the colour of Cydippe's cheeks); Kenney (1970) 411 n. 42 'her blushes ... no doubt figured in the Callimachean narrative', with Dietzler (1933) 37. *Sensi* is a perfect 'shifter' from narrative to *Icherzählung*.

50. Catullus would be saying 'even if my sorrow keeps me away from poetry (but could also promote a different kind of poetry, a new elegiac vein) don't think that I have forgotten your request about *carmina Battiadae*'; then the simile, while picturing a situation of oblivion, confusion and loss, simultaneously proves – through content and style – that Callimachus is being offered and the request is not forgotten. Of course we have great problems in assessing Catullus' relationship to the addressee, Hortensius Hortalus (see Citroni [1979] for this line of enquiry), but I assume that a poetical strategy should be understandable even without this substantial information.

51. This kind of 'double motivation' – writing elegy around a personal loss, writing elegy in a literary tradition – is parallel to a double motivation typical of Augustan elegy: the genre is both (either) dictated from love at first sight, and (or) inspired by Callimachus' Muses. I have tried to show that this duplicity is important for the Acontius epistle.

6. Tropes of intertextuality in Roman epic

1. The assignment was 'Intertextuality in epic' (the conference is mentioned below, Chapter 7, note 1).

1a. Simonides (PMG 59) already cites by name his predecessors, Homer and Stesichorus; cf. also the explicit Homeric quotation in *FEG* 20.14 and 19.1-2 West ([2]).

2. Apolline revelations and prophecies play an almost obsessive role in Valerius, as if a heightened sense of belatedness and imitation lead the Roman poet to over-stress and make explicit the prophetic passages from Apollonius. Valerius' ship is from the proem onwards endowed with clairvoyance (1.2: *fatidica*). The Argonauts even have two competing Apolline prophets on board, Mopsus and Idmon. Valerius represents himself in the proem as a *quindecimvir* (1.5ff.), one of the priests in charge of preserving the Sibylline Books, and his invocation to Phoebus (1.5) is at once a submissive bow to Apollonius (1.1) and a declaration of his professional expertise. The prophet Phineus, already present in Apollonius but kept in check by a mysterious censorship, appears in Valerius as a repository of almost bookish knowledge, like a reader who has learned the plot beforehand

(4.438ff.: *novimus ... legens ... sensi ... vates ... Apollo*). The poem's clear prophetic consciousness is thus also a way of living within – and resigning oneself to – the shadow of a fully written and hence restrictive model. Important pages in Feeney (1991) 315-18. On the connection between prophecy and intertextuality in Virgil, see also below, n. 16.

3. In reality, as far as I can see, this is more a cunning move than a naïve acknowledgement of debt. I am forced, for reasons of space, to resist the temptation to include in my overview the *Achilleid*. Narrating Achilles' education – his apprenticeship, his becoming a hero through heroic song – transforms into a narrative plot the very conditions of the work's own production, that is, Statius' assimilation of the epic tradition. This Achilles, who learns heroic songs transmitted by his teacher Chiron, is among the richest 'figures of intertextuality' in Rome.

4. If you feel the need for a new treatment of our sense of guilt with respect to writing and our nostalgia for lost orality, see Dupont (1994), which casts books, Romans, and philologists in the part of the bad guys, and as the good guys, symposia and *mouvance*.

5. The analysis of Barkan (1986) 243-7 has already become a classic.

6. The irony is even stronger in this case if Conrad's novel is indeed an allegory of reading as a search for an absent centre, as it appears to Todorov (1993) 202.

7. Most (1992) 1014-25.

8. See e.g. Smith (1990) 133-4; Hardie (1997).

9. See e.g. Lynn-George (1988).

10. Assuming, as seems correct for numerous reasons, that Naevius had not already staged an erotic encounter after Anchises and Aeneas disembark in Africa. But this is not a question that can be dealt with in a footnote.

11. Perutelli (1974) has well noted the function of the 'incipit-like' signals in Hector's speech as retold by Aeneas.

12. See Hardie (1993) 102-3, which has inspired this whole paragraph.

13. On the dream appearance, compare *Aen.* 2.270, *in somnis, ecce* with *Ann.* 2 Sk., *somno leni placidoque revinctus*; and 2.271: *visus adesse mihi*, with *Ann.* 3 Sk., *visus Homerus adesse poeta*.

For weeping, compare *Aen.* 2.271, *largosque effundere fletus* with Lucr. 1.124-5, *lacrumas effundere salsas / coepisse.*

For the exclamation, compare 2.274 with *Ann.* 442 Sk. On the possibility of fragment 442 being part of the dream, see Skutsch (1985) 600-1, and for the reconstruction of the dream, see pp. 153-8. Petrarch in his *Africa* takes the same path in reverse, when he writes at 9.175: *aspice, qualis erat quondam cum vixit Homerus.* Aware of the Ennian model from Virgilian glosses, he adapted Hector's apparition to his own apparition of Homer, thus resuscitating in his own way the shade of Ennius. See Hardie (1993) 103 n. 22.

14. Once again, for weeping, compare *Aen.* 6.686, *effusaeque genis lacrimae* with Lucr. cit.

For *pietas*, compare 6.688, *tuaque expectata parenti ... pietas* with *Ann.* 4 Sk., *o pietas animi.*

For the destiny of souls, see *Ann.* 5 Sk., *desunt rivos camposque remanant.*

15. One can compare the oblique and indirect character of programmatic suggestions in the *Aeneid*'s 'proem in the middle' (see Conte [1992] 153; Thomas [1983] 92ff.).

16. Virgil presents the prophecy as a real text requiring interpretation: the voyage of Book 3 begins as an effort to decode, through misreadings and with the help of marginal notes, the 'Homeric' voice of Delian Apollo.

17. For the historical implications of this textual reshaping, see e.g. Gruen (1993) 12-13.

18. I accept the interpretation of Williams (1978) in his comment ad loc.

19. See Heyworth (1993) 255-7; Barchiesi (1994b) 438-43.

20. For Callimachus' presence at the end of Book 3, see Geymonat (1993) 323ff.

21. For the sake of brevity, I refer to my discussion of this episode in Barchiesi (1994c) 109-24.

22. 2.268ff.: *longa est series, sed nota malorum / persequar* (compare *Aen.* 1.341-2); 1.7: *longa retro series*; *series* is a fitting term for both the chain of crimes and tragedies that is the history of Thebes, and for the form of the necklace, a weaving and joining together of threads, scraps and fragments of various sorts.

23. See *Aitia* fr. 1 Pf.; *amica / certatim iuvere manu* (2.274-5) is a disingenuous definition. These evil creatures collaborate for once with unusual benevolence, but only because the created object is both epic and ominous, as well suits their poetic and personal tastes.

24. Feeney (1991) 363ff.

25. Dazzled by the symbols of the solar cult, and aware of being in a sanctuary of Apollo-Helios (5.407-9), the heroes visit the temple as if it were a palace of the Sun. In this way Valerius alludes to the great ecphrasis of the doors of the Sun's exotic palace in Ovid's *Metamorphoses* (2.1-18), making Ovid one of his main models in this phase of narrative which focuses on the 'oriental despotism' of barbarian Colchis (see *Met.* 1.778-9, on Phaethon's march to the Far East). On the other hand, Valerius may have learned much from the use of ecphrasis in Apollonius, whose strategy of inserting digressions into the poem – clearly influential on Virgil as well – is in Valerius even more complex and charged with programmatic value (see Hunter [1993] 53-4, 149).

26. The Argonauts are perplexed and the Colchians, even if they do not comprehend (*nondum noscentibus*, 5.452) the obscure prophetic object (*caelarat*, 434, perhaps contains a pun on *celare*, to hide), turn aside their gaze out of disgust at the image of Medea flying over Corinth (5.454: *odere tamen visusque reflectunt*).

27. 5.448, *omnes secum dequesta labores*, makes one think that Medea will have to pass from epic to Ovidian elegy and then tragedy before the plot comes to an end.

28. On these lines, which are almost a *recusatio*, cf. Clauss (1993) 20-1.

29. Fowler (1996) insightfully examines this highly original passage.

30. There do not appear to be other examples of this formula as openings for description (see M. Barchiesi [1962] 275). There are no other cases in poetic ecphrasis apart from Virg. *Aen.* 6.26, *Cnosia tellus: hic Minotaurus inest*, in which however *hic ... inest* is a 'secondary determination' (ib.), that is, it refers to a space internal to the image rather than, as in Naevius and in Silius, to the relation between artistic object and the space of the depictions. In addition to the parallel examples of this formula in Greek collected by Barchiesi and by Mayer (1887) 267ff., I would suggest Eur. *Ion* 1146ff.: *enên d' 'huphantai grammasin toiad' huphai; ouranos ....*

31. For Lutatius at 687-91, see fragments 46-7 B. from Naevius Book 7. For Venus (the last line of the description) see 6.697: *Haec Eryce e summo spectabat laeta Dione*. For a possible connection between Naevius (fr. 16 B.), the cult of Aphrodite / Venus / Astarte in Sicily, and the foundation of the Capitoline temple of Venus in 217 BCE, cf. Feeney (1991) 109-11.

32. Naturally Naevius might exist as a poet for Silius even if he did not read him directly. At any rate, Silius' style makes it difficult to detect borrowings even from the more modern Ennius, an author Silius surely read. I bring to attention moreover that direct awareness of Naevius is still attested in Nero's time through Caesius Bassus. In cultural formation if not in time of writing, Silius is for all purposes a Neronian author.

33. Silius signals to educated readers that this is a blatant historical falsehood at vv. 390-2: *sed vos, Calliope, nostro donate labori | nota parum* [!] *magni longo tradantur ut aevo | facta viri, et meritum vati sacremus honorem.* Perhaps this has precedent in Virgil, who stylized his warrior king Messapus as a worthy ancestor of a future poet of heroic deeds (see my observations in Barchiesi [1995] 5-18).

34. The tradition according to which Naevius fought in the war and had mentioned this fact in his poem goes back to Gellius 17.21 and to the first book of Varro's *De poetis*.

It is worth noting moreover that the temple is at Liternum near Capua. Silius, a collector of Roman memorabilia living in Campania, might well have known that Naevius came from that area (see Gellius 1.24.2, where *Campanus* means 'from Capua'; Rowell [1949] 17-34). The idea of a temple decorated with poetic images and located in the very homeland of the poet may have a pertinent parallel in Virgil *G* 3.13ff., the temple in Mantua that Virgil evokes to celebrate his own future poetic glory and his Roman epic project. On the other hand, the choice of Liternum must also contain a reference to Scipio, future hero of the new war and of the *Punica*, see Nesselrath (1986) 213. Hannibal eradicates the memory of the war from the very site that will be consecrated to the new conqueror – *his* conqueror.

35. The fundamental introduction to intertextual acoustics is Hollander (1981).

36. As will be clear, my discussion is in harmony with Bonanno's survey of the tradition as it concerns Theocritus, Virgil and Propertius (1990) 195-201. I am glad that our contributions share the same acoustic dimension and echo one another. Further reflections on the echo and intertextuality in Hinds (1998).

37. Nicander, fr. 48 Schneider, took the important initiative of transforming Hylas into an echo (presupposing that we can trust Antoninus Liberalis' [46] reference to Nicander). See also Fedeli (1980) 482-4, who explains how in Prop. 1.20 the *nomen* is indeed the echo of the name 'Hylas' that Heracles cries out.

38. Cf. Malamud-McGuire Jr. (1993) 213 (noted also by Hollander [1981] 13).

39. 'Once again' expresses both the phonic and intertextual reiteration of the name; *reclamat*, coming after the Virgilian *clamassent*, is a gloss on this process of replicating what has already been said/written. The forceful repetition, *Hylan ... Hylan*, called out by Heracles in a thundering voice, is paradoxically the acoustic source from which Virgil offered a fading echo (with the rare prosodic effect *Hyla Hyla*, on which cf. Traina in Traina-Bernardi Perini [1992] 280, not strictly pertaining to my theme, but too fine not to quote in full: 'in the prosodic languishing of the repeated word one almost hears a cry of farewell trailing off into absolute silence'). The end result is that the Virgilian model becomes, so to speak, an echo of its imitation.

40. I.e. 'Intertestualità. Il dialogo fra testi nelle letterature classiche' (*Lexis* 13 [1995]). The importance of the connection between poetic song and the production of echoes had already been announced in *Ecl* 1.5: *formosam resonare doces Amaryllida silvas*, where the agreement with Longus 2.7.6, 'I used to praise Echo because she joined me in calling the name of Amaryllis', noted by Clausen (1994) 37, is worth considering. If Longus depends on a Greek model also known to Virgil, this might mean that in the 'proemial' space of the *Eclogues* Virgil too was playing with the proximity of acoustic and textual repetition. In that case it would be even clearer that there is no natural and absolute separation between the self-consciousness of a latecomer and that of a 'classic' poet. (On the question of the relationship between critical value-judgments and the study of intertextuality see below, Chapter 7, point 7.)

41. For etymological puns on Hylas/*hule*, cf. Opelt (1966) col. 807; Arg. *Orph.* 645 (with comments of Agosti [1994] 179 n. 17); and especially Strab. 12.4.3:

ἑορτή ... καὶ ὀρειβασία θιασευόντων καὶ καλούντων Ὕλαν, ὡς ἂν κατὰ ζήτησιν τὴν ἐκείνου πεποιημένων τὴν ἐπὶ τὰς ὕλας ἔξοδον.

7. Some points on a map of shipwrecks

1. Even a short paper must make room to acknowledge debts and thefts. My thanks, first, to Stephen Hinds, who promoted and animated the conference in Seattle and allowed me to preview his important new book (see below, n. 4); to Don Fowler for his generous production of ideas in his reviews, which have for some years made *Greece and Rome* my starting point for critical investigations; to Gian Biagio Conte; to Maria Grazia Bonanno, Lowell Edmunds, and Pierre Judet de la Combe, for their contributions to the discussion at a conference on intertextuality held in Cagliari and coordinated by V. Citti (1994; cf. *Lexis* vol. 13, 1995).

2. Wills (1996a) 33.

3. Conference proceedings originally published in *MD* 39 (1997).

4. This idea of intertextuality can be seen, e.g., in the use of the term 'effetti' in the subtitle of my book on Homer and Virgil (*Effetti omerici nella narrazione virgiliana*; see Barchiesi [1984]), or in the subtitle of Stephen Hinds' book on the art of allusion (*Dynamics of Appropriation in Roman Poetry*; see Hinds [1998]), or finally in the bivalent use of 'possession' in Nagy (1990), *Pindar's Homer: The Lyric Possession of the Epic Past*. Also of note is Edmunds' theoretical 'tune-up': 'For intertextuality itself is the code ... These are not facts that can be isolated from the two poems but are always *in a state of transition* from the Greek to the Latin poem. The intertextual code keeps the similarity and the difference in play' (Edmunds [1992] 120; emphasis mine).

5. Among the endless recent bibliography I point to a few works that will lead readers back to earlier research: Tatum (1984); Skulky (1985); Johnston (1987); Conte-Barchiesi (1989) 106-8; Smith (1993); Lyne (1994); Drew Griffith (1995); Wills (1996b).

6. In *Ecl.* 3.40-1, Virgil had already quoted the beginning of the *Lock*, allowing us to see the Callimachean model instead of the Catullan (cf. Cassio [1973] 329-32). Similarly, Hor. *Odes* 1.22.23-4 recalls Sappho (*loquentem*) through Cat. 51.5.

7. Cf. Hunter (1995) 24-5. In his view, Apollonius epicized Callimachean elegy just as Virgil epicized the Catullan tradition of the oath. The lock swears to Queen Berenice 'by your head' in Callimachus and Catullus. Medea in Apollonius swears to Queen Arete, calling to witness 'the light of the sun and the rites of the night-wandering daughter of Perses'. In Virgil Aeneas swears to Queen Dido 'by the stars, the gods, and the Underworld'. In favour of Apollonian influences on the Virgilian context, see also Hunter (1987) 138-9. It is truly surprising that Aeneas finds inspiration in the words of Medea when speaking to a woman who feels betrayed by him, in other words, a sort of new Medea.

8. Koenen (1993) 95 draws perhaps excessive consequences from Callimachus' use of the masculine. It may be of interest to survey various interpreters' comments: Van Sickle (1968) 499 contrasts the masculine Callimachus with the Catullan 'feminization'; Puelma (1982) 240: 'ein lebhaft junges Mädchen ... eine Art Kammerzofe'; Gutzwiller (1992) 374: 'a maiden, an intimate companion of

Berenike'; Koenen (1993) 94: 'Kallimachos' lock is male'. But a more systematic inquiry might be in order. If scholars of this level have reached opposing conclusions, this does not mean that the problem of gender is a false one. I would say rather that the Callimachean elegy poses the problem of sexual identity in very strong and paradoxical terms and tests the connection between reading and identification with the narrating voice.

In addition to this, it is worth noting that the lock's swearing 'by your head' has been transmitted to us on account of its exceptional use of a *feminine* term for head, *sên te karên*. The use of the feminine allomorph in Callimachus and the neoterics, studied from a lexical point of view by Lunelli (1969), also deserves consideration from the perspective of the 'feminization' of literature. On the complex problem of Callimachus' feminized poetic voice, see Bing (1995).

9. The problem of voice and sexual identity is particularly keen when the narrative voice of the Callimachean poem says 'I have left my sister locks who missed me' (fr. 110.51 Pf.). The voice speaking is grammatically ambiguous but a moment before it was part of a female body. Note that the sacrifice of the lock is motivated by Berenice's 'fraternal' love for her husband (on eros and monarchy in the poem, see Gutzwiller [1992]).

10. In the *Fasti* Ovid joins the death of Dido and the Callimachean language of hair and perfume, establishing a continuity between Carthage, Cyrene and Alexandria; see 3.561-2: *mixta bibunt molles lacrimis unguenta favillae / vertice libatas accipiuntque comas.*

11. Fitzgerald (1995) 196: 'Not only is speech in this poem [i.e. Catullus 66] displaced from a human speaker, but this speaker is itself displaced from its natural location. This displacement is appropriate to the function of the translated poem ....'

12. Achilles' newly rediscovered masculine identity still suffers some interferences; *te propter* (*Ach.* 1.654) seems to come from one of Dido's pathetic refrains (*Aen.* 4.320-1).

13. Already in the 1970s G.B. Conte's *Il genere e i suoi confini*, a work on 'intertextual dialogue' that has had no small influence, concluded by calling for a 'sociology of forms' that would connect cultural paradigms to the poetic art of allusion.

14. Rosenmeyer (1997) 123ff.

15. See the perceptive observations of Bonanno (1995) 289, concerning Stephen Greenblatt.

16. See Parsons and Lloyd-Jones (1983) 269: *'turgidus iste stilus et inanium iterationum strepitus'.*

17. Bowra (1957) 21-8.

18. For the use of *anastachuô*, see Ap. Rhod. 4.271; for warriors born from the earth as 'giants', see 3.1054 (compare Melinno's 'powerful and great men in arms').

19. *Le Acque Alte* vv. 1-7, from *Diario del '71 e '72* by E. Montale.

20. See Nisbet (1995) 414-30, the only previously unpublished piece in a volume of selected works.

21. See Fowler (1989) 97.

22. Nisbet seems to want to warn a new generation of critics against the sorrows suffered by Yeats's Fergus after he surrendered to Proteus:

> I see my life go drifting like a river
> from change to change; I have been many things ...
> But now I have grown nothing, knowing all ...

23. Pasquali (1964) 324, when daring a comparison with the ending of Plato's *Symposium*, remarks that one finds 'farewell formulas that I might call symbolic'.

24. It is worth noting that Meleager inspired at least three of the oldest programmatic incipits for Roman poetry collections, Propertius 1.1, and before him Catullus 1, and perhaps also the start of Virgil, *Eclogues* 1 (on which see Gutzwiller [1996] 95-6). Krevans (1984) offers new observations on the programmatic value of 1.38.

25. Moreover the idea of a sumptuous, Persian-style banquet makes one think of the debate that raged in Greece after the victory over the Persians: how should one celebrate the triumph, with moderation or by appropriating the luxury of the defeated? (For ancient testimonies, see the commentaries ad loc. that develop a hint in Lambinus.)

26. This point of view is developed, perhaps excessively, by West (1995) ad loc.

27. Nisbet (1995) 422.

8. Allusion and society: Ovid the Censor

1. See below, n. 18. My chapter is not directly affected by discussions on whether 3,11 is a continuous elegy or twin pieces; 3,11 b (in Kenney's OCT text) begins with a clear reworking of *odi et amo*.

2. Interestingly, the following epigram is an attack on people who steal and sell other people's poems. It is still unclear to what extent the arrangement of poems in book 12 resembles Martial's regular practice in the first eleven books (see Sullivan [1991] 54-5).

3. Possibly also in an edict to the people (Suet. *Aug.* 89.2).

4. I owe the reference to Professor McKeown.

5. See Kassel-Austin (1989) 664-5. The learned editors quote as *loci similes* the Metellan fragment, together with Men. fr. 578 Koerte.

6. It is normally assumed that the censor found immediate parody in Lucilius; see fr. 676-87 M. with Marx ad loc., and the thorough discussion, with bibliography, by Berger (1946) 320-8.

7. Reitzenstein (1896) 213-15.

8. Commager (1974) 71-4. On the passage in 2,30 note also Cairns (1971) 206. I came across the censorial fragment in Commager, but then found out that the parallel is recorded in McKeown's invaluable data-base for his forthcoming commentary to *Amores* book 3. He kindly advised me to write a short paper on the problem, since we had noticed the similarity of the two phrasings independently.

9. Badian (1983) 82-98.

10. McKeown (1987) 74-89. He argues at p. 78 that the *Ars* displays an awareness of political implications of elegiac mores which is absent from the *Amores*, written and published before the crisis of 2 BCE; but at p. 26, after quoting *Pont.* 3.3.29ff., he wonders why the *Amores* should have been considered any more innocent than the *Ars* was.

11. This tallies with two well-known Horatian allusions, to the marriage law in the *Carmen Saeculare*, and to the adultery law in *Odes* 4.5.21ff.

12. Links between the *Amores* and the *Leges Iuliae* have been explored in Stroh (1979) and Davis (1993).

13. See Barchiesi (1994a) 14-25 (poetry and delation); and 79-82 ('censorial' themes in the *Fasti*).

14. Though of course our views of the later poem could be affected by a reading of the *Amores* as a text 'guilty' of reference to the Julian legislation.

15. For doubts on the status of *Amores* 1-5 as a 'first edition' see the Appendix to this chapter.

16. On 2.19 and the *Leges Iuliae* see McKeown (1987) n. 11, 28.

17. On the strong nexus of *censura*, marriage and procreation in Roman political discourse see, e.g., Badian (1983) 95-6; Galinsky (1981) and Galinsky (1996) 128-40. On adultery as the transgression par excellence in Roman culture see Richlin (1981) 379-404; and Williams (1995) 533-5.

18. 3.11.7 *perfer et obdura*! cf. Cat. 8.11 *sed obstinata mente perfer, obdura*; 19 *at tu, Catulle, destinatus obdura*; 3.11.32-6 *luctantur pectusque leve in contraria tendunt / hac amor hac odium; sed, puto, vincit amor; / odero, si potero; si non, invitus amabo: / nec iuga taurus amat; quae tamen odit, habet*; 3.14.39 *tunc amo, tunc odi frustra, quod amare necesse est* with Cat. 85,1 *odi et amo*; 3.14.1 *non ego, ne pecces, cum sis formosa, recuso* with Cat. 76.23-4 *non iam illud quaero, contra me ut diligat illa, / aut, quod non potis est, esse pudica velit*; etc.

19. See in general Edwards (1993).

20. Of course in 3.1 he has already accepted a rehabilitation; Tragoedia has urged him '*cane facta virorum*' [v. 25]. An interesting anticipation of a tragedy called *Medea*.

21. 'Ovid's *Amores* is perhaps the only certain case of a revised ancient poetry book' (Cameron [1995] 115; but note his n. 55 'Ovid's juvenilia may have been less successful than generally supposed ... which might explain why no trace of the five-book edition has survived').

22. Both incipits can be related to a wider background of epigrammatic formulas, but what is really impressive is that those two introductory four-liners are both followed by the incipit *Arma* ... (*Aen.* 1.1; *Am.* 1.1.1); *this* analogy is not likely to be based on commonplace; note also the use of *edere* in *Am.* 1.1.2 (contrast Call. *Ait.* 1.21 Pf. 'as soon as I first took my pad ...'; Virg. *Ecl.* 6,3 'while I was singing ...'); *edere* is a technical word for author's publication, not just production, so *parabam/edere* implies that an Ovidian epic was ready before the malicious copy-editing of Cupid.

23. *Ille ego* presupposes as a model the sphragis of *Georgics* 4 and constructs itself as a sequel and integration of that model.

24. A valuable alternative hypothesis, suggested by one of the anonymous readers of the *American Journal of Ancient History* (where this chapter first appeared), is that the new collection was much the same as the previous one, but three books instead of five; longer books, but three of them, instead of shorter books, but five! This gives point to the epigram, but only if the audience was able to compare the two versions of the text and spot the joke. For another sceptical approach to the 'first edition' problem, see the second chapter of Holzberg (1997).

Bibliography

Adamietz, J. (1984) 'Zu Ovids Dido-Brief', *Würzb. Jahrb.* N.F. 10: 121-34

Agosti, G. (1994) 'Ila nella caverna (su Arg. Orph. 643-8)', *MD* 32: 175-92

Alter, R. (1975) *Partial Magic* (Berkeley-Los Angeles-London)

Anderson, W.S. (1973) 'The Heroides' in *Ovid*, ed. J.W. Binns (London-Boston) 49-83

Arcellaschi, A. (1990) *Médée dans le théâtre latin d'Ennius à Sénèque* (Rome)

Baca, A.R. (1971) 'The themes of *querela* and *lacrimae* in Ovid's Heroides', *Emerita* 39: 195-201

Badian, E. (1983) 'A phantom marriage law', *Philologus* 129: 82-98

Baldo, G. (1989) 'I *mollia iussa* di Ovidio', *MD* 22: 33-47

Barchiesi, A. (1984) *La traccia del modello: Effetti omerici nella narrazione virgiliana* (Pisa)

———— (1986) 'Problemi d'interpretazione in Ovidio: continuità delle storie, continuazione dei testi', *MD* 16: 77-107

———— (1989) 'Voci e istanze narrative nelle Metamorfosi di Ovidio', *MD* 23: 55-97

———— (1994a) *Il poeta e il principe: Ovidio e il discorso augusteo* (Rome-Bari)

———— (1994b) 'Immovable Delos', *CQ* 44: 438-43

———— (1994c) 'Rappresentazioni del dolore e interpretazione nell'*Eneide*', *A&A* 40: 109-24 (English tr. in *Virgil* ed. Ph. Hardie [London-New York, 1999] III 324-44)

———— (1995) 'Genealogie: Callimaco, Ennio e l'autocoscienza dei poeti augustei', in *Studia classica Iohanni Tarditi oblata*, ed. L. Belloni, G. Milanese and A. Porro, I (Milan) 5-18

———— (1999a) 'Venus' masterplot: Ovid and Homeric Hymns', in *Perspectives on Ovid's Metamorphoses*, ed. P. Hardie, S. Hinds and A. Barchiesi, *PCPS* Suppl. 23 (Cambridge) 112-26

———— (1999b) 'Vers une histoire à rebours de l'élégie latine: les *Héroides* "doubles" (16-21)', in *Elégie et epopée dans la poésie ovidienne (Heroides et Amours). En hommage à Simone Viarre*, ed. J. Fabre-Sarris and A. Deremetz (Lille) 53-67

———— (2002) 'Narratology in the Metamorphoses', in *The Cambridge Companion to Ovid*, ed. Ph. Hardie (Cambridge)

Barchiesi, M. (1962) *Nevio epico* (Padua)

Barkan, L. (1986) *The Gods Made Flesh* (New Haven-London)

———— (1991) *Transuming Passion* (Stanford)

Berger, A. (1946) 'A note on Gellius *NA* I.6', *AJPh* 67: 320-8

Bing, P. (1988) *The Well-read Muse* (Göttingen)

———— (1995) 'Callimachus and Hymn to Demeter', *Syllecta Classica* 6: 29-42

Boas, H. (1939) *Aeneas' Arrival in Latium* (Amsterdam)

Bömer, F. (1969-86) *P. Ovidius Naso: Metamorphosen* (Heidelberg)

Bonanno, M.G. (1990) *L'allusione necessaria* (Rome)

—— (1995) 'Tavola rotonda', *Lexis* 13: 289

Bonner, S.F. (1949) *Roman Declamation in the Late Republic and Early Empire* (Liverpool)

Bowra, C.M. (1957) 'Melinno's Hymn to Rome', *JRS* 47: 21-8

Brink, C.O. (1982) *Horace on Poetry III* (Cambridge)

—— (1985) *Horace on Poetry II The 'Ars poetica'* (Cambridge, 2nd ed.)

Brückner, C. (1983) *Ungehaltenen Reden ungehaltener Frauen* (Hamburg)

Büchner, K. (1957) *Humanitas Romana* (Heidelberg)

Burke, P. (1992) *The Fabrication of Louis XIV* (Cambridge)

Cadoni, E. (1982) 'Noterelle ovidiane', *Sandalion* 5: 191-203

Cairns, F. (1969) 'Propertius I 18 and Callimachus, Acontius and Cydippe', *CR* 83: 131-4

—— (1971) 'Propertius, 2.30 A and B', *CQ* N.S. 21: 204-13

—— (1984) 'Propertius and the battle of Actium', in *Poetry and Politics in the Age of Augustus*, ed. T. Woodman and D. West (Cambridge) 129-68

Cameron, A. (1991) 'How thin was Philitas?', *CQ* 41: 534-8

—— (1995) *Callimachus and His Critics* (Princeton)

Casali, S., ed. (1995) *P. Ovidii Nasonis Heroidum epistula IX* (Florence)

Cassio, A.C. (1973) 'L'incipit della Chioma callimachea in Virgilio', *RFIC* 101: 329-32.

Castiglioni, L. (1908) 'Studi Alessandrini I – Arianna e Teseo', *Ann. Sc. Norm. Pisa* 21: 1-60.

Citroni, M. (1979) 'Destinatario e pubblico nella poesia di Catullo: i motivi funerari', *MD* 2: 43-100

—— (1986) 'Le raccomandazioni del poeta: apostrofe al libro e contatto col destinatario', *Maia* N.S. 38: 111-46

Clausen, W. (1968) 'Catullus and Callimachus', *HSCP* 74: 85-94

—— (1994) *A Commentary on Virgil, Eclogues*, ed. W. Clausen (Oxford)

Clauss, J.J. (1988) 'Vergil and the Euphrates Revisited', *AJP* 109: 309-20

—— (1993) *The Best of the Argonauts* (Berkeley-Los Angeles-Oxford)

Clay, D. (1988) 'The archaeology of the temple to Juno in Carthage', *CP* 83: 195-205

Commager, S. (1974) *A Prolegomenon to Propertius* (Cincinnati)

Conte, G.B. (1984) *Virgilio: Il genere e i suoi confini* (Milan)

—— (1985) *Memoria dei poeti e sistema letterario* (Turin, 2nd ed.)

—— (1986) *The Rhetoric of Imitation* (Ithaca, NY)

—— (1990) 'Insegnamenti per un lettore sublime', Introduction to *Lucrezio, La natura delle cose* (Milan)

—— (1992) 'Proems in the middle', *YClS* 29: 147-59

—— and A. Barchiesi (1989) in *Lo spazio letterario di Roma Antica* I, ed. P. Fedeli, G. Cavallo and A. Giardina (Rome)

Cornacchia, G.A. (1989) 'Ovidio, am. 3,9,58', in *Mnemosynum. Studi in onore di A. Ghiselli*, ed. G.G. Biondi (Bologna), 101-2

Courtney, E. (1992) *The Fragmentary Latin Poets* (Oxford)

Davis, J.T. (1993) 'Thou shalt not cuddle: Amores 1 & 4 and the law', *Syllecta Classica* 4: 65-9

Dee, J.H. (1981) '*Iliad* I 4 and Catullus LXIV 152 f. Further considerations', *TAPA* 111: 39-42

Degl'Innocenti Pierini, R. (1995) 'Numerosus Horatius', in *Atti del Convegno 'Orazio'*, ed. A. Setaioli (Perugia), 101-16

Della Corte, F. (1973) 'I miti delle Heroides', in *Opuscula IV* (Genova)

—— (1980) *Tibullo: Le elegie* (Milan)

Dietzler, A. (1933) *Die Akontios-Elegie des Kallimachos*, Diss. (Greifswald)

Diller, H. (1934) 'Die dichterische Eigenart von Ovids Metamorphosen', *Hum. Gymn.* 45: 25-37

Dilthey, C. (1863) *De Callimachi Cydippa* (Leipzig)

Dörrie, H., ed. (1971) *P. Ovidii Nasonis Epistulae Heroidum* (Berlin-New York)

Drew Griffith, R. (1995) 'Catullus' Coma Berenices and Aeneas' Farewell to Dido', *TAPA* 125: 47-59

Due, O.S. (1974) *Changing Forms: Studies in the Metamorphoses of Ovid* (Copenhagen)

Dupont, F. (1994) *L'invention de la littérature* (Paris)

Easterling, P.E. (1984) 'The Tragic Homer', *BICS* 31: 1-8

Eco, U. et al. (1992) *Interpretation and Overinterpretation* (Cambridge)

Edmunds, L. (1992) *From a Sabine Jar: Reading Horace, Odes 1, 9* (Chapel Hill and London)

Edwards, C. (1993) *The Politics of Immorality in Ancient Rome* (Cambridge)

Fantuzzi, M. (1980) '*Ek Dios archomestha.* Arat. Phaen. 1 e Theocr. XVII 1', *MD* 5: 163-72

———— (1985) *Bionis Smyrnaei Adonidos Epitaphium* (Liverpool)

Fedeli, P., ed. (1980) *Sesto Properzio: Il primo libro delle elegie* (Florence)

———— (1985) *Properzio: Il libro terzo delle elegie* (Bari)

———— (1986a) 'Properzio e l'amore elegiaco', in *Atti Conv. Studi Properziani* (Assisi) 275-301

———— (1986b) 'La matrona di Efeso', in *Semiotica della novella latina*, ed. L. Pepe (Rome) 9-35

———— and Dimundo, R., eds (1988) Petronio Arbitro, *I racconti del 'Satyricon'* (Rome)

Feeney, D. (1986) 'History and revelation in Vergil's underworld', *PCPA* 212: 1-24

———— (1991) *The Gods in Epic* (Oxford)

Ferri, R. (1993) *I dispiaceri di un epicureo. Uno studio sulla poetica oraziana delle Epistole (con un capitolo su Persio)* (Pisa)

Fitzgerald, W. (1995) *Catullan Provocations* (Berkeley)

Fowler, D. (1989) 'First thoughts on closure: problems and prospects', *MD* 22: 75-122

———— (1993) 'Postscript: images of Horace in twentieth-century scholarship', in Martindale and Hopkins, 268-76

———— (1996) 'Even better than the real thing', in *Art and Text in Roman Culture*, ed. J. Elsner (Cambridge) 57-74

Fraenkel, E. (1957) *Horace* (Oxford)

Fränkel, H. (1945) *Ovid: A Poet Between Two Worlds* (Berkeley-Los Angeles)

Frangini, G. and Martinelli, M.C. (1981) in *Prospettiva* 25 (April) 4-13

Gabba, E. (1967) 'Considerazioni sulla tradizione letteraria sulle origini della Repubblica', *Entr. Hardt* XIII (Vandroeuvres-Geneva) 135-74

Galinsky, G.K. (1975) *Ovid's Metamorphoses: An Introduction to the Basic Aspects* (Oxford)

———— (1981) 'Augustus' legislation on morals and marriage', *Philologus* 125: 126-44

———— (1996) *Augustan Culture: An Interpretative Introduction* (Princeton)

Geisler, H.J. (1969) *P. Ovidius Naso, Remedia amoris, mit Kommentar zu Vers 1-369*, Diss. (Berlin)

Genette, G. (1976) *Figure III* (Turin)

———— (1980) *Narrative Discourse: An Essay in Method*, tr. J.E. Lewin (Ithaca NY)

———— (1983) *Nouveau discours du récit* (Paris)

Geymonat, M. (1993) 'Callimachus at the end of Aeneas' narration', *HSCP* 95: 323-31

Gilbert, C.D. (1976) 'Ovid, Met. 1.4', *CQ* N.S. 26: 111-12

Giomini, R. (1959) 'Per il testo delle Heroides', *Riv. Cult. Class. Med.* 1: 79-82

Goff, B. (1990) *The Noose of Words* (Cambridge)

Goldhill, S. (1986) 'Framing and polyphony: readings in Hellenistic poetry', *PCPA* 32: 25-52

——— (1991) *The Poet's Voice* (Cambridge)

Goold, G.P. (1965) 'Amatoria Critica', *HSCP* 69: 1-107

Gomez Pallarès, J. (1993) 'Sobre Ovidio, Tristia II 471-92', *Latomus* 52: 372-85

Grafton, A.T. and Swerdlow, N.M. (1986) 'Greek chronology in Roman epic: the calendrical date of the fall of Troy in the Aeneid', *CQ* 36: 212-18

Gruen, E.S. (1993) *Culture and National Identity in Republican Rome* (London)

Gutzwiller, K. (1992) 'Callimachus' Lock of Berenice: fantasy, romance, and propaganda', *AJP* 113: 359-85

——— (1996) 'Vergil and the date of the Theocritean epigram book', *Philologus* 140: 92-9

Habinek, T.N. and Schiesaro, A., ed. (1997) *The Roman Cultural Revolution* (Princeton)

Hainsworth, J.B., ed. (1982) *Omero, Odissea, II* (Rome)

Halleran, M. (1988) 'Repetition and irony at Sophocles' Trachiniae 574-581', *CP* 83: 129-31

Hardie, Ph. (1985) '*Imago Mundi*: cosmological and ideological aspects of the shield of Achilles', *JHS* 105: 11-31

——— (1986) *Virgil's Aeneid: Cosmos and Imperium* (Oxford)

——— (1990) 'Ovid's Theban History: the first anti-Aeneid?', *CQ* 40: 224-35

——— (1993) *The Epic Successors of Virgil* (Cambridge)

——— (1997) 'Questions of authority: the invention of tradition in Ovid "Metamorphoses" 15', in Habinek-Schiesaro 1997, 182-98

Harrison, E.L. (1972-3) 'Why did Venus wear boots? Some reflections on Aeneid 1.314 f.', *Proc. Virg. Soc.* 12: 10-25

Haupt-Korn-Ewahld-von Albrecht (1966) *P. Ovidius Naso, Metamorphosen* (Zürich-Dublin)

Heinze, R. (1960) 'Ovids elegische Erzählung', in *Vom Geist des Römertums* (Stuttgart [1919[1]])

Henderson, A.A.R., ed. (1979) *P. Ovidi Nasonis Remedia amoris* (Edinburgh)

Heyworth, S.J. (1993) 'Deceitful Crete: Aeneid 3.84 and the Hymns of Callimachus', *CQ* 43: 255-9

Hinds, S. (1985) 'Booking the return trip: Ovid and Tristia I', *PCPS* N.S. 31: 13-32

——— (1987a) *The Metamorphosis of Persephone: Ovid and the Self-conscious Muse* (Cambridge)

——— (1987b) 'Generalising about Ovid', *Ramus* 16: 4-31

——— (1993) 'Medea in Ovid: scenes from the life of an intertextual heroine', *MD* 30: 9-47

——— (1998) *Allusion and Intertext: Dynamics of Appropriation in Roman Poetry* (Cambridge)

Hollander, J. (1981) *The Figure of Echo: A Mode of Allusion in Milton and After* (Berkeley-Los Angeles-London)

Holleman, A.W.J. (1988) 'Zum Konflikt zwischen Ovid und Augustus', in *Saeculum Augustum II*, ed. G. Binder (Darmstadt) 378-93

Hollis, A.S. (1977) *Ovid, Ars Amatoria, Book I* (Oxford)

——— (1983) *Ovid, Metamorphoses Book VIII* (Oxford, 2nd ed.)

Holzberg, N. (1997) *Ovid. Dichter und Werk* (Munich)

Housman, A.E. (1899) 'Review of Palmer', *CR* 13: 172-8

Hopkinson, N. (1984) 'Callimachus' Hymn to Zeus', *CQ* 34: 139-48

––––– (1988) *A Hellenistic Anthology* (Cambridge)

Hross, H. (1958) *Die Klagen der verlassenen Heroiden in der lateinischen Dichtung*, Diss. (Munich)

Hunter, R. (1987) Medea's flight: The Fourth Book of the Argonautica', *CQ* 37: 129-39

––––– (1989) *Apollonius of Rhodes, Argonautica, Book III* (Cambridge)

––––– (1993a) *The Argonautica of Apollonius* (Cambridge)

––––– (1993b) 'Callimachean echoes in Catullus 65', *ZPE* 96: 179-82

––––– (1995) 'The divine and human map of the "Argonautica"', *Syllecta Classica* 6: 13-27

Jocelyn, H.D. (1986) 'Propertius and archaic Latin poetry', in *Atti Conv. Properziano* (Assisi) 105-36

Johnston, P.A. (1987) 'Dido, Berenice, and Arsinoe: Aeneid 6, 460', *AJP* 108: 649-54

Kannicht, R. (1969) *Euripides Helena* (Heidelberg)

Kassel, R. and Austin, C., ed. (1989) *Poetae Comici Graeci VII* (Berlin-New York)

Kenney, E.J. (1958) 'The *praestantissimus Puteanus* again', *SIFC* 30: 172-4

––––– (1959) 'Notes on Ovid, II', *CQ* 9: 240-60

––––– (1970) 'Love and legalism: Ovid, Heroides XX and XXI', *Arion* 9: 388-414

––––– (1976) 'Ovidius prooemians', *PCPS* N.S. 22: 46-53

––––– (1982) 'Ovid', in *Cambridge History of Classical Literature. II. Latin Literature* (Cambridge) 420-57

––––– (1983) 'Virgil and the elegiac sensibility', *Ill. Class. Stud.* 8: 44-59

––––– (1986) Introduction and Notes to *Ovid: Metamorphoses*, tr. A.S. Melville (Oxford-New York)

Kennedy, D.F. (1984) 'The epistolary mode and the first of Ovid's Heroides', *CQ* N.S. 34: 413-22

––––– (1992) *The Arts of Love* (Cambridge)

Kiessling, A. and Heinze, R. (1968) *Q. Horatius Flaccus. Oden und Epoden* (Dublin-Zurich)

Kirfel, E.A. (1969) *Untersuchungen zur Briefform der Heroides Ovids* (Bern)

Kirkwood, G.M. (1965) 'Homer and Sophocles'Ajax', in *Essays Presented to H.D.F. Kitto* (London) 51-70

Knox, P. (1986) 'Ovid's Medea and Heroides 12', *HSCP* 90: 207-23

Koenen, L. (1993) 'The Ptolemaic king as a religious figure', in *Images and Ideologies*, ed. A. Bulloch, E.S. Gruen, A.A. Long and A. Stewart (Berkeley) 25-115

Kraus, W. (1950-1) 'Die Briefpaare in Ovids Heroiden', *Wiener Studien* 65: 54-77

Krevans, N. (1984) *The Poet as Editor* (Diss. Princeton)

Labate, M. (1980) 'Ulisse, Eurialo e le armi di Achille', *Atene e Roma* 25: 28-32

Labate, M. (1984) *L'arte di farsi amare* (Pisa)

La Penna, A. (1963) *Orazio e l'ideologia del principato* (Turin)

Lazzarini, C., ed. (1986) *Ovidio, Rimedi contro l'amore* (Venice)

Lechi, F. (1979) 'Testo mitologico e testo elegiaco. A proposito dell'exemplum in Properzio', *MD* 3: 83-100

––––– (1993) 'Introduzione', in *Ovidio, Tristezze* (Milan) 5-44

Lefèvre, E. (1988) 'Die grosse Florus-Epistel des Horaz', in *Saeculum Augustum II*, ed. G. Binder (Darmstadt) 342-59

Lehrs, K. (1863) 'Adversarien über die sogenannten Ovidischen Heroiden', *Neue Jahrb.* 9: 49-69

—— (1869) *Q. Horatius Flaccus: Mit vorzugweiser Rücksicht auf die unechten Stellen und Gedichte herausgegeben von K. Lehrs* (Leipzig)

Lenz, F.W., ed. (1965) *P. Ov. Nasonis Remedia Amoris, Medicamina faciei* (Turin)

Littlewood, A.R. (1967) 'The symbolism of the apple in Greek and Roman literature', *HSCP* 72: 147-81

Luck, G. (1961) *Die römische Liebeselegie* (Heidelberg)

—— (1962) 'Ovidiana', *Philologus* 106: 145-50

Lunelli, A. (1969) *Aerius* (Rome)

Lyne, R.O.A.M. (1979) 'Servitium Amoris', *CQ* N.S. 29: 117-30

—— (1987) *Further Voices in Vergil's Aeneid* (Oxford)

—— (1994) 'Virgil's Aeneid: subversion by intertextuality', *G & R* 41: 187-204

Lynn-George, M. (1988) *Epos: Word, Narrative, and the Iliad* (Basingstoke-London)

Maas, P. (1902) 'Studien zum poetischen Plural bei den Römern', *Arch. Lat. Lex.* 12: 479-550

Maass, E. (1889) 'Alexandrinische Fragmente', *Hermes* 24: 520-9

Macleod, C. (1983) *Collected Essays* (Oxford)

Malamud, M.A. and McGuire jr, D.T. (1993) 'Flavian variant: myth. Valerius' Argonautica', in *Roman Epic*, ed. A.J. Boyle (London)

Marg, W. (1960) 'Ovid. Heroides X, 95-6', *Hermes* 88: 505-6

Martindale, Ch. (1993) 'Introduction', in Martindale-Hopkins 1993, 1-26

—— and Hopkins, D., ed. (1993) *Horace Made New* (Cambridge)

Mayer, M. (1887) *Die Giganten und Titanen* (Berlin)

McKeown, J. (1987) *Ovid: Amores*, vol. I: *Text and Prolegomena* (Liverpool)

—— (1989) *Ovid: Amores*, vol. II: *Commentary* (Liverpool)

McNally, S. (1985) 'Ariadne and Others: images of sleep in Greek and Roman art', *CA* 4: 152-92

Melville, A.D., tr. (1986) *Ovid. Metamorphoses* (Oxford-New York)

Most, G. (1992) 'Il poeta nell'Ade: catabasi epica e teoria dell'epos tra Omero e Virgilio', *SIFC* 10: 1014-25

Nagy, G. (1990) *Pindar's Homer: The Lyric Possession of the Epic Past* (Baltimore)

Nesselrath, H.G. (1986) 'Zu den Quellen des Silius Italicus', *Hermes* 114: 203-30

Nisbet, R. (1995) 'Tying down Proteus', in *Collected Papers on Latin Literature*, ed. S.J. Harrison (Oxford) 414-30

—— and Hubbard, M. (1978) *A Commentary on Horace: Odes, Book II* (Oxford)

Nugent, S.G. (1990) 'Tristia 2: Ovid and Augustus', in Raaflaub-Toher 1990, 239-57

Opelt, I. (1966) entry in *RAC* VI col. 807

Owen, S.G. (1924) *P. Ovidii Nasonis Tristium Liber II* (Oxford)

Paduano, G. (1982) *Tragedie e frammenti di Sofocle*, 1 (Turin)

Palmer, A., ed. (1898) *P. Ovidi Nasonis Heroides, with the Greek Translation of Planudes*, (Oxford)

—— ed. (1967) *P. Ovidi Nasonis Heroides, with the Greek Translation of Planudes*, (Hildesheim)

Lloyd-Jones, H. and Parsons, P.J., ed. (1983) *Supplementum Hellenisticum* (Hildesheim-New York)

Paschalis, M. (1986) 'Virgil and the Delphic oracle', *Philologus* 130: 44-68

Pasquali, G. (1964) *Orazio lirico* (Florence, 2nd ed.)

Perrotta, G. (1931) 'Il carme 64 di Catullo e i suoi pretesi originali ellenistici', *Athenaeum* N.S. 9: 177-222; 370-409 (= *Cesare, Catullo, Orazio e altri saggi* [Rome, 1972] 63-147)

Perutelli, A. (1974) 'Commento ad alcuni sogni dell'Eneide', *Athenaeum* 52: 241-67

Platnauer, M. (1951) *Latin Elegiac Verse* (Cambridge)

Phillips, E.D. (1953) 'Odysseus in Italy', *JHS* 73: 53-67

Puelma, M. (1982) 'Die Aitien des Kallimachos als Vorbild der römischen Amores-Elegie, I', *Mus. Helv.* 39: 221-46

Raaflaub, K.A. and Toher, M., ed. (1990) eds, *Between Republic and Empire*, (Berkeley-Los Angeles)

Reeve, M.D. (1973) 'Notes on Ovid's Heroides', *CQ* N.S. 23: 331-8

Reitzenstein, E. (1931) 'Zur Stiltheorie des Kallimachos', in *Festschrift R. Reitzenstein* (Leipzig-Berlin)

Reitzenstein, R. (1896) 'Properz-Studien', *Hermes* 31: 185-220

Renehan, R. (1979) 'New evidence for the variant in Iliad 1.5', *AJP* 100: 473-4

Richlin, A. (1981) 'Approaches to the sources on adultery at Rome', in *Reflections of Women in Antiquity*, ed. H. Foley (New York) 379-404

Ronconi, A. (1958) 'Quaeque notando', *Par. Pass.* 13: 143-8

Rosati, G. (1983) *Narciso e Pigmalione: Illusione e spettacolo nelle 'Metamorfosi' di Ovidio* (Florence)

—— (1989) *Ovidio, Lettere di eroine* (Milan)

—— (1990) 'Note al testo delle *Heroides*', *MD* 24: 161-5

Rosenmeyer, P. (1997) 'Her Master's Voice: Sappho's Dialogue with Homer', *MD* 39: 123-50

Ross, D.O. (1975) *Backgrounds to Augustan Poetry* (Cambridge)

Rossi, L.E., ed. (1977) *Due seminari romani di Eduard Fraenkel* (Rome)

Rousset, J. (1976) *Forma e significato* (Turin)

Rowell, H.T. (1949) 'The "Campanian" origin of C. Naevius and its literary attestation', *MAAR* 19: 17-34

Russell, D.A. (1983) *Greek Declamation* (Cambridge)

Schiesaro, A. (1984) '*Nonne vides* in Lucrezio', *MD* 13: 143-57

Schmid, W. (1934) *Geschichte der griechischen Literatur* I.2 (Munich)

Schmidt, E.A. (1967) 'Ariadne bei Catull und Ovid', *Gymnasium* 74: 489-501

Schubert, W. (1985) '*Quid dolet haec?*', *Antike und Abendland.* 31: 76-96

Scivoletto, N. (1976) *Musa iocosa* (Rome)

Segal, C. (1981) *Tragedy and Civilization* (Cambridge, MA)

—— (1986) *Interpreting Greek Tragedy* (Ithaca-London)

—— (1989) *Orpheus: The Myth of the Poet* (Baltimore-London)

Sharrock, A.R. (1994) 'Ovid and the politics of reading', *MD* 33: 97-122

Skulky, S. (1985) ' "Invitus regina ...": Aeneas and the Love of Rome', *AJP* 106: 447-55

Skutsch, O. (1959) 'Notes on Metempsychosis', *CP* 54: 114-16

—— ed. (1985) *The Annals of Quintus Ennius* (Oxford)

Smith, A.R. (1990) *Allusions of Grandeur: Studies in the Intertextuality of the 'Metamorphoses' and the 'Aeneid'* (Pennsylvania)

Smith, A.R. (1993) 'A Lock and a Promise: Myth and Allusion in Aeneas' Farewell to Dido in Aeneid 6', *Phoenix* 47: 305-12

Solodow, J.B. (1988) *The World of Ovid's Metamorphoses* (London)

Stégen, G. (1960) 'Notes de lecture', *Latomus* 19: 360

Sternberg, M. (1978) *Expositional Modes and Temporal Ordering in Fiction* (Baltimore)

Stinton, T.C.W. (1965) *Euripides and the Judgment of Paris* (London)

Stroh, W. (1971) *Die römische Liebeselegie als werbende Dichtung* (Amsterdam)

—— (1979) 'Ovids "Liebeskunst" und die Ehegesetze des Augustus', *Gymnasium* 86: 323-52

Sullivan, J.P. (1991) *Martial: The Unexpected Classic* (Cambridge)

Suter, A. (1989) 'Ovid, from image to narrative: Amores 1, 8 and 3, 6', *CW* 83: 15-20

Syme, R. (1978) *History in Ovid* (Oxford)

Tarrant, R.J. (1985) 'Two notes on Ovid's Heroides', *Rhein. Mus.* 128: 72-5

Tatum, J. (1984) 'Allusion and interpretation in Aeneid 6, 440-76', *AJP* 105: 434-52

Thomas, R.F. (1979) 'On a Homeric reference in Catullus', *AJP* 100: 475-6

———— (1983) 'Callimachus, the Victoria Berenices, and Roman poetry', *CQ* 33: 92-113

———— and Scodel, R. (1984) 'Vergil and the Euphrates', *AJP* 105: 339

Todorov, T. (1993) *I generi del discorso* (Florence) (= *Les genres du discours* [Paris, 1978])

Traina, A. (1991) *Poeti latini (e neolatini) II* (Bologna, 2nd ed.)

———— and Bernardi Perini, G. (1992) *Propedeutica al latino universitario* (Bologna, 4th ed.)

Van Sickle, J. (1968) 'The unity of the Eclogues. Arcadian forest, Theocritean trees', *TAPA* 99: 491-508

Venini, P. (1965) review of Lenz (1965), *Athenaeum* 43

Verducci, F. (1985) *Ovid's Toyshop of the Heart* (Princeton)

West, D. (1995) *Horace: Carpe Diem: Odes I* (Oxford)

Wiedemann, T. (1975) 'The political background to Ovid's Tristia 2', *CQ* N.S. 25: 264-71

Wilkinson, L.P. (1956) 'Greek influence on the poetry of Ovid', in *L'influence grecque sul la poésie latine de Catulle à Ovide* (Vandoeuvres-Geneva)

Williams, C.A. (1995) 'Greek love at Rome', *CQ* N.S. 45: 517-39

Williams, F. (1978) *Callimachus: Hymn to Apollo* (Oxford)

Williams, G. (1978) *Change and Decline* (Berkeley-Los Angeles)

———— (1991) 'Conversing after sunset: a Callimachean echo in Ovid's exile poetry', *CQ* 41: 169-77

Wills, J. (1996a) *Repetition in Latin Poetry: Figures of Allusion* (Oxford)

———— (1996b) 'Divided allusion: Virgil and the Coma Berenices', *HSCP* 98: 277-306

Wimmel, W. (1960) *Kallimachos in Rom* (Wiesbaden)

Wiseman, T.P. (1969) *Catullan Questions* (Leicester)

Wlosok, A. (1967) 'Die dritte Cynthia-Elegie des Properz', *Hermes* 95: 330-52

Wyke, M. (1989) 'Reading female flesh: Amores 3,1', in *History as Text*, ed. A. Cameron (London)

Zanker, P. (1989) *Augusto e il potere delle immagini* (Turin)

Zetzel, J.E.G. (1978) 'A Homeric reminiscence in Catullus', *AJP* 99: 332-3

———— (1983) 'Re-creating the canon. Augustan poetry and the Alexandrian past', *Crit. Inq.* 10: 83-105

Index Locorum

This index is selective. References to the pages of this book are in bold type.

General Index